Saint Katharine Drexel

Apostle to the Oppressed

❧

By Lou Baldwin

The Catholic Standard and Times
Philadelphia, PA

The Catholic Standard and Times
222 N. 17th Street
Philadelphia, PA 19103-1299

Library of Congress Catalog Card Number: 00-106990

Baldwin, Lou
Saint Katharine Drexel: Apostle to the Oppressed

ISBN: 0-9618073-1-8

Cover photo courtesy of the Sisters of the Blessed Sacrament

DEDICATION

This book is dedicated to the uncanonized saints in St. Katharine Drexel's family.

First of all to Frank, Emma, Lizzie and Louise, all of whom contributed to her formation.

Secondly, and most important, to her spiritual daughters, the many hundreds of courageous Sisters of the Blessed Sacrament, who, ever faithful to her vision, shaped it to their times and situations.

ACKNOWLEDGEMENTS

The publication of this book would not have been possible without the support and encouragement of Msgr. Paul A. Lenz, executive director of the Bureau of Catholic Indian Missions. For more than 125 years the bureau has collected and distributed funds in support of the Indian missions and represented the missions in government relations. Msgr. Lenz is also executive director of the Black and Indian Mission Office that is the trustee of funds for Black and Indian missions in the United States. His support for this biography of St. Katharine Drexel is deeply appreciated and a fitting tribute to the work of the Sisters of the Blessed Sacrament.

The author also gratefully acknowledges the advice and input of many in this work. Among them are:

Bishop Joseph F. Martino, author of the positio, the official documentation for the cause for canonization of St. Katharine Drexel; Sister M. Patricia Lynch, historian of the Sisters of the Blessed Sacrament for her advice, review, and corrections; and several other Sisters of the Blessed Sacrament including Sister M. Thomasita Daley, Sister Maria E. McCall, Sister Faith Okerson, Sister Margaret O'Rourke and Sister Ruth Catherine Spain.

At *The Catholic Standard and Times*: Elena Bucciarelli and Father Paul S. Quinter, copy editing and proofreading; Virginia Durkin-Asti, layout and design; Joseph Kirk Ryan, chapter titles; Frank Coyne, proofreading; and Martha Osgood, indexing.

FOREWORD

Why St. Katharine Drexel? For that matter, why does the Roman Catholic Church make saints?

It doesn't really — saints make saints. Catholics believe saints are persons who have died, and because of the merit of their lives, are now in Heaven. It is hoped there are not thousands of saints nor millions of saints, but billions of saints, most of them very ordinary people who lived unassuming lives.

When the Catholic Church, through the intricate canonization process, declares an individual a saint, it gives recognition to the heroic virtue of his or her life, and says, "Beyond a doubt, this wonderful person has achieved what should be the goal of everyone — salvation."

While canonization bestows a certain amount of honor and glory on the newly named saint, the real purpose is to present that holy man or woman as a worthy example for those of us still on earth.

Katharine Drexel cannot be dismissed as a social worker in religious garb. Nor is she merely the foundress of a religious congregation for women. Her "heroic virtue" shines through on several levels.

First of all, there is her own formation in an extraordinarily pious family, which looked beyond wealth to man's duty to man.

There is also her own complete renunciation of money and the things it buys for service to others. There is her great love of God, best exemplified by her devotion to the Eucharistic Christ. There is her deep empathy with people of color, flying in the face of the prevailing prejudices of her day.

And ultimately, there is her determination to help these same persecuted people know Jesus Christ, a commission accepted by all too few of her own co-religionists.

Katharine Drexel became a saint, not by fiat of the Pope, but by showing others a road to sanctity. Her path might be different than that of a St. Isaac Jogues, a St. Paul or a Dorothy Day — ultimately we choose our own path. But her example is one of the shining guideposts that can guide us as we journey in this new millennium.

— *Lou Baldwin*

Table of Contents

❧

Chapter One
The Challenge

A merica, by reputation, too often confuses fortune with virtue. In fact, the two rarely go hand-in-hand, as a glance at almost any newspaper or magazine will show. Still, it is possible to be both endowed with wealth and graced with virtue.

Three young Americans who traveled to Rome in 1887 prove the point. Through the recent death of their parents they had inherited a huge fortune, yet not a shadow of scandal had ever (or would ever) touch any of them. On this particular day, January 27, they would assist at the private Mass of Pope Leo XIII and have an audience with him. This would be a high point of the European trip for the three pious women, even if it was just a minor event on the calendar of the Pope, a kindly man who met with many people from around the world every day.

Pope Leo, who presumably had been briefed by his aides, would know these were the Drexel sisters from Philadelphia — Elizabeth, 31; Katharine, 28; and Louise, 23. They were devout Catholics in a land where most of the wealthy were Protestant, and they were unusually generous, especially to orphans and to Church missions for the African- and Native-American minorities of their land.

The audience proceeded in the usual manner — a bit of small talk in French, a language that the three sisters well understood. There was a papal blessing, of course, and to their request for a blessing for their loved ones, a nod of his head and a gracious, "Tout! tout! est accordé."

Before they were dismissed, Katharine asked if she could speak to His Holiness in private, and he granted her wish. Katharine had been sending large sums of money to the Indian missions, but a major difficulty was the need for missionaries. It was not a cause that attracted many American priests. Her spiritual advisor, Bishop James O'Connor of Omaha, Nebraska, had asked her to try to obtain European missionaries while in Rome, but she had been unsuccessful so far. Now she pled the case with Pope Leo and was quite animated in her presentation, because the bringing of Christ to the unchurched Native Americans was a cause very close to her heart. In her own words, 34 years after the fact, she recalled that conversation: "Kneeling at his feet, my girlish fancy thought that surely God's Vicar would not refuse me; so I pleaded missionary priests for Bishop O'Connor's Indians."

Leo was impressed by her zeal. "Why not, my child, yourself become a missionary?" he asked. In confusion, she could say only, "Because, Holy Father, Sisters can be had for the missions, but no priests." Leo gave her his blessing without further comment, and in a state of agitation, she left the audience chamber. She felt visibly sick, and as the group left the Vatican, she burst into tears.[1] She did not tell her sisters of the Pope's suggestion. Rather, she kept it in her heart and would reveal it only in later years.

Truth to tell, the desire for a religious vocation had been growing within Katharine for the past six years. But a missionary? She wasn't sure. The life of the cloister, especially as a contemplative before the sacred Host, had immense appeal to her.

Was Pope Leo's suggestion to Katharine an inspiration of the Holy Spirit, or was it simply the kind of offhand remark a wise pastor of souls would make to any young person who has a possible religious vocation? This we cannot know. What we do know is that this brief conversation would be a factor as this extremely religious young woman pondered her own future. There were other factors, too, and not the least of them was her own deep spirituality. It was a spirituality not entirely self-developed. The soul of St. Katharine is a blossom that had been nurtured and watered by the sum of the experiences and insights of the generations that preceded her. Just as nature's flowers are quite different from the various substances that contribute to their full bloom, Katharine gloriously stands alone, a person of rare inner beauty and purity of values in a world where such treasures are too seldom seen.

Chapter Two
In The Beginning

Before there was a Katharine, there were Hookeys, Langstroths, Drexels, and Bouviers; the first three were related in blood, the last in spirit. These families and their co-related branches can claim some measure of her fame, for all of them live through her memory.

On her father's side, Katharine's American genealogy begins with her grandfather — Francis Martin Drexel — artist, astute financier, adventurer and yes, draft dodger. Francis Martin was born in Dornbirn, the Austrian Tyrol, on Easter Sunday, April 7, 1792 to Franz Joseph and Magdalen Wilhelm Drexel.[1]

Franz Joseph was a merchant of sufficient means to send his 11-year-old son to Italy for schooling. Within a year, financial reversals caused by war forced the boy's return home. When Francis Martin showed little interest in business, his father permitted him to apprentice himself to an artist in a nearby village whose specialty was the painting of the outdoor wall murals so typical of the region. War was still a threat when, at age 17, Francis Martin approached the age for conscription. With his father's help, he quietly decamped for neutral Switzerland. He spent the next five years wandering through Europe honing his skills as an itinerant artist. When Drexel was 22, the region was at peace and it was safe for him to return to Dornbirn where he tried to establish himself as a portrait painter. But there was insufficient work to support an artist in the somewhat rural region.

After a short time, he left Dornbirn to try his fortune in America, arriving in Philadelphia on July 28, 1817.[2] Drexel's 72-day crossing aboard the *John of*

Baltimore had not been easy, but he was hoping to make a quick killing and then return home. This was the first dream of many immigrants to America. Like so many who came before and after, Francis Martin Drexel never returned to his native land. He would travel far and wide, but always, at journey's end, he would come home to Philadelphia.

Drexel set up a modest studio at 131 South Front Street, obtained several commissions for portraits, and exhibited at the Pennsylvania Academy of Fine Arts. To make ends meet, he also taught at Bazeley's Female Seminary, a small Catholic-oriented school near St. Joseph's Church. He was, for a time, betrothed to a Miss Mary Fisher, but not uncommon for the age, the engagement was cancelled by her death.

On April 23, 1821, Drexel married Catherine Hookey, the daughter of a prosperous grocer and member of one of Philadelphia's oldest German Catholic families. The wedding took place at St. Mary's Church, with Bishop Henry Conwell presiding.[3] Over time they would have six children: Mary Johanna, Francis Anthony, Anthony Joseph, Joseph Wilhelm, Heloise, and Caroline. Francis Anthony, the second child and eldest son, was born to the Drexels January 20, 1824 and was baptized at St. Joseph's Church on March 4 of the same year.[4]

All the other children in the family would be baptized at Holy Trinity Church, which had been founded for ministry to German Catholics. Francis Martin Drexel was for a time a trustee at Holy Trinity, where his father-in-law, Anthony Hookey, was a founding trustee.[5]

Holy Trinity was a parish that for three decades would be at serious odds with Philadelphia's bishops, including St. John Neumann. The bone of contention was conflicting rights of clergy and laity, complicated in Holy Trinity's case by the congregation's attempt to maintain a German identity in Philadelphia, where the Irish increasingly dominated the Church.

In Federalist America, most Catholic churches were established the same way Protestant denominations formed congregations. Because there were no local dioceses, groups of concerned individuals would come together, build a church and, they hoped, obtain the services of a priest or priests.

To accomplish this, a corporation would be formed and trustees, who would conduct the parish business, were elected. While collections were taken up at Masses, the chief source of revenue was pew rental, and it was the renters of pews who elected the trustees. After the Church became more firmly established in places such as Philadelphia, the bishops sought to exercise greater control. It wasn't merely a case of trying to govern the financial affairs of the parish; spiritual matters were at stake, too.

The trustees, again following a Protestant mode, often claimed the right to hire and fire clergy for the parish. This democratic process may sound fine in theory, but practice was something else again. At the time, before established American seminaries, virtually all the clergy were immigrants, and some of the priests had questionable credentials. Philadelphia's St. Mary's Church (where Charles Bazeley, Drexel's employer, was for a time, a trustee, as was Bernard Gallagher, Drexel's brother-in-law) was a case in point.

Father William Hogan, an Irish immigrant, was hired for ministry at St. Mary's in 1820. Although he had a charismatic personality and was an able preacher, he was man of doubtful orthodoxy and character. When Bishop Conwell tried to suspend him from priestly ministry, it touched off a firestorm among the parishioners of St. Mary's, including the majority of the trustees.

Hogan left Philadelphia — and eventually the Church — in 1823, but the acrimony would remain for decades.

Whatever may have been Francis Martin Drexel's role in the trustee controversy, he had domestic problems of his own. In one important sense, the family prospered — Catherine bore the first three of their six children in the first five years of the marriage. But there were problems with Catherine's family. Bernard Gallagher, husband of Catherine's eldest sister, according to family histories, slandered Drexel; allegations of the slander have not been preserved in Drexel histories.6 Francis Martin Drexel filed suit against his brother-in-law, and Gallagher settled out of court, retracting the slander. But the damage was done. Drexel lost many of his portrait commissions as well as his position with Bazeley.

In order to repair his damaged fortunes, Drexel decided upon a trip to South America where he proposed to sell portraits of the Great Liberator, Simon Bolivar. Drexel had never met Bolivar, but that didn't matter; he had a likeness of him. In that era before photography, a competent painter could make a living by simply copying and recopying a picture or portrait that was in demand.

Even though Bolivar fell from power shortly after Drexel's arrival, he stayed, traversing the continent, experiencing colorful adventures, and earning a bit of money to send home to Catherine and the children. Meanwhile, Catherine Hookey's relatives helped the young family, too, showering them with little kindnesses during Francis Martin's absence.

After four years, Drexel returned to his family in Philadelphia. Because it was still difficult to earn a living solely as an artist, he supplemented his income through other ventures. For a time he operated a brewery, aided, according to his personal memoir, by "three Irishmen and a blind horse."7 He was also a dealer in ribbon, including funeral crepe. Records show he provided the crepe for the funeral of his predecessor as Philadelphia's leading financier, Stephen Girard.

In 1835, Drexel made another foray into the world of art, this time through a two-year tour through Mexico. This trip, too, was not particularly successful. Had he died at this point, Francis Martin Drexel would be remembered, if at all, as an artist of modest talent and an unsuccessful businessman. But then he discovered finance, not art or trade, was his true forte. It came in the wake of a national crisis. President Andrew Jackson withdrew federal support from the nation's leading financial institution, the privately held Bank of the United States, touching off a financial panic. Any currency in the world was preferable to the American greenback.

Whatever else he had accomplished, Drexel had learned a thing or two about currency trading during his years as an itinerant artist. Taking advantage of the situation in 1837, he set up a currency trading business in the Ohio River port of Louisville, Kentucky.[8] He prospered to such a point that he decided to transfer the operation to Philadelphia, and so one of the greatest banking fortunes in American history was born.

Drexel's two oldest boys, Frank and Anthony, were 13 and 11 respectively, old enough, by 19th-century standards, to begin an apprenticeship. Francis Martin took his two sons under his wing. During these early years as his father's apprentice, Frank learned the banking business well; he would at times pack a cold dinner in a basket and stay overnight, sleeping under the counter of the little shop at 34 South Third Street. If banking was his vocation, music was his avocation. To augment the modest salary given him by his father, Frank took a position as organist at St. John the Baptist Church in Manayunk, then well beyond the city limits. Each Sunday he would walk the eight miles to Manayunk for the weekly services. For this he was paid $150 a year, a fair salary at the time.[9]

The family business received a major boost in 1848 with the Mexican War, when Francis Martin Drexel was instrumental in the floating of a vast quantity of government bonds to finance the war. He remained in Philadelphia until 1849, a remarkable length of time in one place for him.

With the discovery of gold in California, he left the firm of Drexel & Co. in the hands of his sons and traveled to the coast, where he established an allied banking house, Drexel, Sather & Church. He remained in the West until the panic in 1857. When he returned to Philadelphia, he found his capable sons had the business well in hand. Francis Martin Drexel died as the result of a railroad accident in 1863, by which time Drexel & Co. was firmly established as one of the nation's leading investment banking houses.[10]

Spiritually, there is not a great deal we can say about Francis Martin Drexel. He lived and died a Catholic, which is more than can be said of many of his descendants. He was, at various times, an active participant in his parish. One might seriously question his tendency to leave his family for years at a stretch, albeit for the purpose of earning a living. Katharine Drexel, who was five when Francis Martin died, certainly knew him. It would be difficult to attribute any of her spiritual qualities to her footloose grandfather. However, financial ability is quite another matter.

Frank Drexel inherited every bit of his father's financial ability, but Anthony Drexel went a step further: He had financial genius. While Frank was the titular head of the company, Anthony was the engine that drove it. The two worked amicably and well in tandem; Frank's conservative streak complemented Anthony's daring. Younger brother Joseph was dispatched to Paris to open another allied branch, Drexel, Harjes & Co. With this company established, he relocated to New York, where he teamed with J. Pierpont Morgan to found Drexel, Morgan & Co.

Anthony Drexel left Catholicism after his marriage to Ellen, an Episcopalian. While it would be unfair to assume his motives were less than pure — he was a deeply spiritual man — such a move would not hurt the family business. Philadelphia, despite a growing Catholic population, was virtually controlled by a network of well-established Protestant families. Catholics might do very well in the trades, but in finance, connections were essential. Anthony Drexel moved in the highest circles both locally and nationally. He was a personal friend of Ulysses S. Grant. As a matter of fact, the former president was living in a cottage in the Adirondacks owned by Joseph Drexel at the time of his death.

Auxiliary Bishop of Philadelphia Joseph F. Martino, who in the 1980s prepared the positio, the official document that promoted Katharine's cause for beatification, suggested that Anthony may have embraced Episcopalianism as a result of the trustee controversy, particularly as it affected Holy Trinity, Philadelphia's first German parish.[11] It is true that many prominent Catholics left the Church during that era, and this perhaps explains why there is no record of any relationship between the rising Drexels and St. John Neumann, Philadelphia's bishop (1852-1860). The Drexel's Austrian heritage should have afforded a natural kinship to the Bohemian-born bishop. But it was under Neumann that the Holy Trinity trustee question was finally settled in the civil courts through a total victory for the bishop and a total defeat for the lay trustees. Neumann was still bishop of Philadelphia when Frank Drexel donated funds to put the roof on Philadelphia's Cathedral of SS. Peter and Paul, a building project begun under Bishop Francis Patrick Kenrick and continued by Neumann. But it must be noted that Frank's donation came after the arrival of Bishop James Frederic Wood as coadjutor to Neumann (1857-60), and in time, Philadelphia's bishop and archbishop, (1860-1883). It was during Wood's administration that Frank Drexel achieved prominence in the affairs of the diocese.

The business and personal relationship between Frank and his brother, Anthony, would be well captured in Frank's obituary, as published in the Philadelphia Public Ledger on February 15, 1885: "Mr. Francis A. Drexel was the senior of the two Drexel brothers who give title to the bank bearing their names, but by the senior's desire, Mr. Anthony J. Drexel has been the directing head. The elder had an almost reverential love for his brother and though a man qualified for his business, he preferred that his brother should lead." The accuracy of this assessment is probably unimpeachable; George Childs, publisher of the Public Ledger, was a close friend to both brothers; they were the financial backers of his newspaper. It would be presumed that Childs, a co-executor of Frank's estate, approved the obituary before it was published.

The Drexel firm was primarily a financial underwriting house. It supplied and placed hundreds of millions of dollars in government, corporate, railroad, and other securities. These were all investment grade stocks and bonds. Unlike a modern descendant institution bearing the Drexel name, it did not deal in speculative issues, which today we call junk bonds. "Sound and sure transactions are the invaluable rule," a 19th-century historian said.[12]

While his father was in California, Frank, at age 30, took a wife. She was Hannah Jane Langstroth, a young woman of 28. Hannah was the youngest of the four children of Piscator and Eliza Lehman Langstroth of Germantown, an old North Philadelphia neighborhood. The Langstroths could trace their American lineage to 1684 and to some of the oldest families in Pennsylvania. Like most Drexel spouses, Hannah Jane was not Catholic. Her family were of the sect called Dunkards, named for their practice of baptism by triple immersion. Today, they are known as the Church of the Brethren. The Dunkards, originally of German origin, were a gentle, God-fearing, pacific, and socially-conscious people; they make fitting ancestors for a future saint. One Langstroth forefather, Huson Langstroth, had given his life ministering to the sick of Philadelphia during the terrible yellow fever epidemic of 1793.

Frank and Hannah Jane were united in marriage at Philadelphia's Church of the Assumption of the Blessed Virgin Mary on Spring Garden Street on September 28, 1854. Father Charles Carter officiated, and Frank's brother and sister, Joseph and Caroline, were the witnesses. They took up residence at 433 Race Street, and the following year — on August 27 — their first child, Elizabeth, named for her maternal grandmother, came into the world and was duly baptized at Assumption Church.[13] A second child, Catherine Mary, named in honor of her paternal grandmother, Catherine Hookey Drexel, was born November 26, 1858. Through her life she would use many variations of her name — as a child she was called Katie, Kitty, and Kate; Katharine as an adult. Legal documents were invariably signed Catherine or Catharine. Now, of course, she is "St. Katharine Drexel."

Her entry into the world came at a heavy price: Hannah never recovered from childbirth. She gradually slipped into delirium and died on December 30. Frank took her to the graveyard of the little Dunkard church in Germantown where her family worshiped and she was laid to rest there.[14] On December 29, as her mother wavered between life and death, little Katie was taken by her uncle, Joseph Drexel, and aunt, Mary Drexel Lankenau, to Assumption Church. Here, Father Carter poured the sacred waters of baptism on the infant and welcomed her into the Mystical Body of Christ, a union that would be the dominant factor of her life.[15]

Assumption Church ceased to exist as a parish in 1995, but the antique wooden baptismal font at which St. Katharine Drexel received her first sacrament, along with a copy of the baptismal record, is lovingly displayed in the Chapel of the Blessed Virgin Mary at Philadelphia's Cathedral Basilica of SS. Peter and Paul.

Many years later, after most of the Drexels had been entombed at the Shrine of the True Cross in Philadelphia, St. Katharine Drexel's Sisters of the Blessed Sacrament petitioned Cardinal Dennis Dougherty for permission to bring Hannah's remains to the shrine. Under Church rules in force at the time, non-Catholics could not be buried in consecrated ground, but in their petition, the Blessed Sacrament Sisters cited a Drexel family tradition that said Hannah was a catechumen, having received instruction from Father Carter at the time of her death.

If Hannah was indeed a catechumen, it is puzzling. Her death was not sudden; the illness was prolonged over the period of a month, although the last three weeks were in a state of delirium. One would presume, if she had in fact been a catechumen, Catholic conditional baptism would have been administered by Father Carter when death became probable, and burial would have been in a Catholic cemetery. Where did the story come from?

Katharine told the Sisters of her congregation she had heard this from Johanna Ryan, her childhood nurse. Johanna had told her that her mother, when dying, had remarked that if she "knew more about the teachings of the Catholic Church she might come into it."[16]

But Johanna did not enter the employ of the Drexels until Frank remarried; she could not have firsthand knowledge, and in other instances, was not a reliable source. One suspects Katharine, to whom the Catholic faith was of paramount importance, was willing to accept a pious story that would make her mother a Catholic by desire. Cardinal Dougherty, who had great respect and affection for St. Katharine Drexel, acceded to her congregation's request and permitted the transfer of Hannah's remains to the family crypt at the Shrine of the True Cross.[17]

In any event, St. Katharine Drexel was not alone among the descendants of Eliza and Piscator Langstroth to enter religious life. Hannah's older sister, Elizabeth, married a Portuguese wine merchant, Fortunato J. Figueira. Two of her grandchildren entered religious life. They were the children of Elizabeth's daughter, the Viscountess de Villa Verde. One of them, Eugenia, had carried the Blessed Sacrament to prisoners at a time of religious persecution. It was her wish to enter Carmel, but her mother objected.

At the time of St. Katharine's own reception into religious life, Eugenia would write to her cousin: "When Jesus calls us we cannot but obey his sweet and loving voice, and truly it is only in his pure love that we find peace which the world cannot give and consolation in this valley of tears." Ultimately, Eugenia entered a Carmelite cloister in Pamplona, Spain, as Sister Isabela Maria de Jesus. Her younger sister, Luiza, like Katharine, would found a religious congregation; it was based in Portugal and called the Order of Our Lady of Fatima.

By the time of their second child's birth and the death of his first wife, Frank Drexel may have resolved a crisis in faith of his own. Responding to condolences from a cousin after Hannah's death, he wrote:

> After three weeks intense suffering, although she may have been unconscious of it, having lost her reason, my beloved one was taken from me. If I know myself I am resigned to the disposition of the Almighty. His will in all things be done, for he ordereth all things wisely and well. He has not left me comfortless for I have been since my marriage, received into Mother Church, wherein is my consolation. I have every assurance my beloved one has gone to her father.[18]

This implies a previous estrangement from the Church, but if so, it does not appear to be serious. As noted, Hannah and Frank had been married in the Church, and the two children had received Catholic baptism in a timely fashion.

After Hannah's death, Aunt Ellen and Uncle Anthony Drexel took the two little girls into their own home to care for them until such time when Frank could do so himself.[19] This would come about through Frank's marriage, on April 10, 1860, to Emma Bouvier, a young woman nine years his junior. Emma, a woman of extraordinary personal piety, had ancestry curiously similar to Frank's.[20]

Michel Bouvier was a Frenchman, and like Francis Martin Drexel, left home because of the Napoleonic wars. But while Francis Martin fled to escape military service, Michel took a ship for America to avoid the possible unpleasant consequences of his service in Napoleon's army. Bouvier was born in 1792 in the Rhone River village of Pont St. Esprit. His father, Eustache Bouvier, according to family lore, was no stranger to America. He served with the French army under Rochambeau at Yorktown. Michel Bouvier joined Napoleon's army during the emperor's ill-fated comeback attempt in 1815 and participated in the Battle of Waterloo. After the French defeat, he fled to New York where he remained for two years before settling in Philadelphia.[21]

While Francis Martin Drexel was an artist, Michel Bouvier was an artisan. He was a skilled cabinetmaker; some of his finer pieces are of museum quality. Among his clients were Stephen Girard and Joseph Bonaparte, the exiled brother of Napoleon who had settled in Bordentown, New Jersey.

In 1822, Bouvier married Sarah Pearson. Like Hannah Langstroth, she died four years later, after the birth of their second child.[22] Michel, who by this time had Anglicized his name to Michael, remarried within two years. Just as Francis Martin Drexel had done, Michael Bouvier prospered, although certainly not on the same scale. In his case, wealth came through dealing in marble and hardwoods, products needed for his furniture business, and finally, in land speculation.

Through his 1828 marriage to Louise Vernou, eight more children, including Emma, were added to the family. Louise Vernou, a woman of stability and dignity, was a perfect mate for her mercurial husband. In all probability, Michael was no more religious than the next person. We know that he was warden of his Masonic Lodge — Catholics, then as now, were forbidden to join the Masons. Most of the next generation of Bouviers would leave Philadelphia for New York, where, greatly helped by the Drexel family connection, they would continue to prosper. If old Michael would have been amazed to learn that one of his granddaughters through marriage would some day be a saint of the Church, he would be equally astounded if he knew another descendant — Jacqueline Bouvier Kennedy (the great-granddaughter of his son, John) — would be the wife of the first Catholic president of the United States.

After their wedding, Frank and Emma departed for a six-month wedding trip to Europe. There were obligatory stops at the ancestral villages of Dornbirn and Pont St. Esprit in Austria and France, as well as leisurely trips through England, Ireland, Switzerland, and Italy. Rome, with a brief private audience with Pope Pius IX, was a highlight.

In his journal, Frank recorded the visit. After going through several antechambers, he and Emma, "wearing the appropriate attire," entered the audience chamber. According to protocol, they knelt at the entrance of the room, again at the center of the chamber and finally before the throne. Pius IX received them standing, presented his hand to be kissed and "inquired about his children in America." He blessed their marriage and signaled them to retire, which they did by walking backward so they wouldn't present their backs to the Pope. "This visit was one which left us with a feeling of pleasure," Frank wrote.23

This was Frank's first visit to Europe; for Emma, it was a return to familiar places.

In 1853, Michael Bouvier had made a sentimental journey to his homeland, including an excursion to Rome and Florence. He took with him his three eldest unmarried daughters; Elizabeth, Louise, and Emma. The girls had been educated at academies conducted by the Religious of the Sacred Heart, a French congregation. These schools, the Academy of the Sacred Heart on Walnut Street in Philadelphia and Eden Hall, in what is now the Torresdale section of the city, would play an important role in the lives of Frank and Emma's children.

Most of the Bouvier daughters, including Emma, had considered a religious vocation. One child, Louise, decided to enter the Religious of the Sacred Heart. Michael was adamantly opposed to the idea and refused to give his permission. When Louise became of legal age, of course, he would have no say in the matter. Perhaps the European trip was a peace offering, and perhaps it was Michael's secret hope that his daughters might meet suitable French lads during the trip and forget this convent business. If so, the plan backfired. The family had hardly arrived in Paris when Louise fled to the convent of the Religious of the Sacred Heart. Because she was now of age, there wasn't a thing her father could do about it. Michael and his two remaining daughters reluctantly continued their tour and returned home without her.24 After her novitiate, Louise, now Madame Bouvier, was sent back to Eden Hall, where she would have a critical, if sometimes indirect, influence on the Drexel children, including little Katie. Emma and her sister had a close relationship, and it is probably no mere coincidence that the Drexel's two principal residences during Katie's formative years were within walking distance of the Convent of the Sacred Heart and Eden Hall.

Chapter Three
Prayers and Industry

When Frank and Emma returned to Philadelphia, they established residence in a spacious three-story brownstone at 1503 Walnut Street in Center City Philadelphia. This home, which would be their residence of record throughout their marriage, was elegant but not extravagant. When one considers their growing wealth, this branch of the Drexel family definitely lived below their means. With a home established, Frank retrieved his two little daughters from Aunt Ellen and Uncle Anthony. Emma took Lizzie and Kate and raised them as her own.[1]

On October 2, 1863, when baby Louise was born to Frank and Emma, the family was complete. The two older girls truly accepted Emma as their mother. In later years, St. Katharine would tell the sisters of her congregation that whenever anyone referred to Emma Drexel as her stepmother, it was like piercing her heart with a sword. Never once, Mother Katharine said, did Emma show the "slightest shade of preference for Louise than she did for her other daughters."[2]

Johanna Ryan, a young Irish girl, was an important member of the household. Johanna had been a novice with the Ladies of the Sacred Heart, but her state of health was not up to the rigors of convent life. At the time, most religious congregations for women had two classes of Sisters: choir Sisters, who would be given the more intellectual pursuits of the convent, and house Sisters, who would assume the humbler duties. Johanna was probably a house sister. When the decision was made that she should leave the convent, the problem remained as to where she should go. Her nearest living relative was a sister in the Dakota Territory, and the Sisters were loath to send a young girl on what was, at the time, an arduous journey. Aunt Louise placed her in the Bouvier household as a servant.[3] When Emma married, Johanna came with her. She would be a colorful addition to the family and devoted servant and friend over a lifetime.

Curiously, Katharine, in that more innocent age, appears to have been unaware that Emma was not her birth mother until she was 13. It was not until then that she realized it is impossible to have three sets of grandparents. If Lizzie had any memories of Hannah, she kept them to herself.[4]

Emma Drexel was a woman of deep piety and of a personal austerity, which suggested, in a good sense, a Jansenist streak. Early in her marriage she followed the lead established by her own mother by setting up a little oratory in her home.[5] It was here that members of the family, collectively or individually, would repair for a few moments of prayer. The family was also mindful of Christ's admonition in Matthew 6:6: "But when you pray, go to your inner room, close the door, and pray to your Father in secret. And your Father who sees in secret will repay you." This private piety was recounted by Mother Katharine many years later in a short memoir written at the request of members of her congregation:

> My father would come home from the office and go right up to his room and kneel down beside a chair — one of those chairs that I think are now in our sacristy, the round ones, you know — and there he would pray — the oratory would have been too public — there he would have been seen — but in his room he would not have been seen by the help. Then he would go to the organ and play — oh, he would play so beautifully. Yes, it is the same organ we have at St. Elizabeth's.
>
> Prayer was like breathing...there was no compulsion, no obligation...it was natural to pray....
>
> Night prayers were always said together. We were usually in bed by eight o'clock when we were children. Then in our little night dresses we would go to the top of the stairs and call down, 'Mama! Papa!'
>
> Then Papa (we did not call him 'Dad') would leave his organ or his paper and Mama her writing, and both at the call of the children would come up and kneel for night prayers in the little oratory. Sometimes, Mama would be sleepy...yes, she would be worn out from her work with the poor...and would doze off and say, 'Hail Mary, Mother of God.' No matter how often this would happen she would begin all over when Papa would gently say, 'Dear, it is Holy Mary, now, Holy Mary, Mother of God....' Yes, he knew she was tired after her day.[6]

The "work with the poor" St. Katharine recalled was a central fact in Emma's life. Three days a week, literally hundreds of people would gather at the Drexels' back gate on Moravian Street. "I often think my mother had no human respect," St. Katharine recalled. "She never seemed to wonder what the neighbors would think or say when they saw a crowd gathered day after day during the winter months."[7]

This wasn't just a couple of sandwiches and "come back next week." There was a certain method to Emma's charity. She employed a woman, Miss Bilger, as a social worker, well before the term was invented. As Emma's assistant, she would visit the poor tenements seeking out cases of want that could be relieved. These people were given a ticket that could be presented to Mrs. Drexel.

At times, Emma and her assistant would disagree on need, with Miss Bilger being a bit more tough-minded. In one exchange of letters in 1877, Miss Bilger emphasizes she had not given one particular supplicant $40 as directed by Emma. "I could not think of giving so large a sum to the old...without your expressed command," she wrote. Emma, she ruefully says, will never be a philosopher "for you lack one great, great ingredient in the character of a philosopher, namely that of hardheartedness." Emma gave the $40 to the woman in spite of this.[8]

Day after day, Katharine would later recall, "the front door and the back door was besieged by a crowd of beggars, who at last became so clamorous that Mama had to scare them off with the face of a policeman. The poor man was at wit's end as to how the crowd was to be diminished."[9]

Katharine went on to recount a typical encounter between Emma and her deserving poor. "It is astonishing how humble the old people are when arriving in Mama's presence," Katharine wrote. But some of the meetings could be quite funny. For instance, there is the woman who begins, "I have none but auld shoes on me feet." She asks for shoes for herself and gets them. She asks for shoes for her five children and receives these also. Then she asks for coal. This is followed by a request for flannels. There is the rent of course, because she is about to be evicted. Then "a bit of food for Jimmy, he's so sick." And, she informs Emma, "little Mary needs a dress." Finally, Emma sends her off with the hint she may be asking too much, but gives her everything she asked for anyway.[10]

If this suggests Emma was a pushover for any hard luck story, it isn't necessarily so. As St. Katharine also explained, her mother kept careful books as to what was given to whom.

> Mama knew if the same need was brought to her again very soon it was because the right use had not been made of the thing given before. Or they might have sold or traded it for drink or something else, and then Mama would be able to inquire and the records gave her the informa-

tion she needed. In this way Mama took a personal interest in them. And they knew it and she was able to direct them. She got to know them and know their needs. And her sympathy was unwearying.[11]

If Emma tried to make certain (but not always successfully) that her generosity was not being abused by the recipients, she was doubly careful that tradespeople did not overcharge. Witness this entry from her journal:

> Mr. Lewis' charges for grave-digging are five dollars. But Mr. Lewis, presuming on the charitable disposition of Mrs. D., presents her with a bill for seven dollars and a half for his services in preparing the last resting place of poor black Emily. Mrs. D., being a sensible woman, even if she is charitable, sends Lewis away in hot haste. Lewis is astonished and begins to see things from a different standpoint, and walks off feeling considerably cheaper than if he had demanded and received the five dollars which were his due. Mr. Lewis as a martyr-grave digger lays the case before his friend, Mr. M., who quietly cons a lesson therefrom, which operates to Mrs. D's advantage, for on the very next occasion of seeking employment from Mrs. D., Mr. M. with affected modesty, but knowing that he will receive no more, is careful to ask the usual price of wages. Because a man is poor he need not necessarily be mean, nor is it true charity to encourage him in his meanness by indolently or goodnaturedly permitting him to compromise his manhood. If a man is poor and despite his poverty, is above the temptation of littleness, he is nobler than a monarch.... Look not then, foolish man, upon the benevolent lady as an imbecile whose soft heart receives every impression, but regard her rather as one who in the exercise of her vocation calls forth all the powers of her mind as well as heart and who possesses the keenness of a knave, the kindness of a fool and the judgment of her philosopher.[12]

Emma's journal suggests she is a woman of charity determined to do the right thing. But there is also a little bit of class superiority in all of it. Servants take advantage of one; the poor are not always deserving; and tradespeople are grasping. Noblesse oblige is not always easy. "How often," she philosophizes in her journal, "is the benevolent lady, but practical woman, God bless her! keen to detect imposture and abjectness, and accordingly, reject such as an offense against heaven, and an insult to her better judgment...."[13]

Lest the impression be given that Emma was unnecessarily hard on those who were in a subordinate position, the records are full of incidents of her forgiving faults in others, some not so petty. Johanna Ryan's case is a perfect example. In one of her later letters to her daughters, Emma remarks,

> It is an axiom of theology that all created things have their purpose and so I suppose a benignant Providence had in view the case of cantankerous old Joe, the great danger of stagnation in the existence of a quiet, happy family, for she is opposed to calms and can raise a flurry from a slight gale to a heavy storm....14

Emma's personal charity was called the Dorcas, after Dorcas or Tabitha, the holy woman in the Acts of the Apostles who ministered to the poor. Emma encouraged her children to take their place beside her in this noble effort. But it was done with the proviso that they do so at personal sacrifice, using their own little bit of money to alleviate the sufferings of the poor. When the children accompanied Emma on a errand of mercy to a poor family, they would be directed to dress simply so as not to suggest any degree of superiority. Emma's corporal works of mercy were done with the full knowledge and consent of her husband. This is made clear in an 1863 New Year's Day letter that Frank writes to his wife. He speaks of the many blessings they have received:

> My dear and affectionate wife: It is well at the beginning of another year to give expression to the thoughts that have been active in the mind during the one just gone by, as well as to form resolutions which may govern us in the one to come.
>
> Many various blessings have been conferred upon us the time we have been united — a special Providence it has been that brought us together, and if we operate according to its designs it will be the means of amending much in us that needs correction.
>
> A similarity in feeling and disposition unless regulated by mutual love and forbearance, does not in general produce perfect accord — what each of us offends in we are less liable to forgive in the other — mutual forbearance is necessary for both of us and for my part I feel that you have shown it toward me in a greater degree than I have returned it. Had I performed my religious duties with more seriousness and attention I should probably not now stand self-convicted.
>
> We have received many and various blessings. Let us not be forgetful of them but in the time to come may we show by our punctuality in approaching the Blessed Sacrament and the attention and devotion that we manifest in preparing for it, that we appreciated the means of salvation which have been designed to sustain our spiritual life. May

our hearts be continually directed towards Him who suffered and died for us and gave us His flesh for our life — when tempted let us instantly call on our Blessed Mother — she is our friend and helps us. God has also bestowed on us abundance. Continue your charities in His name. Be the dispenser of His gifts and let us also extend the charity of thought towards those who offend us.

In conclusion my dear, dear one, let me wish you a happy New Year indeed, a strength to bear all the little trials that may befall you. May your warm, tender, loving heart beat yet more tenderly toward your own loving and affectionate husband, pardoning him his faults and sustaining him in his trials, and thus make home a heaven here below.[15]

Frank's letter is interesting on several levels, once one gets past the rather flowery style of 19th-century epistles. This is 1863, yet in his year-end retrospective letter, he does not mention the horrible war that is raging, a war that was contributing to that abundance that has been bestowed upon them. Nor does Frank even mention the two little girls (Louise would not be born until October) who were so much a part of the family.

No, this is an intimate letter written by a man to his spouse that focuses only on themselves in union with the God whom they mutually adore. We are perhaps intruding by sharing something that was never intended to be shared. Yet it is important, because through this letter we learn of a family devotion to the Blessed Sacrament, Katharine's "Prisoner of Love," and a willing commitment to service to the poor.

Emma's role in teaching the children by example is fundamental to an understanding of St. Katharine Drexel, but one must not discount the part Francis Drexel played. He did more than simply encourage his wife in her charities. Francis sat on virtually every charitable board connected with the Philadelphia Archdiocese, and of course, was a major contributor as well. His charitable works were conducted the same way his business was conducted — quietly and behind the scenes, unlike Emma's hands-on work among the poor. The mature Katharine Drexel would have preferred to follow in the footsteps of her mother, dealing directly and personally with the poor and downtrodden. However, the circumstances and responsibilities of her life as foundress and superior of a religious congregation forced her into the more administrative role of her father. She guided and encouraged others to do the work she longed to do herself.

Under the customs of the time, Francis Drexel's generosity to the diocesan charities conferred upon the family certain rights. For instance, they could — and did — nominate candidates for the children's asylums. In that era before the existence of social safety nets, Emma would hear of a child who had been mistreated or abandoned and send one of her employees to fetch the little one for presentation to the Archbishop for permission to be entered into one of the institutions.

When Johanna Ryan was delegated to social-service duties there could be interesting consequences. In one instance when she was sent to investigate the circumstances of a family, she found the parents intoxicated and neglectful of their child. Ever impetuous, Johanna simply took the child and placed him in the orphanage. The parents never objected. Archbishop Ryan heard the story and laughingly called Johanna "the kidnapper."[16]

Another incident had more embarrassing results. Johanna was sent to the tenements to pick up a recently orphaned little girl. She went, made brief inquiries, picked up a little girl, and took her to the orphanage. It was only later that evening, when very angry parents showed up at the Drexel residence, that it was discovered she had taken the wrong child. Poor Emma kept the episode secret from Frank, who would not have been amused.[17]

At first, Emma appears to have wished her daughters to be educated as she had been — by the Religious of the Sacred Heart, in this case at the Academy of the Sacred Heart on Walnut Street in Philadelphia. When she reached the proper age, it was here that Emma would take Lizzie every day. Lizzie, as a small child, was high-spirited. On average twice a week, poor Emma would have to wait outside with Katie, because recalcitrant Lizzie was being kept after school. Little Katie wasn't above throwing a tantrum now and again either. Witness one trip to New York. Emma, who was on a shopping excursion, took the two little girls with her. When she would not give them their way, they made a scene while riding with her on a street car, much to Emma's mortification. Saints are not born saints. They become saints through practice.[18]

At a point before Katie was ready for school, Emma decided the children would be educated at home. To this end, instructors who were prominent in various fields of knowledge were hired. Michael Cross taught English; Professor Allen and his daughter Bessie, Latin; and Justine Clave, French.[19] When Louise was five, once again through the good offices of Aunt Louise, the final element of their education was put into place. Mary Bernice Cassidy, an educated Irish woman, had emigrated to the United States with her family. They settled in Camden, New Jersey, across the Delaware River from Philadelphia. When her father died shortly after the family arrived, Mary Cassidy became the sole support of her family. Somehow Aunt Louise — Madame Bouvier — learned of her talents and recommended her to Emma for employment. Mary Cassidy, affectionately known to the Drexels as "Bern," would take over the general supervision of the children's education, with a special emphasis on history.

Most of the letters that survive from St. Katharine's childhood are really because of Mary Cassidy. Letter writing, essays, and journal keeping were techniques she used in teaching her three pupils.[20]

Mary Cassidy became much more than governess. In other capacities she would be an assistant to Emma in a variety of undertakings, and a confidant and friend to the girls long after they didn't require the services of a teacher.

As a family of increasing affluence, the Drexels followed custom by maintaining a summer residence away from the heat of the city. Again, it was not an extravagant lifestyle. During the first few years of their marriage, Frank and Emma rented a three-acre property containing a little farmhouse on Fisher's Lane in Nicetown, a section of North Philadelphia that was then countrified. This farm, which the children christened "the nest," came complete with a barn suitable for romping, chickens, and assorted animals. There was a donkey cart, too, and little Lizzie and Katie would be permitted to drive to a nearby store for kerosene for the lamps or cookies for themselves.[21] On Saturdays, in that more tranquil era, they were allowed to drive the cart to nearby Germantown to visit Grandma Langstroth, where one could usually count on a fair number of Langstroth or Figueira cousins to play with. Perhaps not as much fun were the sewing and piano lessons Grandma provided for the little girls.

Grandma Langstroth was very loving, but very proper. She never quite approved of the Drexel fondness for nicknames. To her, Elizabeth was Elizabeth, not Lizzie, and Katharine was Katharine, most certainly not Katie or Kate.

Grandma Langstroth had a special room full of toys that the children could play with when the outdoors was inhospitable. This room was filled with just about anything the 19th-century toy maker could dream up. While the children could play to their heart's content, orderly Grandma insisted everything be returned to its proper place at day's end.[22]

Almost everyone was older than Katie, which meant she didn't get first pick of the playthings. Her favorite toy, her cousin Bessie Langstroth Jardin recalled years later, was "a Negro coachman who sat in state driving a very sumptuous carriage. He would get a new velvet suit each year. As no one appeared to particularly want him, Mother Katharine adopted him as her own." Of course, one reason Katie took to the coachman was because cousin Bessie had taken six dolls and Lizzie took 17. When Grandma Langstroth discovered this, she made them share with Katie.[23]

At one point, there was very nearly a rupture in relations between the Bouvier and Langstroth families, caused by childhood innocence.

"I'm so sorry you can never go to heaven," Lizzie said one day.

"Why can't I ever go to heaven?" Grandmother Langstroth asked.

"Because you are Protestant, and Protestants never go to heaven," Lizzie said.

Needless to say, Grandmother Langstroth was very upset; what in the world was being taught to her grandchildren? When this got back to Frank and Emma, it was discovered that it was Johanna who had explained this somewhat biased theological point to the children. Lizzie and Katie were told this certainly wasn't true, and family relations were straightened out. Nevertheless, the Drexel children always prayed for the conversion (or reconversion) of their many non-Catholic relatives.[24]

Another incident Mother Katharine would later recall was a mealtime visit to her Langstroth grandparents. A guest was an elder from Grandma's congregation. Quite naturally, she asked him to offer grace. This created a dilemma for her pre-ecumenical grandchildren. How could they participate in Protestant prayer? Lizzie solved the problem. The two children held rosaries in plain sight, so it would be clearly understood they were Catholic.[25]

Sunday mornings for the little girls were spent visiting Grandmother Bouvier, who is recalled as calm and serene, quite different from her mercurial husband; and as a woman who was waited on by her adoring daughters. Sunday afternoons were spent with Grandmother Drexel, who also delighted in her little granddaughters.[26]

There is some suggestion that relations between Catherine Drexel and her daughter-in-law Emma were less than cordial, not that anyone in the family or any of the authorized biographies have left a record of this. For an indication of this, we must turn to the last will and testament of Katharine's Drexel grandmother, who died in 1870.

In her will, Catherine Drexel names her second son, Anthony, not the older Francis, as executor. After generous bequests to charity and to her daughters (her sons didn't need any money), Catherine Drexel turned to her grandchildren, leaving a sum of money to "all of my grandchildren living at the time of my death, excepting Mary L.B. Drexel, daughter of my son, Francis A. Drexel, by his present wife, and excepting also any other child or children he may have had by her...."[27]

This rather cruel provision in the will is obviously not aimed directly at Louise (Mary L.B. Drexel), who was only 6 years old. It is clearly aimed at Emma, but how she had offended her mother-in-law we can only speculate. We do know that Emma, for all of her charity, was not comfortable in social situations and often remained at home while her husband and children visited, a practice which invites misunderstanding or injured feelings.

Whatever Grandmother Drexel might have thought, baby Louise had one adoring, lifelong friend and that was Katharine. Perhaps in the very beginning, it didn't appear that way. Little Katie, not much more than a toddler herself, was fascinated by this new family member. She would pinch the little one, just to see all the adults come running to see why the baby was crying.[28] Needless to say, this stopped very quickly. The three little girls had a close bond, but while Katie was closer in age to Lizzie, her younger sister was most special to her. Louise, to Katie, was always "my little sister," or "my angel's gift." And so it would remain even when they were both elderly women. Emma dedicated baby Louise to the Blessed Virgin, and during her childhood she was always dressed in blue and/or white in honor of Mary. This would change only with Emma's death, when Louise, as did her sisters, donned mourning black.

One of Emma's charities was the Good Shepherd Sisters, and a practical way to support their work was to have the children's clothes made by the Magdalens, a related congregation comprising mostly girls and young women who had been rescued from degradation by the Sisters. While Lizzie and "Petite Louise" were content with the simple styles chosen for them by Emma, it was little Katie who would, as the family was leaving, slip away from her mother, run back, and clasp the hand of the Sister who had measured them and say, "Please do put lots of lace and ruffles on my dress, just like Mama's."[29]

This femininity of little Katie was evidenced in one of her childhood class exercise letters to Emma, in which she wrote:

Dear Mama,
I hope this letter will be an improvement on my others for I am going to take great pains to do it well. Will you have my ears pierced, for I am in such a hurry to have my ears pierced? Everybody loves earrings.
Love, Katie Drexel.[30]

Another letter hints at a need for money, but more important, a solicitude for her mother and love for her father.

"I have three dollars and 19 cents," Katie writes. "I must have 11 dollars and 81 cents."

She commiserates on her mother's headache on the first day of Lent and is thrilled by a cold snap.

"I am happy it is cold today," Katie writes, "as I can go skating with Papa. Every time that we go skating he says it is the last time."

In a note written about age 8 concerning a future excursion, Katie's budding piety is beginning to emerge.

"I am highly delighted to go to the (Delaware River) Water Gap," she records. "I suppose we will stay a week or two and every day have a big bunch of flowers. I will take a picture of the Blessed Virgin with me and let her enjoy the flowers."[31]

The devotion to the Blessed Sacrament Frank alluded to in his New Year's letter was passed on to the children, not by written word, but by example. Emma, who certainly needed no prodding from her husband on that score, would often, along with her little daughters, visit the chapel at Sacred Heart Convent on Walnut Street for meditation before the tabernacle. It was not necessarily quiet meditation. Her naturally exuberant children would at times scamper about, something that would cause eyebrows to be raised by some of the more sedate Sacred Heart Sisters.[32] But the lesson was being learned. No greater honor can be shown to God than devotion to His Presence through the Eucharist. No greater honor can be shown to man than reception of this same Presence through holy Communion.

Lizzie and Kate (and Louise in turn) received formal religious instruction and their sacraments at the Sacred Heart Convent. Lizzie was 12 in 1868 when she received first Communion. It was administered by Bishop Wood, who at the same ceremony, confirmed the first Communion class. At the time, 12 was the typical age for reception of holy Eucharist.

Even before Lizzie was permitted to approach the table of the Lord, Katie was pleading for this privilege. At age 9, she wrote a Christmas letter in French to her mother as a school exercise. Translated in part, it reads:

> I am going to make the Stations of the Cross for you, my darling Mama, and for Papa and Louise, too. I am trying to study hard so that I may make my first Communion this year. Mama dear, my letter is nearly finished. A thousand thanks, my dear Mama, for all of the Christmas presents you will give me. Nothing in the world could please me more than if you like this letter. I am hoping it will please you as much as your presents will please me.[33]

In a previous letter she had said,

> Dear Mama, I am going to make my first Communion and you will see how I shall try to be good. Let me make it in May, the most beautiful of all months.[34]

Katie, probably because of Church rules, did not make her first Communion that year. She received the sacrament from Bishop Wood on June 3, 1870. She was 11, a year younger than Lizzie had been when she received and a year younger than Louise would be when she received. As in the case of Lizzie, Katie received the sacrament of confirmation on the day of first Communion. When the cause for St. Katharine's beatification and canonization was opened in the 1960s, a diligent effort was made to locate an official sacramental record of her confirmation. No such record exists, other than family tradition and testimony of the Sacred Heart Sisters. The Sisters speculated that the records, along with many others, were lost in transit after the Sacred Heart Convent on Walnut Street closed.[35]

Katharine's focus appears to have been on the Eucharist, not confirmation. Her letters at the time do not mention being confirmed. As a matter of fact, Aunt Louise, writing from Eden Hall, was dissatisfied with a letter Katie sent her on the day of her first Communion. Emma and Frank, as was their custom, treated the bishop and the entire Communion class to a catered breakfast. Katie wrote to her aunt, regaling her with all the delights of the celebration.

Madame Bouvier, in a return note, wrote:

> I am disappointed. I did not want or care to know about the breakfast, but I did want to know your thoughts and feelings as you received our dear Lord.[36]

Katharine never forgot the rebuke. Many years later in a retreat note she wrote:

> I remember my First Communion and my letter on that day. Jesus made me shed many tears because of His greatness in stooping to me. Truth made me feel the mite I was. I did not realize nor was I ashamed of my sensuality....[37]

When the Sacred Heart Sisters closed their Walnut Street convent, they presented the Drexel family with the little altar where the three children had received their sacraments, and on which, each in turn, had been dedicated to the Blessed Virgin. At different times, it graced the family oratory, served as a temporary altar at St. Francis Industrial School (founded by the Drexel sisters in memory of their father), as the altar for Mother Katharine's first novitiate, and as the chapel altar for Mother Katharine's St. Francis de Sales School in Rock Castle, Virginia. It is now a precious heirloom cherished by the Blessed Sacrament Sisters in their Bensalem, Pennsylvania, motherhouse.

If Katie had waxed poetic about the delicacies of her first Communion breakfast, it may be because, in spite of her family's affluence, this was not her usual fare, and she had not yet conditioned herself to welcome the austerity that would be so much a part of her later life.

Returning to her 1867 Christmas letter, Katie had pleaded with Emma:

> Oh! What fun I shall have enjoying bonbons and receiving so many

lovely things. Mama dear, before going any further with this letter, I must ask you to let Louise have some bonbons, too. You were saying that she does not know the taste of bonbons. I assure you that she knows the taste of them very well. Now that she knows almost the whole alphabet, you will let her have some bonbons? She is just a little girl, so intelligent and sweet, you really cannot refuse her some sweets.[38]

Later, Mother Katharine would confide to Sisters in her congregation that she would as a child wish for more sweets and fewer useful gifts for Christmas. It was, she said, the only time of the year Emma permitted the children to have candy. The Drexel family lifestyle was full of such contradictions. There was the handsome townhouse in the best part of town. There were the servants, and at times, lavish entertainment, so necessary in the professional life of a captain of commerce. There were possessions.

But while the Drexels owned "things," they resisted the temptation to allow possessions to own them. Emma's china closet was well stocked with rare and delicate examples of the potter's craft, such bric-a-brac people of wealth give as gifts to other people of wealth.

Emma was fond of her china, but within reason. The same cabinet displayed a placard: "If thou hast a piece of earthenware," says Epictetus, "consider that it is a piece of earthenware and therefore fragile and easily to be broken. Be not therefore so devoid of reason as to be angry or grieved when this comes to pass."[39]

Francis Drexel, throughout his lifetime, transacted many successful business ventures. None were of greater impact, in the eyes of his family, than one negotiated in 1870. This was the year he purchased a 70-acre farm in Torresdale, along the Poquessing Creek at the northeastern edge of Philadelphia. This certainly pleased Emma, because it was within a mile of Eden Hall, the convent school of her childhood days, where her sister, Madame Louise, was now in residence, and was not far from "Fairview," the summer home of the Bouvier family. It had a comfortable if unassuming farmhouse that Frank expanded into a suitable summer home. It pleased the children, too, because it was a great place to romp and play, and it held a lifelong attraction for the Drexel sisters. This new home was christened St. Michel, in honor of the patron of Emma's father. A statue of the archangel, carved from imported French stone, was placed above the lintel.

As at Walnut Street, Elizabeth and Katharine shared a bedroom; Louise slept in her mother's room, and Frank took a back bedroom because he preferred its coolness. Emma installed an oratory here, too; it was located between Elizabeth and Katharine's room and the spare bedroom. Here, Archbishop Wood, during his annual stay with the Drexels, would celebrate Mass. He also granted permission for periodic Masses by visiting priests.

One neighbor was General Thomas Kilby Smith who had fought under General Grant during the Civil War. General Smith was a convert to Catholicism, and like the Drexels, his family often worshiped at Eden Hall. His children, Walter, Theodore, Dehan, Adrian, and Helen Grace, became fast and lifelong friends with the Drexel sisters.

Life at St. Michel was less structured than at Walnut Street, but Mary Cassidy would still visit to keep the girls under a somewhat lighter regimen of studies. Then, too, there was the little Sunday school that Emma established. Because there was no Catholic church in the immediate neighborhood, many of the children had no formal Catholic training. The Sunday school was at first intended for the children of employees, but it grew until its heyday when more than 50 children were attending. It lasted until 1888.

The school was Emma's idea, but it was Lizzie (by now a more elegant Lise), 14, and Kate, 11, who did the work.

Louise gives a delightfully humorous account of the school in operation in a "St. Michel Daily Bulletin," which she wrote to keep her vacationing older sisters informed of the doings at St. Michel. Because the girls were away, Emma was the substitute teacher, but she had delegated duties to Louise and to servants and older children.

It was mooted that Mrs. D. would come down to San Luigi and become preceptress to the juniors, Louise writes. The scholars heard of this. At one time, Mr. Wheelan was heard to exclaim, "Here she comes, Mrs. Drexel's comin'." A rush for benches and a sudden howl from Mr. Buckley: "I'm sick."

This was a lucky excitement, as the order not before of the best, was immediately restored. Mr. Wheelan endeavored to secrete himself behind the door, which endeavor was nipped in the bud. Miss Tobin was in her sphere: "Boys, I am ashamed! Oh, what would Miss Kate say?" and other like expressions escaped from her lips.

Miss O'Neill also rejoiced in her temporary authority, and the editor was witness without being a witness to the box on the ear administered by the hammer (O'Neill's hand). As the editor left, Miss Tobin was gloating over three small children who were kept in! The first class signally failed, but the second was perfect. When asked what saints were, Mr. Wheelan replied that Mel Hagiman was one. He was not committed for contempt of court.

Mr. Buckley was 'devilish' as usual and wanted to know who would teach next Sunday. Was not satisfactorily answered. W. Cox's aside was, "I would love to hear Miss Louise sing."

Atonement was transfigured to astonishment and persons dying in mortal sin were sent to limbo or purgatory.

The associate will in all probability take Miss Tobin's class at San Luigi tomorrow. A neat pile of handkerchiefs will be provided for the time when infantile fountains will be turned on by the ruthless associate.[40]

The limbo referred to by Louise was a small storage room over the kitchen and consequently usually very hot, according to one family account. Presumably, purgatory was an equally uncomfortable section of the house.

Emma encouraged her daughters to take upon themselves some of the household chores, not so much through their own labors as through the supervision of the servants. Lise had general supervision of the kitchen and stables; Kate the general housework; and Louise the barn and grounds.

In addition to their warm-weather and Christmas holiday stays at St. Michel, the Drexels would usually take a fall excursion, perhaps to the White Mountains in New Hampshire or another of America's scenic wonders. While her aging parents lived, Emma was unwilling to travel great distances. The first family excursion to Europe — then almost a must for wealthy Americans — was in the fall of 1874, and they stayed abroad for nine months. It was the traditional grand tour, starting in England and wending through France, Italy, Germany, Austria, and Switzerland. Johanna Ryan traveled with the group.

The sisters sent weekly letters home to Mary Cassidy that told much about their adventures and something about their faith development. For instance, we find Lise and Kate wandering the streets of Vienna for an entire day in a vain search for a priest who can hear confessions in English. Finally, they find a priest whose English is very limited, but at his suggestion, they confess in French, a language they knew very well.

Christmas was spent in sunny Naples, but Kate would have preferred the family Christmas at St. Michel.[41] Another Italian city visited was Bologna. Kate had a lifelong devotion to St. Catherine of Siena, and while in Bologna, a guide told her of a shrine to her patron saint. At the Church of St. Catherine, the guide asked a priest to open a side chapel, where, surrounded by burning candles, the time-blackened but otherwise preserved corpse of St. Catherine was seated in a chair. It was unembalmed, but her guide informed them that it was "just as limber as it had been when placed in the chapel 450 years ago." Kate wrote in her letter to Mary Cassidy, "The whole effect of the shrine was awful."

After kneeling in prayer, the girls were told it was customary to kiss the saint's foot. All of this was much more than Lise and Kate had bargained for, but they respectfully did as they were told.

Only afterward did Kate discover this had not been St. Catherine of Siena, but Catherine of Bologna, a distinguished saint in her own right. "I did not know such a saint existed, did you Miss Cassidy?" Kate wrote.[42]

During their Rome visit they almost missed a chance to see Pope Pius IX, but at the last minute an audience was arranged. In keeping with custom, Louise carried a new white calotte, or cap, in hopes that the Pope would give her his in exchange. After teasing the little girl a bit about how her cap was too thin and too small, the Pope playfully tossed his cap on her head and accepted her gift in exchange. Johanna Ryan, who accompanied the family to the Vatican, was completely overcome with emotion. She threw herself at the Pope's feet, grasped his legs and exclaimed, "Holy Father, praise God and His Blessed Mother. My eyes have seen the Lord Himself."[43]

For Kate, another stop had perhaps had the most profound effect. The anticipation of a visit to Lourdes "was the only thing that reconciled me to leaving Rome," she wrote. She knelt at the grotto to implore the blessing of the Immaculate Conception. Afterward, she wrote to her teacher:

> "I attributed to no superstition the spiritual refreshment that I drank from the clear fountain which she herself caused to flow and which has been the channel of so many wonderful blessings."[44]

The girls returned to Philadelphia with a new sense of the wonders of the world. During the family stays at St. Michel, St. Dominic's, somewhat more than two miles away in Philadelphia's Holmesburg section, would be their parish of residence. In addition to St. Dominic, there was Maternity of the Blessed Virgin Mary in Bustleton, just slightly farther from St. Michel than St. Dominic. It was here, as a change of pace, the two older Drexel daughters would ride on horseback for morning Mass.

"We have become attached to the little church there by this time," Lise wrote in 1878. "There is a little stream outside, that, in concert with the birds, keeps murmuring a chant all Mass."

For Kate, St. Dominic's would have a critical role in her life, through Father James O'Connor, who arrived as pastor in 1872. Father O'Connor, whose brother, Michael O'Connor, was bishop of Pittsburgh, had emigrated to America at age 15 from Queenstown, Ireland. He studied for the priesthood at Philadelphia's St. Charles Borromeo Seminary and in Rome, where he became friends with the future Bishop Wood who also was a student in the Eternal City.

When Father O'Connor was ordained in 1848, he transferred to the Pittsburgh Diocese where he served as rector of St. Michael Seminary. In 1862, he returned to Philadelphia as rector of St. Charles Seminary.

Father O'Connor, who by reputation was something of an idealist and a visionary, eventually had a disagreement with Bishop Wood on the course of study at the seminary and the rector's advocacy of the introduction of athletics, especially baseball. In the end, Father O'Connor resigned his seminary post. If his subsequent appointment to the little country parish of St. Dominic was seen as a form of exile, he never spoke against Bishop Wood. It was a fortuitous exile for St. Katharine Drexel. Father O'Connor, more than anyone else, would influence the form her future religious vocation would take. He remained her spiritual adviser for the rest of his life.[45]

Father O'Connor served as pastor of St. Dominic for only four years, until 1876 when he was elevated to the rank of bishop and named vicar apostolic of Nebraska, and eventually, first bishop of Omaha. His vicariate extended into the Dakotas and Wyoming, as the Catholic population was rapidly expanding. By the time of his death in 1885, Catholics had increased from 30,000 to 300,000 in five dioceses, including Omaha, where he was the founding bishop.

In his four years at St. Dominic, Father O'Connor had developed a spiritual bond with Kate and apparently also with Lise. "I hope that I may be excused for thinking of you as one and the same person," he would write in a 1879 letter, "and for thinking that whatever is said to one is said to both. If this be a mistake your love for each other has led me into it."

At age 17, Kate writes to Father O'Connor, telling him of the happenings in Philadelphia — Sister Julia of the Notre Dame Sisters is trying to establish a school for the Colored. As for herself, she tells of a visit with Miss Cassidy to a synagogue, singing lessons, and the doings of the Sunday School.

She writes:

> I have a class of 16 young gentlemen, hardly one of which has reached the mature age of seven or eight. It is delightful to listen to them whilst they say 'Hail Mary, full of grace,' we expect however, to go to Holy Communion once a week, and I only hope that the grace received in the wonderful sacrament will impart to me a little of its love.[46]

The year 1878 was one of change for Kate. July 2 marked the end of her formal education, an event that she welcomed with neither despair nor hilarity. Writing to Bishop O'Connor, Kate said, "One looks forward so many years to finishing school, and when at last the time comes, a kind of sadness steals over one whose cause is hard to analyze... the future suddenly looks all vague and uncertain."

At this point in her life, Kate is still very much of the world and fully enjoying it. The month after her "graduation," Lise's journal entry speaks in glowing terms of a three-day visit to Cape May, New Jersey, with Papa and Kate. "We met two old friends down there (Emma Andrews & Fanny Paul) but much to Kate's chagrin made no new ones — (I think this is the one regret in the mind of my dear sociable little sister). What a pity our inexorable sire would not have stayed longer."

The following January Kate made her formal debut into society.

As Bishop O'Connor wrote from Omaha:

> Perhaps I ought not to 'Katie' you any longer. ...You are no longer a child, but a young lady.... 'My dear child,' or 'My dear friend,' or 'My dear Miss Katie' or what? It is better to have a clear understanding on this matter. I only hope it may never be 'My dear Condessa,' or 'My dear Marchesa' or even 'My dear Princepessa.' God protect you from the fate that would involve such a title! I have known two and heard of several other young American ladies to whom such titles fell, but I hope and pray that you may never be as unfortunate as they![47]

While there was no apparent danger of Katharine Drexel becoming enamored by a foreign title, we do know that she had a reasonably active social life, even if Frank and Emma took great pains to ensure their daughters traveled in protected circles.

At one point, in early 1883 when she was 24, she received a marriage proposal. She told no one about it at the time other than her father. He had told her he would be agreeable to any decision she made, because he desired her happiness. Katharine wrote of this to Bishop O'Connor, but did not say who her suitor was, and downplayed the proposal, saying, "I have refused the offered heart. I have every reason to believe it was not a very ardent one."[48]

While Katharine never said who the proposal came from, Sister Consuela Duffy, her 1965 biographer, while giving testimony for the beatification process, said, "I have an idea the man was Walter George Smith who married her sister, Elizabeth."[49]

The sole mention of a specific "gentleman caller" in Katharine's papers was written when she was only 17. "Frank Patterson was waiting to pay me a visit when I got home," she wrote in January 1876. In a charmingly innocent visit, the young man stayed until 9 p.m., discussing an electric alarm he had designed and looking at engravings in a Bible. While Frank was a cousin, he was a Bouvier cousin, which meant he was not a blood relative to either Katharine or Elizabeth. He could technically be a suitor, but Katharine was relatively young at that time, and there are no other documents that suggest a special friendship between the two, either then or later.[50]

The year 1876 was a time of joy in Philadelphia. From January 1 on there were parades, balls and other extravaganzas as the nation revisited its birthplace for the centennial of its founding. The Drexel diaries are full of stories of the social doings — attending the grand opening of the Centennial exhibit in Fairmount Park in the company of the German ambassador, the street demonstrations, and the visits, wanted and unwanted, of a multiplicity of cousins.

On the last night of 1875, the family strolled the streets. Kate was disappointed to find that many residents of Walnut Street had ignored the mayor's request that all citizens drape their houses with patriotic bunting and illuminate the windows. The more commercial Chestnut Street was much livelier in its enthusiastic displays.

The two girls had drifted into slumber when the centennial year rang in. Kate writes:

> The joyful ringing of many church bells, the solemn boom of the cannons, the melancholy sound of penny trumpets awakened Lise and me from a sound sleep and admonished us that the Old Year had come to a close and that 1876 our Centennial year at last arrived. We sat up in our beds till the last peal of the bells died away, wished that we were at Independence Hall to see the hoisting of the United States flag, and then I blush to say that we spontaneously sunk on our pillows not even to dream of the old patriots whose heroic love of country caused liberty to be rung throughout the land, nearly 100 years ago.[51]

One souvenir of this glittering year remains, virtually unnoticed. It is a stained glass window in St. Elizabeth Convent, St. Katharine's motherhouse. At first glance, the convent chapel has but four windows in stained glass — portraits of St. Catherine of Siena, St. Elizabeth, and St. Louis of France — the patrons for the three Drexel sisters, and finally, the Bouvier family patron, St. Michael the Archangel. All are rather grim-faced, not the sort of images that reflect the holy joy that was a characteristic of the Drexels. Only four of the side windows were executed in stained glass because two were gifts from Louise, imported from England. World War II intervened before her project was completed, and by war's end, she was dead. Two more were given by Xavier University. Mother Katharine declined to finish the project, reasoning, "the money would be better spent on the poor."

A more careful look reveals another window, high up in the choir loft, especially beautiful in the afternoon sun. It depicts three young women happily at work at various tasks. The title is "Industry."

Where did it come from? At Christmas time in 1876, Emma wished to present Lise with a stained glass window of St. Elizabeth for the bedroom she shared with Kate. No such window could be readily found or crafted on short notice. Then, among decorative items being sold off from the centennial exhibit, Emma found this winsome trio in glass. How similar these three charming girls were to her own daughters — or at least how she wished her daughters to be. Emma bought the window and had it installed in the girls' bedroom. Years later, probably when the Walnut Street property was sold, this beloved memento was rescued. There it is in a convent chapel; a secular allegory to virtue in the company of saints.

With adulthood, Lise and Kate began to spend more time away from the family hearth. Large portions of the summer were spent visiting with the Anthony Drexels, various Bouviers, the Childs family, or other friends and relations at Long Branch or Cape May in New Jersey, or the Hudson Valley and Lake George in New York, but never more than two weeks at a single time.

During these visits, their hosts, as friends and relatives are ever inclined to do, made certain these highly eligible young ladies met suitable bachelors.

"I hope you are careful not to get into deep water either with the beaux or the surf," Frank Drexel cautioned his daughters, who were vacationing in Cape May. Generally speaking, while we see Frank, schedule permitting, joining the girls during these friendly visits, Emma usually remained at St. Michel.[52]

An 1884 letter from Kate to Bishop O'Connor tells of Emma's preference to remain behind, yet never to do anything to hinder her daughters' social development.

> She plainly saw the vanity vanitas, and did not hide the fact from us. She never prevented us from entering society, in fact, she encouraged it, provided us with the means to go into the world abundantly so that our friends marveled at the variety and elegance of our toilets. We loved her dearly, as well we might, and our family union was complete in every respect. Yet we found that if we gave our lives or even a part of them to the world, we could not be in entire accord with her, for she was not 'of the world.' It was because we appreciated close intimacy with her that we left others for her. I do not wish you to think for a moment that Mama ever advised us to keep from society. Indeed, often I have heard her reproach herself because she had not gone more unto the world for our sakes. If, however, she were to devote even a part of her time to visiting, the duties which she must perform at that time must go unfulfilled.[53]

Chapter Four
Trials and Meditation

Even as Katharine gained full womanhood, the first hint of future sadness manifested itself. In the latter part of 1879, Emma Drexel was not feeling well; she was constantly tired with recurring pain. Rather than alarm the family, she consulted a physician privately. Emma had what proved to be a cancerous growth, and the doctor advocated hospitalization for its removal. Emma declined, but rather, while the family was at St. Michel, she returned to the city on a pretext and had the surgery performed in her Walnut Street home. The operation did more harm than good, and in the end her concerned husband and children had to be told.[1]

Emma's illness did not proceed with merciful speed; it continued for more than three years.

Family life revolved around her comfort, and during periods of remission, restful vacations would be taken, but at not so great a distance as to tax her dwindling energy. In 1882, while the Drexels were vacationing at Sharon Springs, New York, Louise also fell ill.[2] While the records do not state the precise nature of her illness, hers was a slow recovery. It may be that she suffered from the first of a series of nervous disorders that would mar her later life.

"God spared us trials for a very long time and we have been exempt from the common lot," Frank wrote in a letter to his friends, George and Emma Childs, "and if His mercy sees fit to afflict us, we must endeavor to bear it with resignation, knowing that it is for our own good.

...Lizzie and Kate have been good and affectionate daughters and most efficient nurses — they take turns in attending. God has blessed us with the best of children."

Emma's two nurses had quite different personalities. Lizzie was a down-to-earth Martha; Kate was an ethereal Mary. Emma's realization of this is manifested by an extraordinary dream she had in 1880 and is related in a letter she wrote to her daughters:

My Own Darlings:
Last night I had a dream in which I saw a painting of a door, such as we have often remarked in the walls of church sanctuaries abroad, the opening of reliquaries and tabernacles all bedecked and bejeweled, and it was locked. I inquired for the key and Kate informed me that the meaning of this painting was that Jesus held the key, as this was the door to His Heart, which He opened only to those who knocked and asked. You, Lizzie, smiled at Kate's pious interpretation, which you denounced as gammon and spinach, and I became alarmed at the thought of your incredulity. At this conjuncturem I awakened with the entire scene impressed upon my mind, but its meaning and origin I have not yet been able to resolve.3

Even the best of children could not spare their mother the pain of her affliction. Emma's primary physician was a homeopath who believed in natural medicines, and as a consequence, painkillers were not prescribed until late in her illness. "Oh Frank," she exclaimed one day, "How I pray that when your time comes you will be spared all this, and I now offer all the pain I suffer for you."

Emma's suffering came to a merciful end on January 29, 1883, when she entered into eternal life. At the time of her death, her magnificent charity was publicized through the newspapers. She had been quietly paying the rent for 150 families, and it was estimated that she had dispensed more than $1 million in charity over the preceding 20 years.4

Emma, whose funeral was attended by many of the poor she had served, was entombed in the Bouvier vault at St. Mary's churchyard. This was a temporary arrangement; in time, Frank obtained permission from Archbishop Wood to build a new Lady Chapel at Eden Hall in her memory which would also contain a crypt for the Drexel family.

The day Emma Bouvier Drexel was buried, Francis Drexel came home and shut himself up in the music room. He played for hours, pouring forth the grief of his soul in heartbreakingly sad music. The effect Emma's illness and death would have on her two stepdaughters is quite interesting, but yet totally in keeping with their individual personalities. Both Elizabeth and Katharine were, at this point in their lives, weighing the possibility of a religious vocation. It was during her mother's illness that a thought of the religious life became most insistent, as Mother Katharine would, in her later life, tell the Sisters of her congregation. Before that, while she loved God and tried to serve Him as faithfully as she could, and while she "admired the religious life," she had "never seriously thought of being a religious."[5]

Elizabeth, however, came to exactly the opposite conclusion. Months after Emma's death, on Good Friday, in "the year of our sorrow," Elizabeth wrote of her personal decision in her diary.

> Sweet it is to weep at the foot of the Cross and there, Thank God! I have found refuge and consolation. But now the finger of the Lord clearly points to me the way of the active life. There I will find my cross if I pick it up and follow Jesus. There will the footsteps of my mother mark out for me a well-beaten path.[6]

A year later, as she would further write:

> Our meditations on the life of Christ would seem to teach us that to suffer patiently the will of God is even more pleasing to Him than even to accomplish great things for the glory of His name. When I resume in my own mind the edifying life of my darling mother, so full of activity and usefulness, so pure in its intention of pleasing God, all her charities which the world at large dwells on so much — all her devotion to duty — her turning resolutely aside from the influence of the world — all, all beautiful as they are, seem to me less than her final sufferings endured (and so hard to endure) at the hand of God and her surrendering herself to Him at His call in the vigor of her age, and in the very middle of her work.

Married or single, Elizabeth would stay in the world and pick up that wonderful burden of charity which, in death, her stepmother had set aside.

Katharine, at this point, wished to pick up a different burden. She was being drawn to the religious life. Would Emma have opposed her choice? In the end, probably not. She was far too pious a woman for that. It was her desire that her daughters, should they wish to enter a convent, put off the decision until they were at least 25 years old. But had Emma lived, family-centered Katharine's decision would have been rendered all the harder.[7]

Katharine would, in later years, speak of the friendly arguments between her mother and her aunt, Madame Louise Bouvier, at Eden Hall, as to which was the better choice, lay or religious.[8]

Although Emma, as a young girl, had considered the convent herself, she was of the opinion women in their station in life could more effectively serve God through direct charity while remaining in the world. It is quite possible her choice was colored by the memory of the drama surrounding her sister's entry into the Religious of the Sacred Heart against their father's wishes.

In any case, Emma Bouvier Drexel had been clearly the most important single religious influence of the formative years of St. Katharine Drexel. She did not — and could not — make her daughter a saint; Katharine did this herself through her unique application of God's graces to her own life. But the Holy Spirit can work in an indirect fashion. Emma, one of the uncanonized saints of the Church, was the conduit for many of the graces which, especially through example, formed St. Katharine.

While the desire for a retreat from the world into the cloister was forming in Kate's mind, it was not her sole preoccupation. The 1870s and 1880s were a time when Americans were becoming more aware of the shameful treatment suffered by the first citizens of America — the Native Americans.

From the time of the first explorers, they had been slowly pushed away from areas of settlement; now they were mostly in the West, more often than not confined to lands too infertile to be coveted by the white interlopers.

Many of the Native Americans, living in a virtually stone age culture inherited and passed down from their fathers, were ill-equipped to compete in a society dominated by the more literate and technologically advanced whites. In spite of many years of evangelization by dedicated missionaries of all denominations, the old, pre-Christian culture prevailed.

President Ulysses Grant was one of the first to implement a policy that was designed to end the cycle of poverty among the Native Americans and draw them into the mainstream culture. Grant, in his 1870 "Peace Policy," proposed to turn the Indian agencies and Indian schools over to the administration of various religious denominations, especially those that had been active in missionary work with the individual tribes. The religious denominations would build facilities and provide personnel; the federal government would provide monetary support to the institutions through contracts. The schools were usually boarding schools where Native-American children, separated from parental and tribal influence, would learn the ways of the white men, and it was hoped, thereafter be able to compete on equal footing. By 19th-century standards, this was considered a humane and enlightened policy. While today it would be considered a politically incorrect violation of parental rights and deliberate cultural genocide, the policy must be judged by its time and its undeniably good intentions.

Grant's policy certainly seemed to bode well for the Catholic Church, because for many of these tribes, their only contact with Christianity had been through Catholic missionaries. There were 72 Indian agencies; by Catholic reckoning, contracts for 38 of these agencies should have been awarded to the Catholic Church because Catholic missionaries had been their first or principal Christian contact. When the contracts were awarded, the Catholic Church received only eight.[9]

Protestants, of course, thought this was perfectly fair. The Catholics had received contracts in proportion to their numerical presence in the American population. It was a case of which opposing arguments had greater weight.

The Catholic position probably had the greater justice for two reasons. First of all, the Peace Policy was supposed to award contracts not by population proportion, but by previous missionary activity. Secondly, no one asked the Native Americans what their view was in all of this. It is estimated that 80,000 previously Catholic Native Americans were placed under the supervision of Protestant missionaries through the policy. A letter in October 1874 by Joseph Paw-Ne-No-Posh, governor of the Osages and 120 others, to Columbus Delano, Secretary of the Interior, protested: "Religion among the whites is a matter of conscience and voluntary choice. It is so among our neighboring tribes and nations in the Indian territory; it is so throughout all Christendom; and why should it not be so among the Osages? Give us, we beseech you, our choice in this matter." Catholic missionaries, he said, "have been among our people for several generations."[10]

Eventually, in 1881, all denominations were granted equal access to the reservations. But there was another complication. Even if the federal government had now done the right thing, from a Catholic point of view, where in the world were the missionaries to come from to minister to the men, women, and children on the reservations? And while the federal government would subsidize tuition, the Church must first build the schools. Later, when St. Katharine became a major force in Native-American (and African-American) evangelization, her single-handed subsidy went a long way toward erecting schools, but scarcity of personnel would be her greatest frustration. She had the money and the zeal; priests and Sisters in sufficient quantity were quite another matter.

The bald fact is, the 19th-century American Catholic Church was not in an evangelizing mode. The bishops in Indian Territory did the best they could with limited resources. Their Eastern brothers were expending most of their energy and resources on serving the ever-increasing numbers of birth Catholics emigrating to America. What evangelization was being done was more likely to be the conversion of Protestant spouses, recovery of backsliding Catholics, or reconversion of former Catholics lost to the Church through a lack of sufficient priests and Sisters in their area.

In 1874, the American bishops established the Bureau of Catholic Indian Missions to combat the inequities of the contract system, to coordinate education and evangelization, and to cooperate with the other denominations in areas of mutual interest. The first director was Father J.B.A. Brouillett. Father Joseph A. Stephan succeeded him in 1884 and served until 1900. The purpose of the bureau was:

> 1) To direct the administration of those agencies as were assigned to the care of Catholic missionaries.
>
> 2) To secure, if possible, the remainder of those agencies to which Catholic missionaries were justly entitled under the terms of the peace policy.
>
> 3) To protect the religious faith and material interests of all Catholic Indians.
>
> 4) To secure the establishment of suitable schools for Indian boys and girls;
>
> 5) To procure for the Indians moral and practical Christian teachers with adequate compensation for their services and to develop a general interest in Indian education
>
> 6) To secure means with which to erect the school buildings, in all cases possible.[11]

The bureau, which continues to this day, received considerable support from Katharine Drexel, both as a lay woman and a nun. Other initiatives, especially through Vatican prodding, would be undertaken for the evangelization of Native Americans, and of equal importance, African Americans.

Bishop O'Connor's transfer to Nebraska Territory in 1876 could only increase Katharine's interest in this apostolate, but it was hardly the genesis of her concern. For instance, in an 1873 school essay written by Katharine at age 15, we see a not-so-subtle suggestion of the future. It is a long Christmas narrative based upon the history of the Ursuline Nuns in Quebec, and especially on their work among the Native Americans in the 17th century.

The tale is loaded with 19th-century melodrama. There is a fire at a convent school, and one of the heroic Sisters loses her life while saving the lives of the young Indian girls in her care. In adulthood one of the Indian maidens becomes the wife of an especially fierce warrior-chief. Through her influence (and indirectly the Ursulines), he is converted to peaceful Christianity.

What is intriguing is the prophetic parallel between the Ursuline nuns of Katharine's romantic narrative and her own future choice of vocation, suggesting at least an unconscious desire at this tender age to serve God through service to Native Americans.

The teen Katharine wrote:

> These ladies born to the mild climate of France, brought up amid all the luxury that wealth with rank could procure, had come to this wilderness to spend a life of unimaginable hardship among poor Indian children in order that these darkened souls should receive that gift of faith which these generous women burned to impart.[12]

Another witness to Katharine's youthful advocacy of the Native Americans is her cousin George Dixon, who, writing in 1929, said:

> My thoughts flew back to the early 1870s, I think. I recall you championing those — just beginning to be downtrodden — owners of the soil (Native Americans) — I remonstrated and said they were blocking our progress and must be subdued.... I ask at this later date pardon for such attitude — our country should force tribute on all constructed organizations drawing profit from forest, soil, ore...all such that be paid to alienate suffering from the owner (real) of the land.[13]

But while Kate had a deep concern for the welfare of Native Americans, and especially to bringing them to God through the Catholic Church, her great preoccupation was on her own spiritual development. This is evidenced through diaries, New Year's resolutions, and letters to her spiritual director, Bishop O'Connor.

In a meditation recorded when she was about 15, Kate writes:

> Vacation has now commenced and I now take the resolution to say prayers, etc. for 3/4 of an hour every day. I will first say the beads for Grandma Langstroth, my Scapular, the Sacred Heart and Cord of St. Joseph prayer for a happy death and that I make a good Confession. Then a meditation and Father Faber 5 pages. I will try to be patient and kind, overcome v. (vanity) and p. (pride), etc., etc. My meditation today is on death. Every single thing we do is making death easier or harder. There are 3 kinds of preparation for death — 1. the entire series of life; 2. a conscious and intentional fashioning of our lives generally with a view to death; 3. viz. the special preparation for death, viz. spiritual exercises, retreats and penances which have death for their object.

Kate's 1874 New Year's resolutions could be taken from a standard school-girls' examination of conscience: "Resolved that during this year '74 to overcome impurity, pride and vanity. To speak French. Attention to prayers, attention to studies." But they also show a certain introspection beyond the mechanical recitation of standard faults:

> Another year has again come 'round, and I will renew my resolutions again for I am but little better than then in purity. I was much better in May than I am now because I suppose I have relied too much on myself. P. and V. is just the same, or a very little better or worse. In impatience with God's help I am a little better although I have not the same occasion for sinning....14

Bishop O'Connor well knew this was a rare soul who had entrusted her spiritual life to his care. She recorded some of his advice that she intended to follow:

> 1. Never to omit my morning prayers, but to devote 5 to 8 minutes in the morning devotions to a prayer-book.
> 2. During the day, and if you prefer, when the hour strikes, offer up all your actions to God.
> 3. Make a meditation in "Following of Christ" or other book for about 15 minutes, or perhaps less time. Read a life of the saint or some good book such as "the Monks of the West" every three months. Novels of the day, etc. every once in a while.
> 4. Examine conscience thoroughly every day to see if the duties proposed have been fulfilled. Never stay over 15 minutes in examining your confession. Take the advice of your confessor for he has more responsibility than you, and believe what he tells you.15

Bishop O'Connor's advice is excellent and reflects common sense. Yes, do pray regularly and read devotional materials. But take time to read lighter things, too — "novels of the day." Don't overdo the examination of conscience, and he later added, "Try to go to confession less as if you were going to execution." He clearly worried lest Kate develop an unwholesome scrupulosity, a trap that has caused so much mental anguish to so many of the truly holy.

Kate was still a young girl, but before Bishop O'Connor departed for Nebraska, he bade her pray daily that she may know her vocation in life.

Love for the Blessed Sacrament, first manifested in her childhood request for the reception of first Communion, continues to mature during this time.

But hers was an era in which casual reception of the Sacred Host was discouraged.

"I wish very much at present to receive dear Jesus," she wrote, "for it has been so long since I have been to Holy Communion. But I'm so awfully unworthy of this greatest of favors, sinning every second...."

In another entry, she writes:

> Lent has commenced and still I am as bad as ever and perhaps worse. How is it possible that I could treat Him so badly after all he has done for me? I hope I will make a good Confession next Saturday and the Bread of Life will strengthen me against all evil. Is it not wonderful to think of that infinite love shown by Him to us miserable sinners?[16]

Self-denial, something Emma had inculcated in her daughters at an early age, dominates Kate's resolutions for 1882.

> Not to think of self but of God in all things. To renounce self. By frequent offerings, by hastily stopping the least vain thought of self.
> No cake for 1882.
> No preserves until June, 1882.
> No grapes, no honey until July 1st.[17]

It is reasonably clear from Bishop O'Connor's parting admonition to Katharine that she pray daily to discover her vocation, that the possibility of her entry into the convent had crossed his mind. But throughout his correspondence he appears to discourage, rather than encourage, such a course. The bishop was her spiritual adviser, however, not her confessor. This he could not be, because of distance. Jesuit Father D.J. McGoldrick was her confessor. He appeared to be much more open to her possible vocation and suggested an Ignatian exercise to her: Write out all the reasons for and against entering religious life, then consider the two arguments.

A long sheet prepared by Katharine in 1883 does just so.[18]

MY REASONS FOR ENTERING RELIGION	MY OBJECTIONS FOR ENTERING RELIGION
1. Jesus Christ has given His life for me. It is but just that I should give Him mine. Now in religion we offer ourselves to God in a direct state; natural motives prompt us to sacrifice self.	**1.** How could I bear separation from my family? I who have never been away from home two weeks. At the end of one week I have invariably felt "homesick."

2. We were created to love God. In religious life we return Our Lord's love for love by a constant voluntary sacrifice to our feelings, our inclinations, our appetites against all of which nature powerfully rebels, but it is by conquering the flesh that the soul lives.

3. I know in truth that the love of the most perfect creature is vain in comparison with Divine Love.

4. When all shadows shall have passed away I shall rejoice if I have given in life an entire heart to God.

5. In the religious life our Last End is kept continually before the mind.

6. A higher place in Heaven is secured for all eternity.

7. The attainment of perfection should be our chief employment in life. Our Lord has laid a price upon its acquirement when He says, "If thou wilt be perfect go sell what thou hast and give to the poor and thou shalt have treasure in Heaven and come follow Me; He that followeth Me walketh not in darkness." How can I doubt that these words are true wisdom, and if true wisdom, why not act upon them?

8. Katharine listed nothing for number 8.

9. If I should leave all I possess, I am sure that my wealth would be employed by my father and my sister to far greater advantage or at least to as great advantage as I myself could employ it.

2. I hate community life. I should think it maddening to come in constant contact with many different old maidish dispositions. I hate never to be alone.

3. I fear that I should murmur at the commands of my superior and return a proud spirit to her reproofs.

4. Superiors are frequently selected on account of their holiness, *not* for ability. I should hate to owe submission to a woman whom I felt to be stupid, and whose orders showed her thorough want of judgment.

5. In the religious life how can spiritual dryness be endured?

6. When with very slight variety the same things are exacted of me day in and day out, year in and year out, I fear weariness, disgust and a want of final perseverance which might lead me to leave the convent. And what then!!

7. I do not know how I could bear the privations and poverty of the religious life. I have never been deprived of luxuries.

Kate sent this very intriguing thesis and antithesis along to Bishop O'Connor for evaluation. This was in May 1883; synthesis would have to wait several years.

To complicate matters, she also includes a list pro and con about marriage. Among the reasons for, we see: "I should like to be loved with that devoted and special affection which (I imagine) a true husband feels for and shows to his wife," and "I think it a glorious destiny to bring forth souls," and further, "I should like the joys of motherhood."

This, too, is an Ignatian exercise, accompanied by balancing reasons why she should deny herself marriage for a life in religion dedicated to God. It was in this letter, too, that Katharine revealed that she had received (and rejected) a marriage proposal. "I think it is clearly my vocation at present to remain an old maid," Kate tells the bishop.

> I have tried to lay open my heart to you. But it is a difficult matter to know ourselves, and I trust I have not been self-deceived. If my papers are all wrong, please tell me, and in what way, and I shall make as many attempts as you may require of me. If you were to tell me you thought that God called me to the married state, I should feel that a great weight were off my mind and yet I should not in the least feel satisfied with the consequence of such a decision, namely — a low place in Heaven. The religious life seems to be a great, risky speculation. If it succeeds I gain immense treasure, but if I fail I am ruined.[19]

That would seem to be a rather dramatic overstatement of the risks, but not when one remembers the attitudes of the era. To enter the convent was a high calling indeed, but woe to the woman who entered and left for any reason other than health or family responsibility. It was more than frowned upon. Hence, Katharine's "if I fail I am ruined," means both in the opinion of others and in the eyes of God.

The good bishop's answer to Kate must have been less than satisfying. His advice was noncommittal. Replying on May 26, five days after her letter, he writes:

> Most of the reasons you, in your paper, for and against your entering the state considered, are impersonal, that is abstract and general. These are very well as far as they go, in settling one's vocation, but additional and personal reasons are necessary to decide it.
>
> The relative merits of the two states cannot be in question. It is of faith that the religious state is, beyond measure, the most perfect. It must be admitted, too, that in both, dangers and difficulties are to be encountered and overcome. One of these states is for the few, the other, for the many.
>
> In the religious state, the young lady becomes the mystic "sponsa Christi (spouse of Christ)." She gives her heart to Him, and to Him alone. If she loves others it is in Him, and for Him she does so. And loving Him with this undivided and exceptional love she seeks to liken herself to Him as perfectly as possible, by the practice of the three virtues that were peculiarly manifested by Him during His mortal life — poverty, chastity and obedience. If she desires this union with Our Lord, and is not daunted by the difficulties to be overcome in acquiring the perfection it implies, and calls for, and there is nothing in her natu-

ral disposition, and no such want of virtuous habits as would make it imprudent in her to aspire to it, she has what is called a religious vocation.[20]

Bishop O'Connor notes the positive reasons Katharine has given in her seven points for *not* embracing the religious life and demolishes them one by one. "Thousands," he writes, "have borne such things and been sanctified by them, but only such as have foreseen them and resolved, not rashly, to endure them for Our Lord." He urges her to "Think over what I have said here, at your leisure, and let me know what conclusions you may have come to."

At this point, Bishop O'Connor's advice appears sound. It is but a few months since Kate has endured the greatest tragedy to date in her young life — the loss of a stepmother as dear as any parent. Is it really the time she should be making a life decision?

Bishop O'Connor puts his finger on something else in Katharine's letter. While he says the reasons she has listed for and against a religious vocation are "abstract and general," the rest of his letter points to the obvious. It is the reasons for that are abstract; the reasons against are concrete.

"Jesus Christ has given His life for me. It is just that I should give Him mine." That's abstract. However, there is nothing abstract about "I hate community life" or "I should like the joys of motherhood."

Does this represent a weakness in Katharine's desire for a religious vocation, as Bishop O'Connor may well have suspected, or is it simply a manifestation of that scrupulosity that he had warned against years before? Katharine is much more prone to admit faults in herself than virtues. Scrupulosity, perhaps. In this case, let's call it humility. But clearly, by her own writings, Katharine's religious vocation has not yet matured. She must pray more.

Then, too, Katharine may have worried about very human feelings for men, because Bishop O'Connor assures her it is a mere natural propensity.[21]

Troublesome in your case, because of your scrupulosity, and your great love of the virtue opposed to it. It is encountered in any state of life and even by the greatest saints. It is one of the chief infirmities by which virtue is perfected. The same must be said of vanity to which all, without exception, are tempted. Your having these propensities proves nothing, one way or another, for no one, in any state or position can hope, short of a miracle, to be without them. When they frequently lead one to grievous sin, then they establish a presumption not to say a proof that she is called to the married life, not the religious state. But this, my dear child is, I well know, not so in your case.

Bishop O'Connor's great hesitation as to her religious vocation is also influenced by his knowledge of the drastic change such a vocation would bring to her lifestyle. "From your home, from your table, to the cell and the refectory of a nun, would be a very great change indeed," he wrote. "And what makes me hesitate, in this matter, should cause you to do the same."22

Katharine confided her vocational struggles only to her spiritual director and her confessor. She said nothing to the family, but of course, they noticed the little things. Kate, Louise would later say, "liked many underskirts so no one could see through her dress, and her dress long and neck high."

Lise, with unintended prescience, would quip, "It's hard having a saint in the family."

Bishop O'Connor tries to soften Katharine's growing asceticism. In one letter, he advises: "As to the theatre go there whenever your good father asks you to do so. He will not ask you too often or take you to a play you should not see. But go, always in a spirit of obedience to him and as an act of self-denial."23

Just as Katharine and Elizabeth were confronted with life-altering decisions after the death of Emma, so was Francis Drexel. With the death of his wife, his three daughters became his natural heirs. In March 1883, Francis Drexel wrote a new will. It was a truly unique document, the full impact of which would not be felt for almost three quarters of a century. Its terms would not become known until his own death. At a later date, Mother Katharine recounted how her father had come home one day, told them he felt he had done a good day's work, and one that was solely for their own good. When questioned, he said, "I have made my will." After the fact, Mother Katharine placed this conversation as occuring in 1884. While it very clearly was earlier, as the date on the will attests, her memory of her father's comment is probably accurate.24

Meanwhile, as the family struggled to overcome their grief at the loss of Emma, Frank decided another European tour, away from the familiar places, would help his daughters take their minds off their mother. In October 1883, they sailed for a seven-month journey that would take them through England, the Low Countries, Germany, Italy, and France.

During this time, Katharine kept up her debate with Bishop O'Connor. The more she leaned toward a religious vocation, the less certain he became. Shortly after the family's departure for the Continent, Bishop O'Connor wrote:

> ...let me acquaint you with the conclusion I have reached in regard to your vocation. It is this, that you remain in the world, but take a vow of virginity for one year, to be renewed every year, with the permission of your spiritual director, till you or he thinks it well for you to omit or make it perpetual. This, I think, is what is best for you to do now, and as

far as I can see, in the immediate future. Your vocation to religion is not pronounced, and without a very decided vocation, one in your position should not enter it. On the other hand, your vocation to celibacy, and perhaps, to a life of celibacy, is sufficiently evident to warrant or even require you to give it a trial. Should the future make known to you that God asks of you the practice of this virtue for only a time, nothing will prevent your entering another state of life. Should you on the other hand feel free to remain the Sponsa Christi to the end, you can do so and make use of the liberty you will enjoy in the world to be of immense service to others, by deed and by example.[25]

Bishop O'Connor asks her to consider this, and if it is pleasing, make a simple vow in any form she chooses at the next shrine to the Blessed Mother she should visit. He is really asking too much of her. Don't become a nun, Bishop O'Connor is saying. Stay in the world as an undeclared nun. Let people think you are a spinster, even though this may well make you an object of pity, and use your money and talents to do good. He also adds, "You need not mention this matter even to your confessor."

Katharine's next letter to him typifies one of the governing principles of her life — submissiveness to those whom she considered to be in spiritual authority over her.

The outlook in the future to a life of perpetual celibacy is contrary to my present inclination to the religious life. If, however, God calls me to remain in the world, to be exposed to its temptations, to be obliged to serve it, to remain in the world and yet not of the world, to know the great beauty of God's house, and yet to have duties which constantly withdraw from it, to feel that God has given graces, which to quote your own words, 'must be used under direction lest they lead from the path of prudence' and yet be deprived of daily direction such as those in religion receive, to be looked down upon as an old maid — if all of this is for God's greater glory — I must drown inclination and say Fiat. Most likely I can, with God's grace, do more for Him in the world.[26]

It is November and the family is visiting Venice. In obedience to the bishop, she went to St. Mark's and there before a much-venerated painting of Mary, the Madonna of San Marco, she has made a private, one-year vow of celibacy. As a memento of this very private vow, Katharine took home with her a little holy card of the Madonna; it remained with her for the rest of a long life.

Bishop O'Connor has ordered Katharine to spend no more than an hour and a half daily in prayer, "Quite enough whilst traveling." Katharine's soul demands more, but she, denied the privilege of a life in vowed obedience, remains obedient nonetheless.

She writes:

> I am going to ask you whether there is to be no exception to the rule for instance on a day when I have to prepare for Holy Communion or confession, or at a place where there is every opportunity to have a 'religious spree' such as, on special festivals and stations at Rome, or at Loretto or Lourdes, etc., etc. You are going to deprive me of a glorious contemplated 'spree' at Padua and Assissium where we are going to make pilgrimages on leaving here. For of course I shall reduce myself to an hour and a half devotions at these places as elsewhere until I hear from you.[27]

In another letter written from England, Katharine lists some of the foods she is abstaining from: ice cream, preserves, cake, grapes, and wine, except for medicinal purposes. In her diet, Katharine is trying to avoid whatever dish is served that she most enjoys, bringing herself down to what she calls "convent rations." And it is not easily accomplished when she is dining with her father and sisters. "Family eye notices and comments," she writes. "Then comes horrid coaxing to eat 'just a little to please me.'" At this point and in the absence of Bishop Bishop O'Connor, Katharine consulted a priest in confession. "Do as the rest of the family," he orders.

Katharine follows another tack. She observes what Elizabeth eats and simply does the same. But apparently, Elizabeth has a small appetite. "I frequently find I go somewhat beyond her limits," Katharine tells Bishop O'Connor. "But I shall continue to follow her example, and this is possible without attracting notice." And as she writes with self-deprecating humor in another letter, "I am not a gourmet because I am a gourmand."[28]

Her regimen of prayer within the bishop's prescribed one and a half hours includes 15 minutes meditation; 30 minutes hearing Mass, or if not possible to attend, reading her missal; 15 minutes rosary; 10 minutes other prayers; and 15 minutes the Children of Mary.

Bishop O'Connor has given her permission to receive Communion three times weekly; now she wants him to add a fourth. But ever-scrupulous, Katharine worries about her own motives.

> Would such a course add to my judgment and condemnation in the future life, or would the precious Body and Blood, Soul and Divinity

of Jesus strengthen me still more in the difficulties of the pilgrimages? Or would a more frequent reception of the sacrament through my weakness lead to pride and vanity?

Bishop O'Connor is Katharine's spiritual mentor, but how greater the pupil appears than the master in these touching exchanges.

The family, while visiting Rome and through the good offices of a friendly monsignor, attends a private Mass celebrated by Pope Leo XIII. Writing home to Mary Cassidy, Lise noted:

> On seeing Leo XIII one is struck with wonder that old, feeble and apparently absentminded man, should be the one to whom the Protestant as well as the Catholic world is turning for support. Truly in Italy just now the vitality of the Catholic Faith is palpably forced on one. The devotion of the people is edifying. New churches are building, new convents are springing up side by side with suppressed monasteries and Humbert (King of Italy) dare not gainsay the *fiat* of the "Prisoner of the Vatican."[29]

How transitory is life. Lise, this vibrant, healthy young woman of 28, could not know that the "old, feeble and apparently absentminded" Pope Leo would outlive her by more than 12 years!

The family spent four days at Lourdes, as Louise wrote, "cool, clear, pious, hard on the knees ones. We prayed at the grotto, we drank the water, we kissed the ground, we lit candles, and we also went to the piscene and bathed in the miraculous spring water. We dressed in our worst clothes (which by this time were just hanging together). In fact, we behaved like holy pilgrims as we were."[30]

The Drexels came home at the beginning of May, shortly before the installation of a new archbishop in Philadelphia. Archbishop Wood, who had relied so heavily upon Frank Drexel for advice in temporal matters, had died in June 1883. His successor, Archbishop Patrick J. Ryan, arrived from St. Louis the following June. Among the papers that greeted him upon his arrival was a memorandum with the late archbishop's will. In effect, it advised his successor that he had always consulted Mr. Francis A. Drexel on the temporal affairs of the diocese.[31]

Katharine was the only one of the three sisters to accompany her father to Archbishop Ryan's installation. Why it was she and not Elizabeth, as the eldest, is surprising. Perhaps Elizabeth was indisposed or out of town. Whatever the reason, Katharine's presence at the installation was auspicious — Ryan would be a further instrument in her continued formation and life work.[32] Another visitor to Philadelphia for the installation was Bishop O'Connor. Katharine once more spoke of her desire to enter religion, and confided that if she did, it would probably be as a contemplative nun. Bishop O'Connor still had serious reservations about her plans for a religious vocation.

By September 1884, the family was off on another excursion. For Frank Drexel it was a quasi-business trip, but for the girls, it was an adventure. The Northern Pacific Railroad desired to float bonds through Drexel & Co., and Frank was traveling west on an inspection tour of their facilities.

Frank brought his three daughters with him, as well as two employees of the firm, and to accompany his daughters, a niece, Mary Dixon, who like the Drexel sisters, had recently lost her mother in death. This was Kate Drexel's first trip to an area of the country that would be central to her apostolate. She would retrace her path many times in the future, but never again in the same style.

This was truly the gilded age, and the Drexel family rode westward in "the Yellowstone," a private rail car loaned to them by the Northern Pacific. As the name of their rail car implied, part of the journey took them to Yellowstone National Park. One misadventure had the family charged with breaking the law by picking up souvenir rocks on federal land, but after a hearing before a local justice of the peace, this was smoothed over. At another stop they barely missed being robbed, Western style. They were in Bismark, Dakota Territory, where they had stopped to attend Mass. The train that was supposed to take them to Gardiner, Wyoming, came and went without them. They arrived in Gardiner 12 hours late and in daylight. It was later discovered, had they arrived at night, a group of robbers had planned to hold up the "rich eastern bankers."[33]

At Tacoma, Washington, they found a little Catholic mission chapel. When they rang the bell to inquire about Mass hours, the priest who answered the door was Father Hylebos, a Belgian missionary whom they had met just months before in Rome. Kate was thrilled to learn Father Hylebos was working with the Indians. When she noticed his little mission chapel, dedicated to Our Lady of Grace, had no artwork depicting its patroness, Katharine promised Father Hylebos she would find such a statue for him. Later, true to her word, Kate found a beautiful statue in the Benziger Brothers catalog and had it shipped to the priest. This was the first of many donations to the apostolate of her first love — the Native-American mission fields.

Frank Drexel had just opened checking accounts for his three daughters with the first monthly deposit of $200 — a rather handsome allowance; in the 19th century working-class families lived on far less. This statue for Father Hylebos cost $100. Kate worried about how her father would regard this extravagance on her part, and it was not without a little trepidation that she confessed to him what she had done with the money. Frank Drexel placed both hands on her shoulders and smiled. "I'm glad you did it, Kitty," he said.34

Kate's statue arrived in Tacoma in a large crate. Father Hylebos and General Red Spot, a member of the Puyallup tribe, took it by canoe to the reservation. When the crate was opened, the statue was truly magnificent, but in the good priest's mind, perhaps too big for his little chapel. He suggested taking it to a larger church and putting a smaller statue in the chapel.

The chief told him:

No, this big statue will speak better to our hearts than a little statue, and now we can think better of Our Mother in Heaven. We never before knew how to think of the Blessed Virgin Mary. Now we learn to think. Now we can think that she had a crown of stars and that the little Jesus has the world in His hands with His cross to save us all. We want to pray now.

Kate would have a continued interest in this early outreach to Native Americans. In time, as Mother Katharine Drexel, she provided major support to a school that grew out of Father Hylebos' little mission. She placed it under the patronage of St. George, the patron of George Childs. It was Katharine's prayer to the great archangel that George would convert to Catholicism. He never did, but nevertheless was a wonderful support to Katharine in many ways. Possibly by no coincidence, when Childs helped develop the Philadelphia suburb of Wayne, the new Catholic parish was placed under the patronage of St. Catherine of Siena, but using her distinctive spelling — Katharine.35

The time would come all too quickly when Katharine and her sisters would be deprived of the advice and consent of their dear father in any matters, and would have to rely upon their own resources and the advice of their solicitous uncles, including Childs, an uncle by choice, not blood.

In early February 1885, Francis Drexel caught a bad cold. It may have been brought on by a visit in inclement weather on the last of January to St. Michel. It might have been during a long walk he took with Louise the following day. In any case, the cold turned to pleurisy. It did not appear to be life threatening, however, and Elizabeth and Katharine, with instruction from his physicians, divided the nursing duties between them.

Their father appeared to improve greatly, and by Sunday, February 15, seemed well on the mend. Katharine was his duty nurse for the day. Francis, as was his custom, devoted some time to private meditation, ate lunch, then passed the time in light reading — Thackeray's "The Newcomes."

Quite casually, he placed the book on a table with his eyeglasses to mark his spot, appeared to rise from the chair, then slumped into the seat.

Horrified, Katharine rushed to him. One look told her that her father was dying. Katharine called for help, then seizing a wrap, she rushed out the door to the nearest rectory — in this case, St. Patrick's across Rittenhouse Square, a fashionable park near their home. Katharine rushed into the rectory, where several of the priests appeared to be having a conference. "Come quick, my father is dying," she said. One of the priests responded to her urgent pleading and accompanied her to the family home.

Meanwhile, as they left the rectory, one of the Drexel servants, Mary Jane, was waiting for them with a cab. Coolheadedly, she had flagged the cab, gone to St. John the Evangelist, another nearby church, fetched a priest to the Drexel home, then went to St. Patrick's for Katharine. When they arrived, Francis had been taken to his bedroom, already dead. The first priest, too, had been too late. Francis' death from a massive heart attack apparently happened almost instantly.[36] Although he died without consolation of the last sacraments, Emma's prayer had nevertheless been answered. During her own long final illness, she had prayed he would be spared such agony. His death had come quickly, without suffering. His exemplary life, his good works and the prayers of his loved ones through Jesus Christ, one presumes, were sufficient for his salvation.

According to most contemporary and later reports, all three daughters were home at the time Francis Drexel died. However, one account in the annals of the Blessed Sacrament Sisters reports that Elizabeth and Louise had gone to New York on a short excursion. If true, this would explain why Katharine's role was so central at the time of their father's death.

Archbishop Ryan celebrated Francis Drexel's funeral Mass at the Cathedral of SS. Peter and Paul, the family's usual place of worship when in residence on Walnut Street. Frank had contributed much to the cathedral, and he would occasionally play the organ there. Among the many mourners were the captains of industry from New York and Philadelphia. Present, too, were the boys from St. John's Orphanage, a charity especially dear to Frank's heart.

In keeping with Frank's wishes, Archbishop Ryan, an orator of recognized skill, preached no eulogy. Francis Drexel's deeds were his memorial.[37] But the archbishop could not let the opportunity pass without saying something about this extraordinary man.

> Every man may be more or less a philanthropist, but only the religious man can have charity, for charity is the love of neighbor for God's sake.... The loss of such a Christian philanthropist to any community is a serious one and no legacies that he may leave can compensate for it, for the daily life of such a man, his personal example to a whole community cannot be estimated by the standard of money.[38]

In the days that followed, the full measure of his charity became known. By final accounting, Frank Drexel's estate was worth $15.5 million, the largest estate until that point, ever filed in Philadelphia. After some minor bequests to family friends, a tithe of the estate — 10 percent — was willed to charity.

Five percent of this $1.5 million was willed to the Cathedral of SS. Peter and Paul; the Conferences of St. Vincent de Paul; St. Joseph's Church, Willings Alley; St. John's Orphan Asylum; St. Joseph's Hospital (Philadelphia); St. Mary's Hospital; the Sisters of St. Francis; St. Charles Borromeo Seminary; St. Joseph's College; the House of the Good Shepherd; and the West Philadelphia (Francis A. Drexel) Industrial School. Three percent went to St. Boniface Church; St. Joseph's Hospital (Reading); St. James Parochial School; St. Peter's Church; The Roman Catholic Society of St. Joseph for Educating Poor Orphan Children; St. Vincent's Home; Catholic Home for Destitute Children; the Little Sisters of the Poor; the Sisters of Mercy; St. Vincent's (German) Orphan Asylum; La Salle College; Sharon Hill Female Academy; and The German Hospital of the City of Philadelphia. Two percent was left to Eden Hall and one percent to St. Catherine's Female Orphan Asylum; St. Mary Magdalene de Pazzi Italian Orphan Asylum, St. Anne's Widows Asylum, and the Institute of the Ladies of the Sacred Heart, Philadelphia.

All 29 charities were located within the boundaries of the Archdiocese of Philadelphia at the time; most were directly controlled by the Archdiocese. Only one, the German Hospital (later renamed Lankenau in honor of Francis Drexel's brother-in-law, John Lankenau) was non-Catholic. It had a Lutheran affiliation.

While $1.5 million divided among 29 charities might sound like a modest sum by today's standards, it was really quite large for that time. Indeed, many of the institutions were able to build entire new facilities, some on relocated campuses, with their bequest.

With charity accounted for, Francis Drexel turned his attention to his three daughters. To them he left the remainder of his estate — $14 million. With the stroke of a pen, they were the richest women in Philadelphia and very likely the entire country. But they didn't receive the money outright. In the 19th century, there were many cases of young heiresses who were victims of fortune hunters and not just in the novels of Henry James. There were even Drexel relatives who would be victimized in this manner, especially in that era when husbands had a great deal of legal control over the assets of their wives. Then, too, Francis had to be concerned about how well his daughters, with very little financial management experience, would be able to handle a very large inheritance. They were women in what was still a man's world.

Of course, it was not just fathers of daughters who had to consider these things. Michael Bouvier, Emma's father, had confronted a similar problem.

Through two marriages he had 12 children, and at his death in 1872, he left sufficient money that each, with proper management, could live quite well. The problem was the eldest son, Eustace. During their litany of childhood prayers, the Drexel children would be asked to pray for Eustace. "He's wild," Mama would cryptically explain. The truth of the matter was, there is no way Eustace could be expected to act responsibly. It was a given that he would run through an inheritance in no time. For this reason, Michael had left his share of the inheritance in a life trust — Eustace could spend only income, not principal.

Elizabeth, Katharine, and Louise were by no stretch of the imagination "wild," but they were certainly vulnerable. Taking a page from his father-in-law's book, Francis wrote what was then known as a "spendthrift will." His residual estate — $14 million — was divided equally among his three daughters. But, in their lifetime, they would receive only the income. Further, they could not anticipate income. As the will stated:

> No one of the beneficiaries under this trust shall have the right to anticipate the payment, sell, assign, encumber or in any way dispose of its income, or any part thereof, or of the principal or corpus of said trust Estate, or any part thereof, before the same shall be actually received by and come into possession or such beneficiary from the trustees.

What this meant was that any of the girls might well promise to give someone a portion of their estate in future years, but the promise would be non-binding in law. They could not spend or give away anything but current income already received.

If they married, their husbands would have no estate rights, except for that income previously received. Should the sisters die, their children would receive their share on the same terms, but outright after the last of the three had been dead 21 years. Should one of the sisters die childless, her share would go to the remaining sisters or their children if the sisters were already dead.

What if all three should die childless? In that case, the trust would be dissolved and the funds distributed to the charities named earlier in the will and in the same proportions as the original bequests.[39]

In March 1883, when Frank Drexel wrote his will, his daughters were 27, 24, and 19. From surviving photographs and letters, they are obviously attractive, intelligent and personable, qualities that could be magnified in the eyes of suitors by their great wealth.

The will, dated less than two months after Emma's death, is also dated less than two months before Kate tells Bishop O'Connor she has received and rejected a proposal of marriage, a disclosure she made to only one other person

— her father.

It is reasonable to suppose that Frank at this point knew his second daughter was being courted. But he was a man of sufficient wisdom to realize it was possible his daughters would never marry, and indeed, any or all three, given their piety, could enter the convent. It was something he had said he would not oppose.

There was a distinct possibility that his children would be childless, and charity would inherit his fortune. But it is just as certain, had he been given the gift to see into Katharine's future, his will would have been written quite differently.

The family crypt beneath the Lady Chapel that Frank had been building at Eden Hall was not yet complete, and so his daughters entombed him temporarily with Emma in the Bouvier vault at St. Mary's.[40]

Uncles Anthony Drexel and John Lankenau stepped in as surrogate fathers to the girls, and Aunt Ellen loaned her nieces a summer home, in order that, away from the home where their father died, they could recover from this second grievous loss. Later in the spring, they took up residence at St. Michel.[41]

Chapter Five
The Most Attractive
of the Three

A s they sorted out their lives, Elizabeth took on the role as leader; but it was really first among equals. "The all three," Elizabeth, Katharine, and Louise would call themselves.

"In a well brought up family," Mother Katharine would later say, "the younger sisters reverence the older. We reverenced her (Elizabeth). We reverenced her because she took our mother's place and she was our elder sister."[1]

It was at this point Elizabeth proposed a suitable memorial for their father. Francis Drexel had been a generous man who gave of his wealth to a variety of benevolent causes. But those to which he gave time and talent tended to be institutions for children in need. He was a board member of St. John, St. Joseph, and St. Vincent Orphan Asylums. As a rule, boys in such institutions were nurtured until their pre-teen years when they would be placed as apprentices with local craftsmen or farmers. It was a well-meaning system, but subject to abuse. All too often the masters treated their apprentices as nothing more than cheap labor, giving very little in return. Elizabeth proposed the founding of a residential training school in their father's memory. This school would provide the orphan boys from the Catholic homes with manual or craft training, with which they could then earn a useful living. To this end, Elizabeth purchased 200 acres in the Bucks County suburb of Eddington, about three miles north of St. Michel. On this property she would erect what would be known as St. Francis de Sales Industrial School (later St. Francis Vocational School and today St. Francis Homes for Boys).[2]

To say this is Elizabeth's charity is not completely true; her two sisters also contributed, just as after Katharine became more active in missionary outreach to Native Americans, her sisters participated. And when Louise chose African-American outreach as an area of special concern, Elizabeth and Katharine shared her mission.3 As a matter of fact, although Louise was the most single-minded of the three in devotion to the African-American apostolate, we find Elizabeth in the 1880s teaching Sunday School to black children at Philadelphia's St. Joseph's Church. And of course, Katharine's apostolate very quickly expanded to include both Native and African Americans. It was at this critical point that two visiting clerics called upon the Drexel sisters, probably at the suggestion of Bishop O'Connor, who had first-hand knowledge of the generosity of the three sisters. By benevolent providence, Katharine was the one to greet them.4

One was Bishop Martin Marty, vicar apostolic for Dakota Territory. The other was Father (later Msgr.) Joseph Stephan, director of the Bureau of Catholic Indian Missions. As noted, the Bureau of Catholic Indian Missions had been a Catholic response to Grant's "Peace Policy." This was the agency that was responsible for coordinating the Catholic missionary effort and seeing to it that schools were built and staffed.

Like so many of the great missionaries to the Native Americans, both were of European birth. Bishop Marty, a Benedictine, was Swiss; Father Stephan was German. Bishop Marty, a former prior and abbot of St. Meinrad Abbey, Indiana, would eventually become the first bishop of Sioux Falls and later St. Cloud. His work among Native Americans was primarily among the Sioux, and through him, Presentation Sisters, Franciscan Sisters, Grey Nuns, Benedictine Sisters, and Jesuit Fathers would open missions on Sioux Reservations. During this visit to the East Coast, Bishop Marty and Father Stephan were trying to raise money for their missions.

Father Stephan, born in Germany, had begun his career as a military officer. According to the annals of the Sisters of the Blessed Sacrament, he underwent a conversion experience as dramatic as St. Paul's. While riding during a storm, he was struck by a bolt of lightning that threw him from his horse, killed his companion, and left him blind. During his convalesence, Stephan vowed to God and the Blessed Virgin, should his sight be restored, he would devote his life entirely to God and the salvation of souls.

He recovered his sight within three months and entered the seminary. As a deacon, he migrated to America and completed his studies for ordination in Cincinnati. During the Civil War, Father Stephan served with distinction as a Union Army chaplain; a wound to his leg left him with a permanent limp.

He became a missionary to the Native Americans after the war and remained in this apostolate for the rest of his life. He was single-minded in his chosen vocation and battled the Washington bureaucracy for the Native Americans with all his strength. He was a staunch ally and friend to Katharine Drexel, whom he called "Mother Katharina."[5]

The Drexel sisters gave them a courteous welcome, but Katharine responded beyond their wildest expectations. First there was a gift of $500. This was followed by a donation to build a frame chapel in Osage territory. The first year it was blown away by a cyclone. Undaunted, Katharine rebuilt — this time more substantially and storm-proof. Very quickly, a virtual river of donations from Katharine was funneled through Stephan for the Indian missions.

* * *

Meanwhile, Katharine's interior debate continued. In the summer of 1885, writing to O'Connor from Sea Cliff Villa, the Childs' summer home in Long Branch, she confides:

> To tell the truth, it appears to me that God calls me to the religious life. But when will it be prudent for me to obey the call? Next week? This Fall? This Winter? — In what religious order? Please tell me, dear Father, what I should do to save my own soul, to save as many souls as possible, to devote myself and all I have to God and to His Church. You know that I have a leaning to the contemplative life — but you and Father Ardia both say no to that; You know that I long to bring the Indians into Mother Church.[6]

Katharine, at this point, knows she wishes to enter religion. Part of her longs for the secluded life of the contemplative; another part yearns to be a missionary. When she says Bishop O'Connor and Father Joseph Ardia, another Jesuit confessor, are both disinclined to see her enter a contemplative order, there is a difference. Her confessor is much more receptive to the general idea of a religious vocation than is Bishop O'Connor, who has hardened his position.

In his answer to Katharine's letter from Sea Cliff, the bishop writes, "The conclusion to which I have come in your case is, that your vocation is not to enter a religious order.

> The only order which I could have thought of recommending you, as I have more than once told you, is the Sacred Heart; but you have not the health necessary to enable you to discharge the duties which would devolve on you as a member of that society. God cannot be presumed to wish us to do what He has not given us the means to perform.

Living in the world, he goes on to say, she can benefit Christ's poor, and the rich also, "who after all are the poorest of the poor." As a laywoman, she can work to bring her relatives back to the church and be a spiritual influence on her sisters. "Much of the good you will thus be able to do in the world," he writes, "you would not be free to perform in religion."7

Was Katharine's wish to enter religion, at this point, colored by her grief at the loss of her beloved parents? In hindsight, she would argue this was not the case. "That's nonsense," she said, during a 1932 interview. "I am, and always have been, one of the happiest women in the world." The only sorrow in her life, she added, was that of "those that outlive many of their loved ones."

The truth may lie somewhere in the middle. The death of both her parents within a few years certainly drove home to her the transience of earthly relationships and made it easier for her to break home ties.

But just as Elizabeth appears to have been the most grief stricken of the three upon the death of Emma, Katharine was most affected by the death of their father. She suffered from jaundice, a general weakening, and a loss of weight, no doubt the result of coming down too zealously to "convent rations." There were temporary remissions, but a year passed, and her protestations to the contrary, her health did not improve.

Elizabeth and Louise were sufficiently concerned to arrange another European tour, but not completely a pleasure trip.8 They sailed on July 31, 1886. Their first stop would be to Schwalbach, one of the German spas, where a five-week combination of spring water, mud baths, and country jaunts appeared to have the desired effect. "The sea voyage already seems to have done her good and the doctors give us hope that this place may complete it," Elizabeth wrote in a letter to Mary Cassidy. 9

"I have gained eight pounds, honest weight," Katharine wrote. "All my clothes are beginning to be too small. Dyspepsia much better."10

Back home Uncle Anthony was handling their financial affairs. One letter confirms his understanding and support of the path of charity they have chosen to tread. "Earthquakes continue in Charleston," he writes. "I think you ought to contribute to the sufferers there. I shall send Archbishop Ryan $500 from your account and have it sent to Charleston for the relief of Catholics there. I think you will approve of this."11

In a follow-up letter, after receiving a letter from Elizabeth in approval, he wrote:

> "I knew there was a great deal of suffering among the Catholics in Charleston and I thought it right to direct your money to their relief. I know you are not sectarian where the interests of humanity are con-

cerned but are always willing to take the Christian view of it and distribute your alms irrespective of creed. This is what I have always done and am glad to have you do the same. Lizzie's letter with the few lines on that subject gave me great satisfaction and pleasure."[12]

In their absence, Uncle Anthony arranged for the laying of the cornerstone at St. Francis in the presence of Archbishop Ryan. "Not a cloud in the sky and just cold enough to be bracing," he wrote. "All I hope, a happy augury for the future of the noble work you have undertaken."

During their continued travel, there was the visit to Rome and its magnificent churches, and of course, the audience with Leo XIII that would leave Katharine so shaken.

In Switzerland, the sisters acquired a creamy-colored St. Bernard puppy of three months, which they wrapped in a shawl and pretended was a baby in order to take him in their first class train compartment. Lizzie sat holding "baby" and innocently praying her rosary when a train official came to the compartment. The "baby" was shipped on ahead to a long and happy life at St. Michel.

In France, visits were made to a number of vocational training schools for boys conducted by the Christian Brothers. These were of special interest to Elizabeth as she planned her own school. Mettray, Fleury, and Igney were impressive, Issy, less so. In any event, the journey played a large part in Elizabeth's decision to obtain Christian Brothers for her new school in Eddington.

Paris was just as famous for its couturiers in the 19th century as in the 20th. Katharine's letters to "Bernadetta" (Mary Cassidy) are full of news of the long sessions with the dressmakers and corset makers and the visits to the salons on Rue St. Honore. If her newly recovered health had given her a few pounds, here was the place to replenish her wardrobe.

But her correspondence with Bishop O'Connor takes on a much more serious note. We know this not from her letters, which have not survived, but rather from his replies.

In a March 5, 1887 letter written to Katharine, by this time in France, the bishop notes the work she has begun for the Native-American missions. "You have the means, you have the brains, you have the freedom of action necessary to do this work well," he writes. "In religion you could direct your income to this or some other good purpose, but your talents and your energies would be directed by others." He tells her, "you are doing more for the Indians now, than any religious, or even any religious community has ever done, or perhaps could ever do for them in this country."[13]

As a counterproposal to her entering religion, perhaps as a missionary, he suggests she fund a novitiate where Sisters could train for the Indian missions.

He proposes (with Katharine's money of course) inviting the Sisters of Providence from Montreal to establish a branch novitiate in Philadelphia. In the end, the plan was shelved. Another proposal of Bishop O'Connor's that did not come to fruition was a plan to have the Jesuits take charge of the college division of Philadelphia's St. Charles Borromeo Seminary. Again, it would be made possible by the Drexel sisters' funding, as a memorial to their late father.

The new Catholic University in Washington, D.C., "may or may not succeed," O'Connor wrote. "I am sorry to think that it is almost certain to fail — but the Seminary of St. Charles Borromeo, under the guidance of the Jesuits, is sure to become the first institution of its kind in the world."[14] The bishop contacted the Father General of the Jesuits in Florence, and for a while the plan seemed to have a green light. When it fell through, the Drexel sisters donated $50,000 to The Catholic University to establish the Francis A. Drexel Chair of Moral Theology.

In an April 1887 letter, O'Connor concedes the religious life is the nobler state. "That was settled long ago," he writes. "But in which you can give more glory to God, be of more service to your neighbor and acquire more merit for yourself." Katharine, he says, is called to be a bride of Christ. "This you can be in the world as well as in religion, and that such is your vocation, I have had for long no doubt."[15]

All of this raises a point. While Katharine Drexel was the daughter of wealthy banker Francis Drexel, Bishop O'Connor treated her exploration of a possible religious vocation with proper caution. "Let's see what develops," he was telling her. Now, with her father's death, Katharine is not a millionaire's daughter; she is a millionaire. Not only that, she is funding some very commendable charities dear to the heart of the bishop. Assuredly, this was for the benefit of the Church and the people of God, not Bishop O'Connor. But the question is still there: Did he allow the very good works she was doing through her inheritance to interfere with his proper role as her spiritual advisor? Was he primarily thinking of the good of the Church and the missions or the good of Katharine Drexel's soul? Had Katharine joined a religious congregation, she could have signed her inheritance over to her sisters or to any charity or charities she chose, including the order she joined. But under her father's will, such a contract would have to be reaffirmed every year — money could not be given away before it was received. It is natural to suppose at some point she may well have been more inclined to support charitable works of her own congregation, rather than the Western missions.

* * * *

With her future still undecided, Katharine returned home from Europe with her sisters in late April 1887. On September 19, at the invitation of Bishop O'Connor and Father Stephan, they left for a four-week tour of Indian country. Here Katharine learned firsthand about the needs of the missionaries and saw the fruits of her donations.

This was quite different from their European tour, traveling first class from one luxury hotel to another. This was roughing it. They traveled by train when possible, but more often than not, Indian reservations were far from the beaten track and iron rail. In these instances, they traveled by coach if they were lucky; otherwise, it was a springless buckboard. Elizabeth and Louise, who were both excellent horsewomen, brought along saddles and rode horseback.

The first stop was the Rosebud Agency in South Dakota, where a school subsidized by Katharine was being conducted by the Jesuit Fathers and Sisters of St. Francis from Stella Niagara, N.Y. This was St. Francis Mission, named in memory of their father. The next stop was at Pine Bluff Agency where the Drexel sisters were introduced to Red Cloud, one of the most important chiefs among the Sioux. At Immaculate Conception Mission in Stephan, South Dakota, they toured the buildings under construction through Katharine's donation. The name of this mission was chosen to memorialize Emma Drexel — the Immaculate Conception had been her favorite devotion to the Blessed Virgin.

At Immaculate Conception, they were treated to an Indian dance. It was a rare honor but somewhat embarrassing, because the participants wore little more than paint and feathers. At the earliest opportunity, the Philadelphia maidens slipped away.

Needless to say, the trip, if grueling, was a grand adventure, and if the purpose was to lead the Drexel sisters to even greater generosity, it worked. Katharine redoubled her efforts on behalf of the missions.[16]

The three sisters made a similar visitation the following year. At Red Lake, Katharine was thrilled to stand as godmother for William, a little Chippewa Indian child. Louise and Elizabeth, too, served as godparents for babies. Several large mission donations came out of this trip — one for the Rosebud Agency, one at Pine Ridge, and another in Wyoming. At White Earth, Montana, where the Benedictine Sisters had been laboring for years, Kate funded a boarding school for 100 pupils. Under the contract system, once the school was built and staffed, the federal government would pay approximately $100 annually for the board and education of each Indian child. While this seems paltry today, it was quite sufficient for the time. However, it would not be too many years before contracts to sectarian schools would be phased out, something that would place a further burden on Katharine's purse.[17]

Building the mission schools was one thing; staffing them was quite another.

To this end, Katharine worked directly with the various religious congregations willing to take on this challenging mission. For example, together with Elizabeth and Louise, she donated $30,000 to the Sisters of St. Francis of Philadelphia, on the condition that they accept and staff 10 Indian missions.

Other donations, great and small, aided a variety of charities. In April 1888, word reached the three sisters that Father Damien de Veuster, (now Blessed Damien), the missionary to the leper colony at Molokai, Hawaii, needed funds to repair his church. They responded with a check for $500. A note from Father Damien assured them he and his faithful would remember the intention requested by Elizabeth that was enclosed with the donation.

* * * *

In late 1888, Louise Drexel became engaged. She also had received a previous proposal; her suitor had been Protestant, and to her devout sisters' relief, she declined. This latest beau, Edward Morrell, was Protestant, too, but he solved the problem by converting to Catholicism.[18]

In May 1888, Bishop O'Connor wrote to Katharine:

> I take all the responsibility for having 'kept you out of a convent' till now. The more I reflect on the matter, the more I am persuaded that you are where God wishes you to be at present. Should I see any certain indications of His will that you should enter religion, I shall not fail to direct your attention to them. The good work in which you are now engaged calls for all your time and your entire freedom and, as far as I can see, they give more Glory to God, and do your neighbor more good than anything you could accomplish in a religious community.

On November 11, 1888, as Louise and Ned's wedding approached, Katharine wrote to her spiritual director:

> I am reduced to reading over all the letters you ever wrote me on the subject of my having no vocation to the religious life. I entreat you, for God's sake, reconsider the matter and see if Our Lord will not give me the grace to enter the perfect state — the religious state.
>
> To serve God is to reign, and the religious always serves Him in those through whom He invests with His authority. With God's help I desire to serve Him, and what a consolation it will be to be sure that I serve Him.
>
> As of now, I am perpetually in trouble of soul, warring as it were with better nature. The peace which I felt last year in obeying you,

gives me an assurance that the same peace and security would overshadow me in obeying a superior. I did not renew my vow of obedience to you because you are so far away that I cannot ask permission in cases where I am almost sure you would, were you present, permit me to make an exception to a rule. I obeyed often and often at times very inconvenient and contrary to my judgment, yet in obeying you for God's sake I found a peace that nothing except the knowledge of being sure I serve God can bring.

In her letter, she further confided that family separation is no longer a great barrier, and as for her dislike for community life, this is not so great as her distaste for participating in a social life "in a world with whose aspirations I feel no sympathy."

Katharine concluded her letter with a confession:

I am so afraid Our Lord will reject me because of my unworthiness. Up to this I have not dared ask Our Lord to give me a religious vocation. I have said, "May the most just, high and adorable Will of God be done." If I have not this religious vocation, can I pray and have prayers said for it?[19]

If there was a reply to this letter it has not been preserved, and as a matter of fact, Bishop O'Connor appears to have been ducking Katharine at this point.

Her next letter, dated November 26, 1888, is possibly the most crucial and poignant in the series:

Rt. Rev. and Dear Father:

Before another word we must say that we scarcely believed our ears when we heard that you were in Phila. and did not call on us who were expecting that pleasure. If it were not for your extreme kindness to us in giving us so much of your time this Fall, our feelings would have been hurt. We trust you have reached home safely and well.

May I trouble you to read the enclosed. It was written more than two weeks ago, and I have stamped it ready for sending to you, then concluded to wait. The sentiments in it remain the same, only I am suffering greater anxiety lest Our Lord should deprive me of a life near Him in union with Him. My God! What can I desire better than this. "If thou <u>wilt</u> be perfect." I <u>will</u> it. Our Lord's words ring in my ears. How I wish to spend my entire life given to Him by the three vows which would consecrate me to Jesus Christ! This night I feel a sadness out of which it is difficult to rally.

It appears to me that Our Lord gives me the right to choose the better part, and I shall try to draw as near to His heart as possible, that He may so fill me with His love that all the pains I may endure in the religious life may be cheerfully endured for the love of Jesus, the Lord of Love. Do not, Reverend Father, I beseech you, say, "What will become of your work?" What is to become of it when I give it all to Our Lord? Will Our Lord at the day of Judgment condemn me for approaching as near to Him as possible by following Him and then leaving my yearly income to be distributed among the Missions, or for the Missions in some way that I am sure could be devised if only Our Lord will free me from all responsibility, save that of giving myself to Him? You allowed Louise to take Mr. Morrell, what about her income to the poor?

Are you afraid to give me to Jesus Christ? God knows how unworthy I am, and yet can He not supply my unworthiness if only He gives me a vocation to the religious life? Then joyful I shall run to Him. I am afraid to receive your answer to this note. It appears to me, Reverend Father, that I am not obliged to submit my judgment to yours, as I have been doing for two years, for I feel so sad in doing it, because the world cannot give me peace, so restless because my heart is not rested in God. Will you, Reverend Father, please disregard the rudeness of this last remark in view of this — I am trying to tell you the truth? You have always been so kind in helping me that perhaps I have presumed on this kindness. Please pardon me and please give your blessing to your poor child in Dno.

K.M. Drexel

P.S. I intend to try and grow in love of Our Lord, so that all sacrifices in the religious life may be cheerfully endured. In your charity, Rt. Rev. Father, pray that I may do God's holy will now and always.[20]

Katharine had finally rebelled, and Bishop O'Connor quickly and gracefully conceded. She did indeed have a religious vocation. Writing to her four days later, he said:

Yours of the 26th is received. I had come to regard it as certain that Our Lord had chosen you for Himself, but for reasons with which you are familiar, I inclined to think He wished you to love and serve Him as His spouse, but in society. This letter of yours, and your bearing under the long and severe tests to which I have subjected you, as well as your entire restoration to health, and the many spiritual dangers which surround you, make me withdraw all opposition to your entering religion.

In all that has passed between us in regard to your vocation, my only aim and anxiety have been to help you discover God's will in the matter, and that, I think, is sufficiently manifest. Something, too, which I heard, when in the East a couple of weeks ago, of the well-meant plans made by your own flesh and blood to entangle you and Lizzie in mere worldly alliances, confirms me in this view of the case. A vocation, like any other grace, may be lost, and they who have it should not be too much exposed, or expose themselves needlessly.

The only matter that now remains to be determined is, which order should you choose? Have you a decided preference for some one of them?...

There are three orders the rules of which it would be worth your while to examine: The Sacred Heart, the Sisters of Mercy, and the Ursulines of Brown County, Ohio. Don't be impatient. The matter to be considered is a serious one for you: so let your motto be Festina lente....21

It is really quite extraordinary. Bishop O'Connor has done a complete about face. Not only is he not advising against her entrance into the convent, he is suggesting possible congregations for her. None of the three suggested by the good bishop, however, was to Katharine's taste.

Replying on December 15, she writes that she would prefer "a missionary order for Indians and Colored People." She is, at this point, leaning toward either the Franciscan Sisters of Philadelphia, a congregation founded by St. John Neumann, or the Benedictines. Fundamental to her choice is the frequency with which the congregation will permit the reception of the Eucharist. Katharine wishes to receive Communion every day, something that was not an accepted practice in the late 19th century. She is leaning toward the Benedictines, because it is her understanding that of the two it is the order more likely to permit daily Eucharist. Whatever Katharine's decision, her target date for entry was May 5, 1889, because on this date there were already plans in place for closing 1503 Walnut Street for the season and for she and Elizabeth to accompany Louise and Ned to Europe. This, she decided, would be the perfect time to break the family ties.22

* * * *

Louise and Ned were wed at the Cathedral of SS. Peter and Paul on January

17, 1889. Bishop O'Connor celebrated the wedding Mass; the vows were exchanged before Archbishop Ryan, and Uncle Anthony gave the bride away. Following the ceremony, the happy couple departed for a honeymoon to the Southwest and Mexico, which would be followed by the European tour.

Morrell had an interesting personal history. Through his mother, Ida Powell, he was a descendant of one of the founding Quaker families of Philadelphia. His father had lost most of his money in sugar speculation and died when Edward was quite young. When Ida Morrell remarried, her second husband, John G. Johnson, was a prominent lawyer and art collector. Edward followed his stepfather's profession and was of sufficient ability to have the honor of delivering the oration at his graduation from the University of Pennsylvania School of Law.

Edward — Ned to the Drexel girls — had social position, brains, and prospects. But he had other qualities that probably made Francis Drexel, in his grave, relieved he had written so restrictive a will.

Edward had the tastes and habits of a true aristocrat. A 1947 *Philadelphia Record* column written by society writer "Rex Rittenhouse" tells something about Morrell. He was, according to the author, "the handsomest man in town with dark curly hair and a long, rakish moustache...all of the girls wanted to marry him." He chose Louise, who had the immense wealth to complement his tastes. After their marriage, the Morrells kept magnificent homes on Philadelphia's Rittenhouse Square and in Torresdale, as well as Newport and Calf Island. A convivial man, he belonged to the 13 smartest clubs in the city, kept show horses, and maintained a handsome "coach and four" that participated in many a parade in Philadelphia and New York well into the age of the automobile. No society dance would start without Edward Morrell leading the way. He served as an officer in the Pennsylvania National Guard for much of his life, and because of this, was known as "Colonel Morrell" and eventually "General Morrell," even though he never served on active military duty.

If all this suggests Ned Morrell was nothing but a social parasite, all is not what it seems. Morrell, who was active in Republican politics, was appointed to fill an unexpired term in Congress in 1900 and was re-elected three times to the Fifth Pennsylvania District, serving until 1907. As a member of Congress, he vigorously promoted the rights of Native and African Americans and was of invaluable help to Katharine Drexel in her apostolate.

By way of example, in 1903, arguing before Congress for the continuation of rations for Indian school children who did not attend government schools, Morrell said, "The question thus presented is: whether in legislating for the Indian tribes, Congress shall discriminate between Indian children attending private schools and those attending public or government schools. I submit that the power to discriminate amounts in effect, to the power to destroy."

In many ways a very practical and forward-thinking man, Morrell was a pioneer in promoting electrification and the telephone when those two modern necessities were mere novelties. Louise Morrell's great work was outreach to African Americans, and in this apostolate the record clearly shows Ned was more than a "me too" partner. He was with her every step of the way. In Congress, he championed voting rights for blacks, a cause that would not gain serious recognition for almost half a century.

While the Johnson fortune was modest compared with the Drexel's, this too aided Katharine's work, along with Ned's eventual inheritance. As an aside, it might be noted that most of John Johnson's wealth was tied up in his art collection, which included some of the finest Renaissance paintings in America. This he willed to the Philadelphia Museum of Art.23 It is easily the museum's finest collection, and given the astronomical increase in the value of fine art, probably is worth many times over the value of the Drexel estate.

* * * *

Kate, of course, had been one of her sister's bridesmaids. The portrait taken of her that day shows an attractive, thoughtful young woman, with no hint of the inner turmoil that had just been resolved. She still had not told most of her relatives of her decision, nor had she determined what congregation she would enter. And, of course, what to do with all that money?

She had already confided her plans to Louise and Elizabeth. They gave their cautious approval, but Louise, with great practicality, said she should make no disposition of her inheritance until she had completed her novitiate.

Hardest of all had been breaking the news to Elizabeth. After all, Louise had Ned. Elizabeth would have no one. Katharine would later remember saying to Elizabeth, "I will leave you all alone if I go into the convent." Elizabeth replied, "If God wants you, go. Don't think of me at all."24

Katharine came up with an interesting proposal concerning her future, which she shared with Bishop O'Connor in a February 12, 1889 letter.

Suppose the American bishops — or, she adds, more realistically — "at least those concerned in the Indian and Colored Missions" were to organize a Bureau for Colored and Indian Missions? Her annual income could be the start-up funding, supplemented by an annual collection taken up in all churches during the first week of Lent.

After she entered the convent, Lise and Louise could act as trustees for her in dealing with the bishops. Her greatest single concern was that there were many more Colored than Indians in the country. "I would have to devise some method to save these 600,000 souls so that the interests of the Colored seven millions would not prevent the speedy help which these 600,000 Indians require in order to fit them for the opening of their reservations in 25 short years," she wrote.

Further, rather than join a missionary order, she would step away from the apostolate and become a contemplative.25

By the time Katharine wrote this letter, Bishop O'Connor, together with Father Stephan, had come up with quite a different idea. It was something that, Bishop O'Connor said, came to him while celebrating Mass. Katharine should found a congregation of her own, a missionary congregation to Indians and Colored. What an amazing leap! Three months earlier, the bishop was telling her not to enter the convent. Now he was telling her to found an order.

In this case, Bishop O'Connor did not trust the mail, so he came to Philadelphia to give the word directly. Katharine told the story years later to one of the Blessed Sacrament Sisters, most likely Mother Mercedes, her successor in office and the compiler of the early annals.

> I was always drawn to the contemplative life. The thought of forming an order was appalling to me. I had written frequently to Bishop O'Connor and told him of my desires for the contemplative life and he would always answer me, "Wait a while." I told this to my confessor and he advised me to write again to His Lordship and tell him of the strong attraction I felt to serving God in the contemplative life and my special attraction to the Order of the Dominican Perpetual Adoration — St. Dominic, and that I did not want to wait any longer and with the advice of my confessor I intended making arrangement to enter this order. This brought the bishop from Omaha to Philadelphia and then he told me of the plan he had, saying that I should found an order for the Christianization and evangelization of the Indian and Colored races, and use the wealth that God had given me for that purpose. I was horrified when the Bishop told me this, but then, had he told me to go to Timbuctu, I would have gone willingly, feeling that he was speaking as my spiritual director and I could only obey.26

On February 12, Father Stephan wrote to Katharine:

> I went to see Bishop O'Connor, found him well and happy. We talked about your future plans in regard to yourself, thoroughly and conscientiously, and I will give you the results. We are both of the opinion and hope it is God's Will that you start a new order for Indians and Negroes alone and therefore I ask you and your sister to meet me here at Omaha at the bishop's residence and we will go to Indian territory to visit our

Indian schools.27

Bishop O'Connor followed up his visit with a letter on February 16 that was somewhat less imperious, but the idea was the same.

> I fear you are likely to suffer from a surplus of advisers. Too many cooks spoil the broth, and sometimes too many doctors will kill the patient, whom the family physician would save.
>
> You have decided to become a religious. The next thing for you to determine is whether you shall establish a new order for the Indians and Colored people, or leaving your income for their benefit, enter an order already established, which will take more or less interest in these races. If you establish a new order, you will need all of your income and ten times more, to make it accomplish the objectives, even partially.
>
> In this hypothesis, then, no need to talk of a committee or administration. Should you enter an order already established, take Louise's advice. Make no final disposition of your income — it would be simply folly to do so — till you shall be ready to make vows. In the meantime, Lizzie and Louise can administer according to your instructions. The more I have thought about your case the more convinced I am that God has called you to establish an order for the objects above mentioned. The need for it is patent to everybody. All the help the established orders can give, in the work, will be needed, but a strong order devoted to it exclusively is also needed. You have the means to make such an establishment. Your social position will draw to it subjects and friends without number. God has put in your heart a great love for the Indians and the Negroes. He has given you a taste and capacity for the sort of business which such a foundation would bring with it. All these things point more clearly, than an inspiration or revelation could, to your duty in the premise.
>
> ...Reflect carefully on what I have told you, and let me know your objections to my decision in your case."28

When Father McGoldrick, her confessor, was apprised of this notion of founding a congregation, he also was in agreement. The three men upon whom Katharine leaned for spiritual advice — Bishop O'Connor, and Fathers McGoldrick and Stephan — were of the same mind; now it was a matter of convincing Katharine.

In her February 24 reply, she asked to be excused from meeting with Bishop

O'Connor and Father Stephan at that time because she would be on a retreat with the Children of Mary. She listed her reasons for questioning the advisability of founding the order Bishop O'Connor and Father Stephan were suggesting:

> 1st. I have never decided whether a life of prayer and contemplation would not be more acceptable to God. And this, because of the merit of prayer and the goodness of God in listening to prayer and the merits of Jesus Christ which are ours through prayer. Then in Contemplative Orders daily Communion is permitted and this is not the case in active Orders, and as the merit of one Communion is necessarily greater that any merit which I could acquire by any work of mine, as one single Holy Communion gives Our Lord more pleasure and God more glory than all the work and toil and labor for God, of all the men in the whole world, then I feel that a contemplative life where daily Communion is usual, would give Our Lord more pleasure than if I were to devote myself to active life in an Order where the nuns communicated but four times or three times each week....
>
> My second reason for not wishing to found an Order for Indians and Colored is that I appreciate that a founder of an order should be animated with every virtue capable of fitting her to carry out the object of her order. If she has not the right spirit, who should have it? I know the self-sacrifice necessary in the missionary life! I know the privations, the trials, the temptations, and I ask myself, could I go through all these things in a manner suitable for edifying the religious of my order? And if the founder were not to set an example, were to shrink from the toils and privations, where could you expect to find this example? I have seen the Sisters of St. Francis. Their spirit is my ideal of what a missionary nun should be. I know that I have not the courage to put into action the Gospel as they do. Why not be taught by them and follow their steps by following their rule (if I am called to an active life) rather than starting a new rule?
>
> Thirdly, is not an old and tried order more efficient in this Indian and Colored harvest; because in making new rules there are necessary delays and oppositions not to be met with an approved order.
>
> Fourth, could not the Indian and Colored work not be better done by employing all the orders? The Orders to be employed by the Catholic Indian Bureau to which Bureau I would leave all my income. What does Father Stephan think? Does he think and you think before God that an order of nuns would accomplish more than the Bureau's em-

ploying all efficient Orders and by keeping in its office the deeds to each of these missions?

Katharine concluded by telling her spiritual adviser she will found an order if it is God's will. "The responsibility of such a call almost crushes me, because I am so infinitely poor in the virtues necessary. Pray for me, I beseech you, that I may know God's will and do it."[29]

Bishop O'Connor's February 28 reply addresses her concerns:

> I was never so sure of any vocation, not even my own, as I am of yours. If you do not establish the order in question, you will allow to pass an opportunity of doing immense service to the Church which may not occur again.
>
> Your objections are simple scruples.... Your love of contemplation is just sufficient to sustain you under the distractions of external occupations. No more.
>
> Daily Communion can well and easily be made a rule of the new institute. It is simply a matter of history, that every great need that arose in the Church, called into being a new order. There are intrinsic reasons why this should have been the case. Is not the conversion and civilization of seven million Colored and a couple of hundred thousand Indians a great and pressing need? The "old and tried orders" have done very little to meet it, and what they may do in the future will be, for each community, a side issue. We will welcome their assistance but it will be far, very far from sufficient to accomplish the work that is waiting for us. We must have an order, and a strong order devoted exclusively to it, and even then, I fear, it will be little more than half done...
>
> An order established for the Negroes and Indian missions will make a much more direct and economical use of your money than an Indian Bureau could.
>
> Even as foundress, you will have your faults, but God not you will do the work. He often makes use of very weak instruments. The question is not will you be all you should be, but does God will you to be His instrument....

If Katharine had doubts, Bishop O'Connor had none, and he insisted it was her duty to found an order. Period. End of discussion. His letter concluded:

> I regard it settled that you are to establish a new order, and I shall go to Philadelphia merely to arrange the details. The Church has spo-

ken to you through me, her unworthy organ, and you must hear her or take the consequences. Do you wish for a decree of a general council in this matter or for a decision ex cathedra from the Pope?...30

Even before Katherine gave her final assent, Bishop O'Connor chose the order where she herself — and her first Sisters — would receive their own formation as religious. It would be with the Religious Sisters of Mercy in his brother's former diocese, Pittsburgh. Bishop Michael O'Connor had first encountered the Religious Sisters of Mercy, an Irish congregation, when, as a student priest in Rome, he translated their proposed rule into Latin for them. When he became a bishop in Pittsburgh, he invited the congregation into his diocese. The Mercy Sisters were an active order with an apostolate out among the people, just as Katharine's congregation would be — if, in a more specialized field — limited to Indians and Colored. Another difference, of course, would be the new order's focus on the Blessed Sacrament, something which satisfied a deep inner yearning of Katharine's. But on the whole, the Mercy Sisters and the future Sisters of the Blessed Sacrament were a good fit.

Katharine gave her final decision to Bishop O'Connor on March 19, a significant feast in the life of the Church. She wrote:

> The feast of St. Joseph brought me the grace to give the remainder of my life to the Indians and Colored — to enter fully and entirely into your views and those of Rev. Stephan as to what is best for the salvation of the souls of these people.
>
> On the 30th of April, Lise said she would accompany me to the Pittsburgh House of Mercy. May I ask you to kindly drop me a line introducing me to the Superior? I wish to ask her what clothing, etc. I must bring with me. We shall not tell Uncle Anthony nor Mr. Childs of the "plan" until Louise's return so please keep very secret. They would have every reason to be angry did they hear the news first from strangers. From my heart we thank you for your extremely kind visit. We thoroughly appreciate it. I had a lovely retreat at home. It was only this morning that I could promise Our Lord to please Him by entering fully into your plan to found an order. As long as I look on self, I cannot. Our Lord gives and will give me the grace always to look at Him. Please, I pray, bless your children.31

Louise and Edward were not due home from Europe until April 15, and Katharine would have preferred to tell Louise of her decision to found a congregation before informing Anthony Drexel and George Childs, the trustees of her father's estate. But there were too many matters which had to be attended to, if she were to enter her own postulancy in May.

Katharine chose March 25, the Feast of the Annunciation, as the date she would tell the two men of her choice. She told Bishop O'Connor:

> Uncle Anthony dropped four or five tears, but he said he would not oppose anything which contributed to my happiness. He thinks, however, that I am making the mistake of my life if I become a religious; yet he consents and so does Mr. Childs. I told them both of your plans relative to my establishing an Order for Indians and Colored. They think I can do so much more good by helping the Orders already established. I have told your plans to no one except to Uncle Anthony and Mr. Childs. They have agreed that it is best to tell the world nothing of this: I am going to pass the summer with the Sisters of Mercy at Pittsburgh. If I like it there I shall remain.[32]

To say no one else knew wasn't strictly true. For instance, Archbishop Ryan had been fully apprised of Katharine's decision and gave his approval. George and Emma Childs, although not Catholic, were personal friends of the Archbishop. They dined with him a few days later, and the Archbishop assured them that should she not be suited for convent life, there would be ample opportunity to change her mind. Archbishop Ryan wrote Katharine of this meeting, while they regretted her action because it will deprive them of her presence, yet they felt that God was pleased with her consecration.

Katharine, accompanied by Msgr. Stephan, paid a courtesy call upon Cardinal James Gibbons in Baltimore on April 2. Cardinal Gibbons, the unofficial primate of the Church in the United States, was well aware of the magnificent work she was doing among the Native and African Americans. In the relatively short time she had funded this apostolate, she had already built 11 missions and was contributing to the support of many others. During this meeting with the Cardinal, ownership of these missions was discussed. He thought ownership should rest with the Catholic Indian Bureau, rather than with the various orders. Plans were also discussed for the financing of education in English and American ways of Benedictines who would come from France and Belgium for the Indian missions.

Finally, Katharine told the cardinal of her plan to enter religious life and to found a congregation specifically for work among the Indians and Colored. Of this he seemed to heartily approve, she told Bishop O'Connor. But as to her entering religion through the Mercy Sisters, that was another matter. He was clearly afraid that once she entered the Mercy Convent she would never leave. "I almost wish that before you enter the novitiate you would make a vow not to make a vow whilst you are there," he told her. "Write to me," he said, "if the Sisters try to persuade you to stay." As a final piece of advice, he warned, "Do not wear their dress; be a visitor."[33]

The next week, Katharine, accompanied by Elizabeth, visited the Sisters of Mercy Convent on Webster Avenue in Pittsburgh. They traveled incognito to avoid publicity, using the name Langstroth. The meeting went well and plans were made for Katharine's reception. The Mercy Sisters thought Elizabeth would soon follow Katharine into the convent. Katharine, however, had other plans for her beloved sister.

Years earlier, Walter George Smith (the same gentleman who may have been Katharine's beau) had proposed to Elizabeth, who had refused his suit. Walter, a childhood friend and Torresdale neighbor, was, like Edward Morrell, a lawyer. While he wasn't as handsome or dashing as Morrell, he had one thing that made him prime husband material as far as Katharine was concerned. Most of the Smiths, like her branch of the Drexel family, were active and committed Catholics, and Walter, as the saying goes, was an apple that didn't fall far from the tree.

Katharine, in one of her last acts before entering religious life, played Cupid by arranging for the two to renew their acquaintanceship, or at least she tried. In her April 6 letter to Bishop O'Connor, an apparent co-conspirator, she wrote:

> The game has been played, and I think ends in platonic affection on both sides. I know you will in charity pray for Lise, asking the Sacred Heart to protect and keep her, since I am to leave her without earthly guardian. Please do not in any way show by word or insinuation to anyone and above all Lise that I have told you about this affair. I cannot help wishing that our Lord would send her a husband whom she could love not platonically; but according to the model laid down by St. Paul to the Ephesians — a man whom she could justly love, fear and honor. Of course I feel no man could be worthy of a character as noble as hers. My heart aches for her in her loneliness....

All of that may be well and true, but Katharine would discover that she was not the only Drexel who could keep a secret. Seven months later, Lise and Walter announced their engagement.

George Childs' newspaper, the *Public Ledger*, reported on Katharine's May 7 departure for the convent:

On Monday morning, Miss Drexel attended Mass at St. John's Church in the city and chose that sacred place to take farewell of her relatives, excepting such as would accompany her and one or two very intimate friends. She was attired all in black and according to custom, knelt in front of the altar and dedicated (herself) to the Virgin Mary. The Mass over, her distant relatives, her old governess and maid and one or two faithful servants crossed from the other aisle and bade her farewell. She kissed them all. Although evidently deeply and greatly affected, she did not shed tears and in this very severe ordeal showed remarkable fortitude.

In appearance she is the most attractive of the three sisters, though not so tall as the other two. She has a good complexion, a sweet expression and was noted for her smile. Her eyes are blue or blue-gray and one of her greatest charms is a wealth of uncommonly beautiful brown hair. It is said to reach far below her waist. One of the sad thoughts in connection with her withdrawal to some of her relatives was that she should sacrifice this part of her personality and "woman's glory," but according to usage, she will not have to sacrifice her hair until she takes her final vows.

The *Public Ledger* account was probably correct for the most part, although Katharine's hair would be cut when she took first vows, not final vows. According to Louise, the leave-taking for her close friends and relatives was at a breakfast at 1503 Walnut Street after the Mass. One does wonder what Louise and Lizzie might have thought, as they read over their morning coffee, "most attractive of the three sisters."

"...by the ring Our Lord plights
to His bride His troth,
and she, receiving it vows
to be faithful to Him.
This done she is no longer
her own,
she is His forever."

SAINT KATHARINE DREXEL

Chapter Six
Mother and Servant

Elizabeth, Louise, and Edward accompanied Katharine to Pittsburgh and her new life before departing on their European vacation. Katharine would have a six-month postulancy, during which, according to custom, she would wear a simple dress and veil rather than a nun's habit. This would be followed by two years in the novitiate, after which she would officially take first vows. The day following her arrival at the Webster Street convent, she wrote a charming letter to her sisters, telling them of her first impressions and assuring them she was adjusting to the religious life:

> Well, in arriving at the convent, Rev. Mother and Mother Hilda and Mother Josephine remained with me in the parlor for a half hour or so, and then I went upstairs and put on the postulant's gown. Now here is the real truth, so don't suspect me. The dress fits me, sleeves and all, length of skirt — everything except that it is just a little too long-waisted. I forgot to bring a tiny looking-glass with me so I don't know how I look, but entre nous there is much more room for vanity in not seeing myself than getting a glimpse of my countenance without bangs. By the time you see me, my aspect will be much improved for I can puff my hair in front, which can't be done at present until the bangs have less of a tendency to stick straight up. You would be pleased with my veil, which is of lace quite as fine and pretty as my Paris lace dress which Lise said she would have altered for herself.[1]

While Sister Katharine would have preferred to be treated in exactly the same manner as any other postulant, the Mercy Sisters made certain exceptions for her. A few were physical, in deference to the greater change in lifestyle she was making and her previous history of delicate health. She was permitted to rise a half hour later. Later being 5:30 a.m. She was permitted to bathe every day and change her garments twice weekly. She was given an orange every day.

"The food is abundant and very good," she wrote in a reassuring letter to Louise. "All the Sisters work extremely hard and it is not thought virtuous for them to unfit themselves for their work by fasting. We have meat three times a day."[2]

Other allowances made for Sister Katharine were practical ones designed to better fit her for her future as superior of a congregation. She was given more time for spiritual reading than the other Sisters received, and the Mercy Sisters made certain her training exposed her to a variety of vocational apostolates from teaching to nursing. She discovered that teaching a class of unruly children could be quite challenging, not quite the same thing as the somewhat relaxed atmosphere of the St. Michel Sunday School.

Convent rules are not inborn. Sister Katharine had tremendous vitality. One of her sister novices later recalled her habit of walking very fast and running down steps. But halfway down, she would remember her new station, stop, stand still for a moment, then proceed at the sedate pace proper for a novice.

Some days would find her at the Mercy Sisters' hospital; here she learned how to move a patient, how to dress a wound, how to disinfect for lice. Along with the hands-on nursing, she was provided with lists of nonprescription medicines and their uses, a handy tool for Sisters working in remote areas far from doctors and civilization.

She tried to put the care of the missions aside; day-to-day decisions were left in the hands of Lise, the Morrells, and Mary Cassidy. But major decisions still had to be made — for instance, where would the new congregation be headquartered? Bishop Marty suggested Sioux Falls; Father Stephan favored either Banning, California, or Washington, D.C. Sister Katharine had already built St. Boniface, a school for Indian children in Banning, but no congregation had been found to staff it. If the novitiate for the new congregation were there, the aspirants could be given practical teaching experience at the school. Bishop O'Connor thought the Philadelphia area would be best. Most American Catholics lived in the East, and that would be the area where a congregation could more easily attract postulants. In all probability, Archbishop Ryan also favored this location because Sister Katharine was barely a month into her postulancy when Edward Morrell began negotiations for a property on Bristol Pike in Cornwells Heights, two miles north of St. Michel.

The location of the motherhouse was of crucial importance for reasons related to the nature of new religious congregations. If a group of pious women (or men) opt to live in community and perform certain spiritual or corporal works of mercy, that is laudable. But it does not make them a recognized religious congregation in the eyes of the Catholic Church. To obtain official recognition, such congregations must draw up rules of conduct in keeping with their stated mission but still within general guidelines issued by the Church. New congregations almost always operate under the direct control of the local bishop. After they have established a record of stability, they may receive official recognition from Rome.

During their period as a strictly diocesan congregation (some congregations remain this way always), they may find a bishop that has a different idea about what their mission should be. For instance, in America's past, there were times when congregations would have preferred an apostolate among the poor or in hospital ministry. But if the bishop thought there was a greater need in the education apostolate, they were ordered to become teachers.

Sisters Katharine's new congregation would have a dual purpose — devotion to the Blessed Sacrament and missionary outreach to Native and African Americans. The practical means to this evangelization was, in most instances, through the educational apostolate, but evangelization remained the primary purpose. It was very important that their bishop, wherever they were located, understood and supported this mission. Sister Katharine would be fortunate; in Philadelphia's Archbishop Ryan and his successors, she would have such bishops.

* * * *

"I try to think just as little as I can about the new order," she wrote in a letter to Bishop O'Connor, "endeavoring to attend solely to my own progress in perfection."[3] All this was made the more difficult by a stream of visitors who could not be denied — Archbishop Ryan, Father Stephan, Bishop Marty. Surely, the other postulants must have wondered why Sister Katharine was called so often to the parlor.

In all things she sought to be no different than her sister-candidates, who at that time had no notion she was aspiring for anything other than the vocation of a Sister of Mercy. All her life, until that point, Katharine had found coffee nauseating and opted for tea. But on her first morning, coffee was served. She drank it without comment and did so for the rest of her life. "I entered to embrace community life," she later explained, "and leave my peculiarities outside the door." Sewing was part of the routine for the aspiring Sisters, and it was noted, when the period was over, it was Sister Katharine who would first leap up to fetch the pan and brush to tidy up the room. But if Sister Katharine strove to be the best possible Religious she could be, it was never done in a spirit of superiority over her other sister-candidates. Afterward, they would remember her for her warm sense of humor as much as her piety and how she would try to teach them the Indian dances she had observed during her visits to the West.

Her outward composure masked a continued inward anxiety. No, there was no doubt in her mind the convent was where she belonged; rather, it was this idea of founding and directing a religious congregation that was unsettling. Her letters to Bishop O'Connor continued to reflect this self-doubt. On May 12, she wrote:

> This convent life is full of joy for me and I take a most unmortified satisfaction in this respite from responsibility, which brings me peace. There is one thought, however, which causes me uneasiness — it is the thought of why I am here viz: — to prepare me for a future life of responsibility, and what is more, a life which is most apt to be one of opposition, trial, subject to criticism even of the Church. Then as it were to have the very salvation of so many to hang as it were upon my instrumentality! The undertaking you propose, Reverend Father, seems enormous and I shall freely acknowledge that my heart goes down in sorrow when I think of it. To be the head of a new order! New orders always, I think, have to pass through the baptism of the cross.
>
> All of these dismal thoughts are not generous to Our Lord, and in the chapel and meditation I am striving to overcome this selfishness and self-seeking, and to look upon the future life you propose for me with cheerfulness since you say it is the will of the Lord....[4]

Her direct superior and mentor during this period of postulancy and novitiate would be the Sisters of Mercy Novice Mistress, Mother M. Inez Casey. Mother Inez would confide at a later date that Sister Katharine was the most outstanding of the novices under her charge. "If I could do such a thing as take from each humility," she said, "that is, if it could be measured or weighed, and I brought the whole stock of these 80 novices into one grand whole it would not begin to equal the simplicity and humility of Sister Katharine." As to her obedience, "as soon as she recognized the voice of authority, her submission was absolute," Mother Inez noted.[5]

In chapel, Sister Katharine was delighted to find her assigned stall was located just under the window of her patron, St. Catherine of Siena. Though she could not receive holy Communion daily, it was permitted four times a week. "I miss the other three Communions," she wrote, "but all is well when we are doing Our Lord's will."

* * * *

Sister Katharine passed her first milestone in religion in November 1889. Her six-month postulancy neared completion, and she prepared to enter the novitiate phase. As a novice, she would receive a name in religion and be clothed in the habit of her new station in religious life.

"What name shall I take?" she asked in a letter to her sisters in Philadelphia. Her first choice was Sister Francis Emma, in honor of her beloved parents, but she worried lest this seem "too linked to family affection." In the end, Mother Sebastian helped her make her choice. She would be Sister Mary Katharine, a simple reversal of her birth name of Catherine or Katharine Mary.[6] It was a very practical choice. She was already known to the world as Katharine, and since it would soon be publicly announced that Katharine Drexel was founding a congregation, it was sensible to keep the name. And of course, from Mother Sebastian's point of view, it didn't hurt a bit that the Mercy Sisters had been founded by another Mother Catherine — Catherine McAuley.

The Drexel family rented a private rail car to take them to Pittsburgh for Sister Katharine's November 7 reception. There was Lise, Louise, and Ned, and of course the Drexel, Lankenau, Langstroth, and Bouvier aunts and uncles, Mr. and Mrs. Childs and assorted cousins and friends. Katharine was dressed in a beautiful white satin and crepe bridal gown. The magnificent diamonds that adorned her neck competed with the glittering rings upon her fingers and the golden bracelets encircling her arms. The ensemble was offset with delicate orange blossoms, and it was as if this wealthy heiress was saying, "See, this is what I am surrendering for God!" An escort of honor of eight pretty little relatives preceded her up the chapel aisle. First in line was cousin Josie Drexel, who as the tallest, was appointed cross-bearer.[7]

At the altar, Archbishop Ryan received her, flanked by three bishops and a score of priests. The only missing person who was important in Sister Katharine's life was Bishop O'Connor; he was ill in Omaha and unable to attend.

"My child, what dost thou demand?" The Archbishop inquired.

"The mercy of God and the holy habit of religion," responded Katharine, in keeping with the prescribed ritual.

She was presented with a folded garment that the Archbishop blessed. She retired to another chamber, where she discarded her finery and emerged clothed in a simple black serge habit and white muslin veil. After the ceremony, there were a few tears and a gala reception for her friends and relatives. Sister Katharine attended, but did not partake of the banquet. In keeping with her new status, she waited upon her guests.

Now that Sister Katharine had been received and clothed in habit, it was time to announce to the world at large that she was founding a religious congregation for service to the Indians and Negroes.

Archbishop Ryan spoke of the plan a few days later when he addressed his brother bishops in Baltimore during ceremonies for the centennial of the American episcopate:

> ...I believe that in the last century we could have done more for the Colored people of the South and the Indian tribes. I am not unmindful of the zeal, with limited resources for its exercise, of the Southern bishops, nor the great self-sacrifice of Indian missionaries, who in the spirit of primitive Christianity gave their lives for the noble, but unjustly treated Indians. But as I believe that Negro slavery and the unjust treatment of the Indians are the two great blots on American civilization, so do I feel that in the Church also, the most reasonable cause for regret in the past century is the fact that more could have been done for these dependent classes. Let us now come in the name of God and resolve to make reparations for these shortcomings of the past.[8]

After this blunt, overdue mea culpa on behalf of his nation and Church, the Philadelphia Archbishop, one of the great orators of his day, waxed poetic:

> On the threshold of the new century, I lately beheld a scene prophetic of this reparation. On Thursday last, in the quiet convent chapel of the Sisters of Mercy in Pittsburgh, I could well imagine along each side of the chapel the representatives of the different races. On the one side the Indians and Colored, on the other the White race that oppressed both. They, the oppressors and the oppressed, gazed on each other with little feelings of fraternal love. And then I saw coming out of the ranks of the White race, a fair young virgin. Approaching midway between the contending lines, she knelt before the illumined altar of the God of all races of men, and offered her great fortune, her life, her love, her hopes, that until the grave shall receive her, all she possesses now or shall possess in the future, may belong to God and to the Indian and Colored races. She hopes that other Christian maidens may unite with her and thus inaugurate the great work of reparation, and help to render it perpetual.[9]

There were two reasons for the delay in announcing Sister Katharine's plan. First, the postulancy period, while it had a degree of formation, was really a time of trial — a time when both she and the Sisters of Mercy could weigh her suitability for convent life. Any announcement of a new congregation before her reception of the habit would have been premature. The second reason had to do with the acceptance of candidates for the congregation. Once the announcement was made, it was presumed young women would apply. As a matter of fact, Bishop O'Connor already had a few candidates in mind. Psychologically, it would be best that Katharine be clothed as a religious when she met her first postulants. By November 16, Sister Katharine could report to Bishop O'Connor that two postulants, "Miss Jennie Clayton (Sister Mary) and Miss McGarvey (Sister Sallie), have been here for two days. We are very much pleased with their dispositions."[10]

Neither Miss Clayton nor Miss McGarvey, both of whom were Philadelphians, would remain in religious life. But one of the pioneer band of postulants was Kate O'Connor of Pittsburgh, the future Mother Mercedes. Before Sister Katharine announced the forming of her congregation, Kate O'Connor had a great desire to enter the convent and work among Native Americans. Her confessor opposed this idea, but finally steered her toward the Franciscans, an order that was missioned both to Native-American and white schools. When she heard the news of Sister Katharine's congregation, Kate wanted to join, but her confessor was adamant that it was the will of God she be a Franciscan. She met Sister Katharine when she accompanied a school companion to an interview with the new foundress at the Mercy convent. Mother Inez, the novice mistress, was the one who convinced her that her confessor was wrong: She should not enter the Franciscans against her own will. Sister Katharine, without comment, promised to pray for her.

In the end, Kate O'Connor's confessor was suddenly transferred to Canada, and her new confessor agreed with her: If the Holy Spirit was telling her to enter this new congregation, that is what she should do.[11] Kate O'Connor entered the Mercy Convent with the intention of becoming a member of Sister Katharine's congregation. Of course, at that point, Sister Katharine had very little to do with her formation — she was a mere first-year novice herself. But on her first night in the convent, Kate was shocked to see her future superior, this millionaire's daughter, darning a stocking that appeared to be long past hope.

"I could never wear darned stockings like that," Kate exclaimed.

Sister Katharine smiled. "Oh," she said, "it will be a long time before you have to. Yours are new now." (That was holy poverty.) The next week, Sister Kate was presented with an example of holy humility. She and Sister Katharine were alone in the community room, working at different tables. Sister Katharine got up and left. Almost immediately, she returned, knelt at the postulant's feet and asked forgiveness for walking out of the room without seeking her leave. The lessons would continue; not by words alone, but by personal example.[12]

In Sister Katharine's personal retreat notes during this period, notes meant only for her eyes, her humility shines through. "I would fear to die because naked before God Who knows the graces He has given me. I know I shall have to give an account for faith, education, fortune, sacraments. Point out one saint in Heaven who has had more aids than I."

Meanwhile, there were joyful tidings from Philadelphia. It was during the train ride home from Sister Katharine's reception that Lise broke her news to the family. She and Walter George Smith were engaged; she had held off telling anyone so as not to upstage Katharine's ceremony.

A few days later, Louise wrote that she and Ned had visited the site of Sister Katharine's proposed convent. The location, Louise informed her sister, "is a beautiful piece of property and so easy of access to the station. The convent will stand on a knoll and have an extensive view."

She also added, "Lise is genuinely in love. Instead of office last night she began to tune up her rosary, and was only brought to by a groan from me."

Prim and proper Walter, too, seems to have been altered by love. In a December letter to Sister Katharine, Lise wrote, "I think you would have the greatest difficulty in reconstructing out of the frivolous lightminded gentleman in the easy chair chuckling over the silly Sunday paper jokes our elegant, nonchalant, classical friend of former days."

Elizabeth's St. Francis de Sales Industrial School was opened by this time, and Sister Katharine, in a letter of Christmas Day written to Lise, asked:

> "Do you remember how I used to fear that you and Louise and I would become separated in our works. And now it seems to me Holy Providence will somehow unite the St. Francis de Sales and Indian and Colored and all our works. I hope with God's help, to be of some use to your boys."

In the 19th century, vows were considered sacred, and marriage was almost always for life. But engagements could be surprisingly short. Walter George Smith took Elizabeth Langstroth Drexel in holy matrimony at St. Dominic Church on January 7, 1890. It was two months to the day since Sister Katharine's reception into the Sisters of Mercy novitiate and Elizabeth's announcement of betrothal. Archbishop Ryan officiated at the wedding ceremony; Walter's brother, Dehan, in religion known as Passionist Father Maurice Smith, celebrated the Nuptial Mass; and Anthony Drexel gave the bride away.

Winter weddings are at best chancy, and poor Elizabeth and George got off to an inauspicious start. The weather was stormy, and worse yet, Philadelphia was in the midst of an epidemic of "the grippe" — in today's terminology — the flu.

Two-thirds of the guests never made it to either the wedding or the breakfast that followed at St. Michel. Lise and Walter were oblivious to these minor disappointments; wed they were.

Walter in love may have mellowed somewhat, but he could never let his hair down completely. Edward Morrell may have been "Ned" to his friends, but it would be difficult to imagine anyone calling Walter George Smith "Wally."

In a letter written after the wedding, Walter told Sister Katharine:

> Elizabeth was more gratified than I can tell you by the spiritual bouquets. I write now that you may know that you are on our minds, and that your letter and all it contained was received. Elizabeth (I do not call her Lizzie) is so busy, that she asks me to write in her stead. But I think she will add some to this scrawl, which, if it serves to assure you of my fraternal affection, will fulfill its office.

Elizabeth did indeed add a note: "Everybody is gone. I am very sleepy and shall have to make an early start tomorrow. I have only time to say I love you and think of you always." And yes, she signed her name "Lizzie."[13]

Among those absent at the ceremony, of course, was Sister Katharine. It would not be proper for a 19th-century Sister to leave the novitiate for something as frivolous as a family wedding. Instead, Elizabeth and Walter stopped off in Pittsburgh to visit Sister Katharine during a trip that took them to Niagara Falls and New York City before leaving for a European honeymoon and travels to Spain, Lourdes, and Monte Carlo. May found them in Florence where Elizabeth became seriously ill. At first, there was simply the nausea that could be attributed to the beginnings of a pregnancy. But then there were ominous liver pains. Her condition was such that last rites were given, but she recovered sufficiently to allay family alarm. The couple lingered in Europe as she recuperated, and in September they finally came home to St. Michel, where Elizabeth and Walter had decided to make their year-round home. It was adjacent to Louise's San Jose and within a few miles of Katharine's planned convent and Elizabeth's St. Francis de Sales School. Elizabeth would be close to everything important to her. She settled into the newly renovated house and awaited the birth of her and Walter's first child. Her mother's daughter in all things, Elizabeth had already purchased a complete layette for the baby from the Magdalen seamstresses of the Sisters of the Good Shepherd.

While Elizabeth and Walter had been touring Europe, Louise was taking care of business at home. The Cornwells Heights property had been purchased, but no announcement was made about its future use as a convent. Mr. Simon, the local coal dealer, came calling to offer the sale of an adjoining property and to pump Louise about what she was going to do with the parcel already purchased. She thanked him for his offer, and "he left no wiser than before," she reported.[14]

Louise represented the three sisters at a ceremony at the new Catholic University in Washington, D.C., and reported the doings in her usual breezy fashion. It rained, and they arrived rather wet. "There was a palpable lack of system, but after an hour of delay, about 100 bishops filed into the chapel and a shoal of clergy. There was a solemn high Mass sung by the Papal Legate, then Bishop Gilmore prosed away for half an hour. On the whole the ceremonies were very creditable, the singing magnificent," she wrote.

Louise also told of progress in Baltimore where she and Ned were building Epiphany College for the Josephites, the congregation she was funding in their work among African Americans.[15] The Morrells were watching out for Katharine's concerns in other respects, too. Louise reports to her sister on developments in the field of the Indian Missions.

General Thomas Morgan, Commissioner of Indian Affairs (1889-93), was no friend of the Catholic Church. "He has," Louise reported, "assigned Protestant missionaries to areas where the Indians are Catholic." Msgr. Stephan was also upset by Morgan's actions. He charged Morgan had dismissed Catholic teachers and superintendents and replaced them by Protestants. Morgan, for his part, dismissed Catholic complaints. "They oppose government schools in Indian Territory," he responded, "for the same reason that they oppose the public school system of our country."

In Pittsburgh, Sister Katharine had been preoccupied with another grave concern. Bishop O'Connor's health had not improved since her reception. In spite of her worry, she kept up a brave front in her letters to him.

She and the Sisters of Mercy had suggested he come to Pittsburgh to recuperate, but so far, he had refused. In a January 14, 1890 letter, she wrote: "...Is it a merciful providence that prevents me from ministering to you at Mercy Hospital? Would I have administered the wrong medicines? Horrible thought! Or would I have scalded the Right Reverend Bishop with a potion of boiling liquid in my eagerness to serve?"

On a more serious note, the convent had five Masses that morning, most of which Sister Katharine must have attended. "You have a share in four of these Masses and every prayer I utter," she wrote. In this letter, too, she ruefully recounted her shortcomings as an inexperienced classroom teacher.[16]

One of the Sisters was ill, and she replaced her in a classroom of Colored children. They knew instinctively that she was a beginner. One child had a tiny whistle in his mouth, and he gave it a short blast. Another boy on the other side of the room did the same. Sister Katharine reached for the rattan switch. "Hold out your hand," she commanded the first miscreant. Instead, he folded his arms and whistled again. Two other boys started fighting. Another built a fire in the fireplace.

Sister Katharine had seen Sister Loyola, her instructor, control a class with a few mild words. She tried that tack. She sat at her desk and said, "Children! No more lessons until there is perfect silence in this room!" With that, the entire class burst into song at the top of their lungs. Mercifully, Sister Emerentia, who had a class in the opposite room, came in and restored order. "The children are very interesting," Katharine, with some understatement, wrote.[17]

By January, Bishop O'Connor had gone to Florida to recuperate, but he continued to decline in both physical health and spirits. In the end, Sister Katharine and Mother Sebastian went South and prevailed upon him to return with them to Pittsburgh's Mercy Hospital. Sister Katharine was permitted to nurse her dear friend and spiritual father. In his illness, he was not a perfect patient. For example, one day, as Sister Katharine opened a closet in the sick room, a large water bug flew out. She screamed. The Bishop banished her from his room for two days "because she had not sufficient control of her feelings."[18]

Sister Katharine overlooked these small outbursts, because she knew Bishop O'Connor was a dying man. "This standing on the threshold of Eternal Life makes the soul exact in keeping perfect purity of heart," she wrote. "I hope I don't forget the silent lessons I received at this holy deathbed. The bishop never speaks of piety — and so all the lessons are silent ones — virtue in practice."[19]

While all this was happening, Sister Katharine was continuing her spiritual formation and making hard decisions as to the form her new congregation would take. This was central to one discussion during a visit to Philadelphia. The new order was to serve Indians and Colored. The question was: Should the congregation also accept Indian or Colored candidates? It was an enormously complicated issue.

Edward Morrell (and probably Louise) thought it should indeed accept Colored candidates. Father John Slattery, superior of the Josephite Fathers, proposed a white congregation with a Colored Third Order that would work directly with the Sisters. From the record, we can gather the others favored a totally white congregation. Elizabeth, who was in Europe, wrote, "This talk of a Colored and white community appears to me nothing but sheer madness."[20]

Bishop O'Connor does not appear to have a part in the discussion. Given Katharine's track record of deference to authority, it is highly unlikely that she did not consult Archbishop Ryan. In any case, the final decision was that the new congregation would, at this time, accept only white candidates. But the discussion was obviously brisk, and the matter was by no means closed for all time.

Katharine wrote to Edward Morrell after the meeting (April 23, 1890), commenting on "the earnest speeches made by all, the room strewn with papers, the loudness of the voices as we heated to the discussion." She also said, "Ned, the more I think of that, the more I doubt whether it would be wise. Let us pray however that the Holy Will of God may be done in all things."[21]

More than a century after the fact, it may be difficult to understand this decision. Why shouldn't African Americans be admitted to the congregation? Context is everything. We must look at this decision as an 1890 decision, just a quarter century after the Civil War. Remember, Lincoln only freed the slaves; he didn't invite them to tea. No African American broke bread at the White House (in other than the servants' quarters) until the coming of the New Deal under Franklin Roosevelt.

In 1890, when plans for the Sisters of the Blessed Sacrament were being drawn up, the reality was that most African Americans still lived in the Old South, where Jim Crow was the law of the land. How could an integrated congregation serve the community if the law clearly forbade blacks and whites to share the same living quarters? As it was, the Sisters would conduct boarding schools for black children, something which in itself was technically against the law in some states if they lived in the same building.

In spite of this obvious disagreement on the issue of Colored Sisters, Edward Morrell continued to be one of Sister Katharine's chief advisers and agents as she laid the groundwork for the new congregation. The arrangement worked very well, and although Archbishop Ryan advised Katharine to take charge of her own affairs after her formation, he encouraged continued cooperation and collaboration with the Morrells, who were already a force in the Colored apostolate. In a September 23 letter, he wrote, "I understand that Bishop O'Connor recommended that Mr. M. should do the work for you whilst you should be a novice in order to prevent distractions of mind. When you come to Philadelphia, circumstances will be changed."[22]

Bishop O'Connor's health did not improve in Pittsburgh. In April 1890, when it became obvious to him that he would not live, he returned to Omaha, determined to die in his own diocese. Death came on May 27, 1890. For Sister Katharine, even though she had known the bishop was dying, the reality of his death was almost too much to bear. It was he who had guided her during her long and torturous journey to the religious life. It was he who had convinced her it was God's will that she found a religious congregation to minister to the Indians and Colored. She had fully expected to lean upon him for guidance as she founded this new order, accepted new candidates, and opened missions for its apostolate.

Now he was gone, and Sister Katharine felt all alone. This was the darkest hour in her young life as a religious. She felt she simply could not do this complicated work on her own. Bishop O'Connor's earlier words, "The question is not will you be all you should be, but does God will you to be His instrument," now had a hollow ring.

Archbishop Ryan traveled to Omaha to officiate at the bishop's funeral, and on the way home, stopped at Pittsburgh's Mercy Convent to console Sister Katharine.

"I can't go on," she told him.

"If I share the burden with you, if I help you, can you go on?" the kindly Archbishop asked.[23]

With his words, Sister Katharine found new courage. She would persevere. As in so many other times in her life, God provided the instrument at precisely the time it was needed. Bishop O'Connor, through sheer force of will, had convinced — literally commanded — Katharine to found a religious congregation to serve African and Native Americans. Once she did so, his task was completed. With his death, the baton passed to a new adviser. Ryan was perfect for the task. The parameters for the congregation had already been set. He would offer advice and direction, which in most cases, was wise and practical. As Katharine's direct religious superior, he would rarely step in, except to apply a steadying brake at such times when inexperience and youthful enthusiasm threatened to take the new congregation on an impetuous course of action.

* * * *

But Katharine's trial was not complete. There would be one final sorrow.

Elizabeth Smith's apparent recovery from the illness contracted during her wedding trip in Europe was illusory. On September 24, 1890, even as she neared the time for delivery of her child, she again became gravely ill. Two days later, she died at St. Michel, and so did her unborn child. So passed the eldest of the Drexel sisters, in all her warm and wonderful manifestations — the proper Elizabeth, the sophisticated Lise, the girlish Lizzie. We can never know what this gifted woman, no longer a maiden, not yet a mother, would have accomplished had she lived.

Sister Katharine, who had been notified of the gravity of her sister's condition, was still en route from Pittsburgh. Louise and Ned, too, were absent. They were on the high seas, on their way home from a European vacation. Walter, of course, was with his wife at the time of her death. His sister, Helen Grace Smith, remembered that sorrowful day: "I can never forget when Walter came downstairs," she would write, "the drawn look on his face, every muscle tense with anguish, and as his gaze fell on me almost beside myself with grief, he took my hand and drew me out on the piazza and pointed to the beautiful serene sky above us, and said, "Grace, God reigneth — His Will, not ours be done." Helen Grace questioned why this should be so. "Don't make the cross harder, little sister," Walter said. "You are forgetting God's way is always the best way."

Elizabeth, with her baby in her arms, was laid to rest with her parents at Eden Hall.

With her death, under the terms of Francis Drexel's will, Elizabeth's trust fund passed to Sister Katharine and Louise. Walter inherited only such income as his wife had already received. He also inherited St. Michel, but Louise, not wishing the old home to pass from the Drexel family, purchased it from him. Walter's monetary inheritance was not great because most of Elizabeth's income to date had been absorbed by the building of St. Francis and her other charities. While the $200,000 construction cost of St. Francis had been covered, the intended endowment of the school had not. Sister Katharine and Louise generously consented to jointly donate $120,000 a year for the next eight years to the St. Francis endowment. Katharine also donated approximately $50,000 from her share of the Langstroth estate, and she agreed to make further donations periodically as needed. The completed endowment was expected to produce an income of $30,000 a year, deemed sufficient at the time to cover the operating expenses of the school when combined with the products of the working farm and shops of the vocational school. For the next half century, Louise managed Elizabeth's school, although her primary focus was always the African-American apostolate.

Walter George Smith never remarried, but he remained a loyal friend of Mother Katharine Drexel and the Sisters of the Blessed Sacrament, serving pro bono as counsel for the congregation for 33 years. He distinguished himself in his field to the point that he rose to the presidency of the American Bar Association and was awarded Notre Dame University's prestigious Laetare Medal.

Letters written by Cardinal Gibbons to Archbishop Ryan tell something of the world's perception of Smith (and coincidentally of Morrell). In 1909, after the election of President William Howard Taft, the Baltimore cardinal wrote to Philadelphia's archbishop informing him that the new president had consulted him as to a possible choice for ambassador to Vienna — the Austro-Hungarian Empire. The two men who came to Gibbons' mind were "Mr. Morell (sic) and Mr. Smith of your city as being persons capable of filling this position."[24] Cardinal Gibbons thought that Smith was the better qualified of the two, "having, I would judge, more poise than Mr. Morell." But Smith, Gibbons suggested, might "lack sufficient means to enable him to accept such a position." Whatever Ryan replied is unknown — a record does not exist in either the Ryan or Gibbons papers. In any case, neither Smith nor Morrell received the diplomatic appointment at this especially critical period in European history.

Through Elizabeth's death, both Sister Katharine and Louise Morrell were able to expand their already magnificent charitable works. There is an anecdotal "might have been" recorded in the annals of the Blessed Sacrament Sisters at the time of Walter's death in 1924.

According to one of the Drexel cousins, Lucy Wharton Drexel, when Elizabeth lay dying with no reasonable hope for recovery, her child, a boy, was so close to birth that baptism was administered on the foot in utero. One of the consulting physicians, Dr. DeCosta, suggested that the baby might live if it were delivered by cesarean section. Walter asked if this would cause Elizabeth even a moment of additional pain. "Yes, there will be some," the doctor replied. Walter refused permission. DeCosta took him aside and reminded him that not only the child's life but millions of dollars were at stake. "Not for one moment would I voluntarily add one degree to her suffering," Walter replied.[25] If the story is true, one has to suspect, had Elizabeth any say in the matter, she would have exclaimed, "For goodness sakes, Walter, try to save our baby."

With the aid and comfort of Archbishop Ryan and the Sisters of Mercy, Katharine overcame this second great loss and went on with her plans for the new order. As foundress of a religious congregation, she was taking on the responsibility not only of the spiritual welfare of the young women who would join with her, but their very lives. There is an inherent danger in missionary work, and this was emphasized in December 1890, when the Sioux Indians, who had been mistreated time and again by the government and white settlers, rose up in one last desperate revolt. It was at the Pine Ridge Reservation, where Sister Katharine had built Holy Rosary Mission, which was staffed by Franciscan Sisters, under the leadership of Mother M. Kostka. During the uprising, there was extensive property damage and some loss of life on both sides. It ended in the bloody massacre of Wounded Knee, which saw the slaughter of several hundred Indian men, women, and children by federal troops and effectively ended all resistance by the tribes.

Several government schools were torched during the uprising, and Holy Rosary was in obvious danger. The Franciscan Sisters had been given a chance to leave, but they refused, relying instead upon the Providence of God. In the end, the danger passed, and only after the fact was it learned that some of the braves had indeed urged the destruction of Holy Rosary and the killing of the nuns.

"I would like to publish it from the highest mountain that prayer and only prayer saved our very dear mission and all the inmates from harm and injury, by the enraged savages, burning, killing, stealing everything in the vicinity," Mother Kostka wrote. Prayers had been answered, according to the Franciscans, through the intervention of Chief Red Cloud, the same chief who was befriended by Sister Katharine and her two sisters three years earlier. Red Cloud told the assembled tribal chiefs of the kindnesses of the Sisters at Holy Rosary, and if this was not enough, he warned that he and his tribe would go over to the government side if the mission was harmed.

* * * *

Even as Sister Katharine and her little band of postulants in Pittsburgh prayed for the safety of the Sisters out West, the days of her novitiate were coming to a close. Soon she would be professed, and with her profession, the new congregation would officially be born. What should it be called? "Sisters of the Blessed Sacrament" was a title that suited Sister Katharine and her followers. Devotion to the Blessed Sacrament would be at the core of their religious life. There was a problem, however. An order with that title already existed. It was Archbishop Ryan who proposed the solution that was ultimately adopted. "Sisters of the Blessed Sacrament for Indians and Colored People." The full title was in keeping with their special apostolate — to bring the Blessed Sacrament to the two races.[26]

A new congregation needed a new habit, one that would proclaim that they were women religious, but set them apart from other orders. Archbishop Ryan, with proper male diffidence, said he would leave the design entirely up to the Sisters. The first design agreed upon by the congregation was less stylized than the Mercy habit, somewhat like the less restrictive garb of the Sisters of Charity and reminiscent of the original Franciscan habit of St. Clare. Contrary to his stated intention, Archbishop Ryan did interfere. According to convent tradition, the young Sister who modeled the proposed habit looked entirely too attractive to suit the Archbishop. "Kate, you can't send these young girls out West in that," he protested. "Make it more severe."

After several tries, the Sisters came up with a habit similar to the Mercy habit in many ways, quite modest, and of course, totally impractical for the wilderness where many of them would be missioned. It is one of the few instances where it can be suggested Archbishop Ryan was dead wrong in the direction he gave Katharine and her Sisters. One of the nicer details of the new habit chosen by Sister Katharine was the inclusion of the Franciscan cord, appropriate for a congregation that to this day adheres to the spirit of the rule of poverty with remarkable scrupulosity.

Archbishop Ryan chose February 12, 1891, the feast of St. Agatha, as the date of Sister Katharine's profession. February 12 was fraught with significance. It was the anniversary day for the profession of Mother Catherine McAuley, foundress of the Mercy Sisters, and, by happy coincidence, it was also the birth date of Abraham Lincoln, America's martyr-president, liberator of the African-American race.

In keeping with Sister Katharine's wishes, there were only the Sisters of Mercy and a very few close friends present for the solemn ceremony of profession. Helen and Walter George Smith were there along with Bishop Marty and Father Stephan. Edward Morrell came, but Louise could not. She was so affected by Elizabeth's death that she could not bear the thought of the profession ceremony, which contained elements of a funeral rite, a metaphor for the candidate's symbolic death to the world. Pittsburgh's Bishop Richard Phelan celebrated the Mass. Archbishop Ryan received from Sister Katharine the vows that would bind her to the Church for the next five years. After that, perpetual vows would bind her for mortal life:

> In the name of Our Lord and Savior Jesus Christ, and under the protection of His Immaculate Mother, Mary ever virgin, I Katharine Drexel, called in Religion, Sister Mary Katharine, this 12th day of February, 1891, do vow and promise to God for five years from this date, poverty, chastity and obedience; and to be Mother and Servant of the Indian and Negro Races, according to the Rule and Constitution of the Sisters of the Blessed Sacrament for Indians and Colored People; nor shall I undertake any work, which may tend to the neglect or abandonment of the Indian and Colored Races; under the authority and in the presence of you, My Most Reverend Father in God, Patrick John Ryan, Archbishop of Philadelphia.[27]

The traditional vows of the Religious — poverty, chastity, and obedience — had been joined by a fourth, which bound Sister Katharine and those who would follow in her footsteps to service exclusively to Native and African Americans.

After receiving her vows, the Archbishop presented her with the black veil and crucifix, symbols of a professed member of the new congregation. Through this ancient ceremony, Sister Katharine not only became a professed religious, but Reverend Mother Katharine, superior of the congregation that was born through her profession. Archbishop Ryan appointed her to a five-year term. In the future, major appointments would be made with the approval of Philadelphia's Archbishop; this would not change until the Blessed Sacrament Sisters received official approbation from Rome.

Now that a congregation existed, there was still the matter of a motherhouse. Plans had already been drawn up for the convent that would be named St. Elizabeth in memory of Elizabeth Smith. It would be built in the Spanish mission style developed by the Franciscan missionaries in the West. Ned and Louise Drexel had visited the California missions the previous year and brought back a selection of mission photographs as examples. However, at this point, the convent was still in the design stage.

Should the Blessed Sacrament Sisters remain in formation in Pittsburgh or move to a temporary convent in their home diocese? One suggestion was that they come to Philadelphia and take up temporary residence near St. Peter Claver Church, an African-American parish that had been funded by Mother Katharine. In the end it was decided, as soon as necessary alterations could be made, to take up temporary residence at St. Michel, vacant since Elizabeth's death.

Chapter Seven
Pioneers with Patience

Mother Katharine and one other Sister took possession of the temporary convent on May 10; others arrived on May 20 and 25. "Nazareth" was the name she gave this temporary home. Just as the young Jesus dwelt in Nazareth, so would they mature in Nazareth. There were a total of 14 novices and postulants in addition to Mother Katharine, at that time the only professed Sister. There were two other important members of the community. One was Mother Inez, on a one-year loan from the Mercy Sisters to serve as the Blessed Sacrament Sisters' Mistress of Novices. The other was Ida Mae Coffey, the first black child placed in their care. She was the forerunner for the thousands of children, African American and Native American, who would follow. A gardener's cottage on the St. Michel grounds had been transformed into a laundry and a temporary home for the children. This house, called "Holy Family Home" by Katharine and her Sisters, would give the young religious in formation hands-on training for their life work. Ida Mae was quickly joined by other children, and one room at Holy Family was made into a classroom under the direction of Sister Mary James. Interestingly, this very first mission of the Blessed Sacrament Sisters was integrated. White children, either from the neighborhood or children of Drexel-Morrell employees, joined the classes. These were day students; the black children were boarders. Since integrated classes were technically against the rule of the Blessed Sacrament Sisters who were vowed to serve Colored and Indians exclusively, Mother Katharine, ever conscientious, obtained permission from Archbishop Ryan before she accepted white scholars.[1]

Another early resident of the school was Josie Garrett, a young woman of 17. Josie was partially paralyzed, given to epilepsy, of ungovernable disposition and covered with sores that made her physically unattractive. Josie needed constant attention so that she would not harm herself during a seizure. Mother Katharine took her into her own cell at night. Josie, she said, "is a little Christ Child."

St. Michel itself had temporarily been rechristened "Nazareth" by Mother Katharine, who likened this period of preparation to the hidden years of Christ before He took up His active ministry. She told her Sisters:

> He did not need the years of preparation, but in His love for us He led an obscure life in obedience and subjection for 30 years to give us an example we should follow. We should, then, Sisters, endeavor to sanctify ourselves during this period of holiness which He has given us. If we desire to build this house of holiness, we must begin by laying a good, firm foundation and the firmer the foundation, the higher we can build.[2]

The surest foundation, she told them, is humility. "If we are not humble, tell me, what use are we in God's service?" In the meantime, she urged, the Sisters should "practice for our future work with the little ones of Christ, the Colored children whom God has given us. In them we shall behold the Lord Himself."[3]

The first Sisters were truly a band of pioneers. While one might assume young women of the 19th century would be adept at the practical arts of homemaking, it wasn't necessarily so. At first, the Mercy Sisters had sent a Sister to act as cook for the community, but she was withdrawn after a short period. They were truly on their own. One of the more amusing stories in the congregation annals tells of a young postulant who was designated cook for the day. Louise Morrell was going to supply the dinner. In the meantime, she should fire up the coal stove. Try as she might, she couldn't get it going — the coal was anthracite, not the easily started bituminous commonly used in Pittsburgh. She was totally frustrated when one of Louise's servants, James, arrived. He quickly saw her problem and expertly lit the stove. The main course was to be planked shad. When it became obvious she didn't know how to prepare it, he planked the shad, whipped up a salad and some milk sauce for the toast. The postulant made the toast and set the table.

When the Sisters came to dinner, everyone profusely praised the postulant's prowess as a cook. She modestly accepted the praise and burst into tears only when Mother Inez suggested she should be made the permanent cook. When the true story was discovered, Mother Inez suggested as punishment for allowing them to think she had cooked the dinner, that she should really be made the cook. Probably because this would have been as much of a punishment to the community as to the postulant, this was not carried through.

As for Louise's servant, James, he volunteered to work for the Sisters, and served them faithfully for the rest of his life.[4] James, it might be noted, was African American. Mention of his race is important only as an indication of the tremendous loyalty of persons of color who came in contact with Mother Katharine, a loyalty both to herself and the Blessed Sacrament Sisters who followed.

These young women learning the serious business of being nuns had their playful moments. Daily recreation was prescribed by Archbishop Ryan, and during one of these periods of recreation, Mother Katharine and a group of perhaps ten of the Sisters, clasped hands and ran pell-mell down a hillside. When they reached the bottom, they were drawn up short by the sudden appearance of a visiting bishop from North Carolina. The startled prelate was not amused by the unconvent-like behavior.

But life at "Nazareth" was certainly not a replay of the convent scene from "The Sound of Music." Mother Katharine Drexel was absolutely serious about her spirituality. Perhaps too serious for ordinary mortals. As part of the continued spiritual development of the Sisters, Archbishop Ryan had recommended Jesuit Father John Scully to them for monthly spiritual conferences.[5] Father Scully, a former president of Fordham College, advocated a harsh regimen of self-mortification. "We should hate our bodies and bring them into subjection," he told the Sisters, "never flattering them in anything, allowing them only as much as is requisite to preserve health." He believed in hair shirts, chains, and disciplines (whips) as means of self-mortification, and advocated their use. He was probably not the best spiritual director for Mother Katharine, a person who needed little encouragement when it came to mortification.[6] It was common knowledge among the Sisters that their superior did indeed use a discipline in the privacy of her cell. Her observable penances during this particular stage of her spiritual journey caused uneasiness among the other Sisters.

Her eating habits became literally a perpetual lenten fast. She refused condiments and always took the hardest crust, the least appetizing portion, as her own. She was observed emptying the dregs from other Sisters' cups into her own.[7] This would be her coffee. Sister James appealed to Father Scully, but he was dismissive. He feared the Sisters were much too afraid of "inflictive punishment." Finally, Archbishop Ryan heard of Katharine's extreme fasts. Binding her by her vow of obedience, he ordered her to take regular portions at meals and include butter and honey in her diet.[8]

Only part of Katharine's abstentions can be attributed to a form of penance.

Another very important element was her absolute commitment to her vow of poverty. This woman who would write checks for many thousands of dollars for her mission of evangelization, would also check the garbage can for usable food. There was nothing quite like seeing Reverend Mother eat a bit of bread that had been thrown out, to impress upon her young Sisters the obligation to avoid waste.

At another time, through this extreme sense of poverty, Mother Katharine had the Sisters stuffing their mattresses with corn husks. Somehow, Archbishop Ryan learned of this. "You ought to have hair beds," he told Mother Katharine.

"Husks are in keeping with holy poverty," she replied.

Archbishop Ryan, always ready with a witty retort, responded, "Let the nuns observe poverty in something else. If they have no hair on their heads, they must have hair in their beds."[9] A Sister of the Blessed Sacrament owned nothing. In all the convent records the expression, "the room given for Reverend Mother's use," "the rosary for Sister's use," "the book for Sister's use," automatically supplants "her room," "her rosary," and "her book."

The Sisters were at St. Michel, but a few months before, Mother Katharine began exploring the possibility of sending some of them out on mission. St. Stephen's, a Jesuit mission that served the Arapaho and Shoshone Tribes in Wyoming, had been receiving considerable financial support from Katharine since 1885. The mission had suffered many reverses, but a school was finally established, at first conducted by the Sisters of Charity of Leavenworth. When these Sisters were withdrawn, lay Protestant teachers were employed, and this also had been a failure. When Mother Katharine learned the school had closed, she wrote to a number of congregations, but could not find one willing to take charge of St. Stephen's. With Archbishop Ryan's permission, she decided to personally visit the mission to determine whether or not St. Stephen School could be taken over by her own Sisters. Accompanied by Sister Patrick, Mother Katharine set out for the mission. At Rawlins, Wyoming, she and her companion joined with Cheyenne's Bishop Maurice Burke, and switched from train to stagecoach for the final 175-mile leg of their journey. At St. Stephen's, almost everything was in place, except children and teachers. Through an interpreter, Mother Katharine assured the parents that the school would be reopened. All that was left to do was stop at Chicago on the way home to order the necessary supplies. She wrote home to her Sisters at St. Michel, "Pray, pray, my dear children, to Our Lord to send laborers into this beautiful vineyard — and a chaplain when we come in August."

In Mother Katharine's absence, Mother Sebastian had paid a visit to St. Michel, where she learned of the proposal to send Blessed Sacrament missionaries to Wyoming. Neither she nor Mother Inez were comfortable with the thought of sending Sisters to the mission fields so soon. These young novices had not yet been sufficiently formed for the work. Mother Sebastian relayed her concerns to Archbishop Ryan. Mother Katharine, on her way home to Philadelphia, stopped at the Mercy Convent in Pittsburgh. She was elated as she told Mother Sebastian of her intended project. The older nun softly hinted that the time was not yet ripe for sending forth missionaries. "I fear the Archbishop will not permit you to send Sisters to St. Stephen's Mission," she said.

Mother Katharine was thunderstruck. The Archbishop had, in fact, already implied consent when he allowed her to travel west, and she had just purchased new furnishings for the mission. What could this possibly mean? Sisters were truly needed at St. Stephen's. This was God's work!

Immediately after her arrival in Philadelphia, she set out for the episcopal residence. On the way, the novice who was accompanying her casually asked her to explain the meaning of the "obedience of the judgment."

The question startled Katharine, who certainly knew the meaning. Her best explanation would be by example of her own submission to the judgment of her superior — Archbishop Ryan — no matter what his decision.

Mother Katharine knelt before the Archbishop and kissed his ring. "Most Reverend Father, do you mean we are not to go to St. Stephen's?" she asked. Archbishop Ryan turned away, casually looking at some papers. It was difficult for him to look her in the eye and say what must be said. "No, I think you had better not go," he responded.

This was hard indeed, but Katharine accepted the judgment of her bishop with humility. It was the will of God. Harder still was breaking the news to the young members of her community.

Sister Kate O'Connor started to cry. Mother Inez, the novice mistress, chided her. "Well, you are audacious to think that you would have been sent to the mission, and you, only a postulant." Katharine's response was more comforting. "Well, child," she said, "I am glad to know that you have such a love of souls, but God does not wish the sacrifice now. God grant that when the real call comes to you to go out into the Master's vineyard to work for souls, He may find the same strong love in your heart."[10]

There was a happy ending. Mother Katharine renewed her efforts to obtain another congregation for St. Stephen, and this time she was successful. First, the Sisters of St. Joseph from Kansas took charge of the mission; the next year they were succeeded by the Sisters of St. Francis of Philadelphia. At a later date, even Mother Katharine would concede that Archbishop Ryan had been absolutely correct in refusing permission for Sisters of the Blessed Sacrament to take charge of St. Stephen's. "Almighty God was certainly good to save us from such a mistake," she said.

Bishop O'Connor thought that the Sisters should study for seven years before going off to the missions. If this seems excessive, there are several factors to consider, and it isn't simply because O'Connor was a former seminary rector, where young men typically trained for that length of time before taking Holy Orders. The mission of the Blessed Sacrament Sisters would take them to remote places and to situations much different from any of their previous life experiences. Further, because the congregation was in its infancy, there would be no cadre of experienced Sisters who could give moral support and practical guidance to the young missioners.

While the Sisters were still at St. Michel, the congregation was extremely fragile. A study done by Blessed Sacrament Sister Patricia Lynch shows 41 women entered the congregation before December 1892, when they left St. Michel for St. Elizabeth. Of this number, almost half left the congregation, most before first vows.[11] That some would leave is understandable; 19th-century convent discipline was strict, much more difficult than seminary training for male aspirants to the priesthood. But the Blessed Sacrament Sisters had an exceptionally high attrition rate, and that may well be the downside of being founded by a saint. Saints, in their goodness, may be naive; they truly think the rest of us are as saintly as themselves. They aren't aware they may be setting the bar too high for ordinary souls.

Many of Katharine's earliest recruits would be dismissed or voluntarily leave her, including her first vicar general. It was a grievous loss; these were good women. But it was a winnowing process, too; those who remained in that pioneer band were not merely good women, they were remarkable women for whom the bar was never too high. They well knew the hardship of their chosen vocation, and they had absolute loyalty to and admiration for their foundress. Of those who left the Blessed Sacrament Sisters, at least two joined other congregations and had long lives in religion.

According to Sister Patricia Lynch's study, 19 of the 22 who persevered were American born; the majority were Pennsylvanians. They entered in ages ranging from 18 to 33, with a median age of 22.[12] They would live an average of 44 years under religious vows. In education, some had nothing more than home schooling, but most had at least a primary school education, a fair achievement at the time. A half dozen or so had a high school education, and one or two the equivalent of two years of college. Many brought with them a variety of work experience, and some had taught Sunday School at St. Peter Claver, the Colored parish in Philadelphia funded by Mother Katharine. None had experience among Indians. All had a zealous desire to serve God. Zeal alone can go a long way, but not nearly as far as zeal tempered by the discipline achieved through a solid formation period.[13]

After Archbishop Ryan refused to give permission to send the Sisters west, Mother Katharine bided her time at St. Michel. The Sisters continued their spiritual formation and practical education. Some were sent to Uncle Anthony Drexel's new institute in West Philadelphia. Anthony Drexel's original idea was to found a school that would give young women a practical education. There were several such free schools in Philadelphia for young men but none for women. At first it was to be located in the suburb of Wayne, but he had changed his mind, perhaps because, as it was a day school, a city location was more practical.14 He eventually built it near the Schuylkill River in West Philadelphia, and it was co-educational — an innovation for its day.

From this rather modest beginning, Anthony Drexel's institute grew into what it is today — Drexel University, one of the great technical and engineering schools in America. Back then, Mother Katharine's Sisters were taking humbler courses: domestic sciences that they could pass on to the young Indian and Colored children at their own future schools. St. Michel itself was still a working farm, and in addition to their Holy Family (later Holy Providence) teaching experiences, the Sisters learned practical skills that could be useful in remote missions, for instance, how to milk a cow.

During the summer of 1891, progress on St. Elizabeth's reached a point where there could be a formal laying of the cornerstone. The ceremony was held on July 16, the same day Archbishop Ryan presented ten of Mother Katharine's novices with the habit of the congregation. Prior to this, all except Katharine had been clothed in the Mercy habit. Through the kindness of the Morrells, the Sisters were driven in carriages to their new, but far-from-completed convent. Here, Archbishop Ryan presided over the simple ceremony of the cornerstone laying.

The inscription was appropriate for a congregation vowed to inviting the outcasts of society to the banquet: "And it shall be in the place where it was said unto them: You are not my people. There they shall be called the sons of the living God. Romans IX."15

The day went without incident, but the Sisters later discovered it was not without anxiety. They were not aware of a rumor that there would be an attempt to disrupt the ceremony, perhaps blow up the grandstand and everyone with it. Not everyone in Cornwells Heights took kindly to this plan for a Catholic convent with a school for Colored children. The day before the ceremony, a stick of dynamite was found near the construction site.

Edward Morrell and Archbishop Ryan agreed that the Sisters shouldn't be told about this. The architect, James Burns, also had a box marked "Danger, Explosives" placed under guard near the stand. It was presumed this ruse kept mischief makers away from the area where the ceremony would be held. It is far more likely that the dozen hired guards Edward Morrell had stationed around the property were the real deterrent. In the end, there was neither vandalism nor an attempt to disrupt the ceremony.

Mother Inez remained with the little congregation until after their August 1891 retreat. She was an experienced novice mistress and had given crucial service to the newly founded Blessed Sacrament Sisters. But she was in poor health, and Mother Sebastian wished her to return to Pittsburgh. With her departure, at Archbishop Ryan's direction, Mother Katharine took on the added duty of novice mistress, an office she would hold for the next 17 years, with only a brief interruption.[16] Mother Inez told her spiritual pupils:

> I am sure that it is for the best that I go. Yours is a missionary order, and Mother Katharine has been especially chosen by God for this work in the Church, and she has the grace and spirit to carry on the work and to train the souls her God calls to labor in it. In my opinion she is more fitted for the work than I.[17]

Mother Inez asked her former novices to keep her in her prayers, a request Mother Katharine took so seriously that a nightly Hail Mary for Mother Inez remained part of St. Elizabeth Convent ritual for many years.

The next month saw a ceremony more important to the congregation than the laying of a cornerstone and building a convent. Three of the Sisters were professed; that is, they pronounced first vows.[18] Two of them, Sister Magdalen and Sister Joseph, had completed their two-year novitiate. The other, Sister Patrick, had been a novice for but a year, and a special dispensation was made in her case because she was ill and Mother Katharine feared she would not live through a two-year novitiate. Sister Patrick had entered at age 25, a late vocation for her day; she had remained in the world until the death of her invalid mother. She had been in poor health even before the Sisters left Pittsburgh. "The grippe" was the common explanation, but the truth was, she apparently contracted tuberculosis during her nursing training at the Mercy Sisters' Pittsburgh hospital. Sister Patrick had been chosen to accompany Mother Katharine on her visit to St. Stephen's with the hope that the western air would improve her health. It did not. By the time the great day for profession came, Sister Patrick was too ill to attend the Mass and ceremony. Archbishop Ryan received her vows from her sickbed.

The following week, as it became obvious Sister Patrick was nearing death, the Sisters kept watch over her bed. Mother Katharine was alone at the bedside when at 11 p.m. death visited the Blessed Sacrament Sisters for the first time. Rather than disturb the rest of the Sisters, she took it upon herself to wash and dress the body in habit; all was done by the time a Sister came at midnight to relieve her. "Our Sister Patrick has gone to her Spouse," she told the Sister.[19]

Now the death watch became a wake. Two by two, the Sisters prayed by Sister Patrick's body until she could be laid to rest in a little cemetery first at St. Michel and finally at St. Elizabeth's Convent.[20] It was an eerie experience for these impressionable young women, even in that era when it was customary to keep a body in the home until burial. It was late at night, and two Sisters were in prayer by the bier. Mother Katharine was one of the two watchers scheduled for the next shift. One of the Sisters quietly went to wake her. Because it would be unseemly to shake Reverend Mother, she gently tugged at a lock of her hair. A startled Mother Katharine screamed. The poor little Sister who had been left alone with the corpse didn't wait to find out what the scream was about; she scuttled off to her bed.[21]

In the lists of seniority for the Blessed Sacrament Sisters, Sister Patrick Flaherty's name is second, preceded only by Mother Katharine. Neither Sister Magdalen nor Sister Joseph persevered in religion. Sister Magdalen's leaving was especially hard for Mother Katharine. As Jennie Clayton, she had been the first to enter after Mother Katharine herself. And in the earliest years she was first assistant, in charge in Mother Katharine's absence, perhaps too overwhelming a responsibility for such a young woman. Sister Joseph, who served for a brief time as novice mistress, did not profess final vows.

But new candidates were coming in. Little St. Michel was bursting at the seams, while construction lagged at the new motherhouse, St. Elizabeth's Convent in Cornwells Heights. It was partly a design problem. The architects had not taken into consideration the immense weight of a mission-style tile roof. Foundations proved to be insufficient, and some walls were in danger of collapse. Much of the work had to be reconstructed or buttressed and given a new, more solid start. On December 2, 1892, ready or not, an exasperated Mother Katharine moved her growing community to this convent named for the patron of her beloved older sister. The building was far from finished, and it would remain under construction through the following year. But at Mother Katharine's insistence, the most important room of all was complete. That was the chapel, and here on that very first day, the Sisters enjoyed exposition of the Blessed Sacrament.[22] This was a precious gift from the Archbishop to the Sisters, but it would be permitted only on First Fridays of the month. It would not be until 1914 that Archbishop Edmond Prendergast would extend the privilege to all year-round.

The Sisters were true pioneers. No lighting, no running water, and a heating system that was woefully inadequate for the mostly stone structure. The only water supply was a pump in the barn, and during that first winter, this was often frozen over. The permanent Holy Providence School on the grounds of St. Elizabeth was not yet ready for occupancy; the children slept in an attic dormitory, christened with perhaps grim humor, "Our Lady of the Snows." But progress was being made. The congregation had reached sufficient size for an elected Council to be named — Sisters who would assist Mother Katharine in the governance of the growing order. In keeping with the customs of the day, the counselors, while in office, were addressed as "Mother." The title "Reverend Mother" was reserved for Katharine as head of the congregation. Mother Magdalen was named vicar general, Mother James, bursar, and Mother Joseph, novice mistress, which was an office Mother Katharine eventually re-assumed.

One applicant accepted at the convent in that same month is of special interest. Georgianna Burton was a convert and a member of the Seneca Indian tribe. She was a guest of the Blessed Sacrament Sisters until she could obtain admission to an Indian congregation. In the end, she was professed as a Blessed Sacrament Sister — Sister M. Elizabeth — and served until her death in 1909. Oddly enough, during most of this time, she labored in the black apostolate rather than the Indian apostolate, as a domestic sciences teacher at Rock Castle, Virginia.[23] She was described as shy and retiring; a lover of flowers, birds, and dogs. The children loved her, and she raised cardinals and mocking birds. They would flock to her as if she were St. Francis of Assisi.[24]

Also in 1893, the question of admitting black candidates to the congregation was raised anew. Mother Mathilda Beasley, foundress of a Third Order of St. Francis community, arrived with a companion from Savannah, Georgia, and stayed several weeks. Mother Beasley, a widow, was African American, as were the handful of members of her little community and the children in the orphanage she conducted. The congregation was desperately poor and had not been able to attract sufficient candidates for their work to flourish.

There was some consideration given to moving these black Franciscan Sisters to Philadelphia and even merging them into the Blessed Sacrament Sisters. In the end, no action was taken either to accept the Franciscans or relocate them, although a limited amount of financial aid was provided by Mother Katharine. Ultimately, the small congregation's position became so untenable that it was suppressed by the Bishop of Savannah. Mathilda Beasley returned to the lay state, a devout and charitable woman until her death in 1903.[25]

One might ask why more wasn't done to encourage the work of Mother Beasley, either through support of her congregation or admission to the Blessed Sacrament Sisters. The generally accepted answer is that there were already two established African-American congregations for women — the Oblate Sisters of Providence, founded in Baltimore by Elizabeth Lange in 1829, and the Holy Family Sisters, founded by Henriette Delille in New Orleans in 1842.

While both were viable, neither was of great size due to a lack of candidates. The Blessed Sacrament Sisters were reluctant to take any action that could harm the existing black congregations, either through the encouragement of another foundation or accepting black candidates themselves. The Sisters of Providence especially would benefit from the policy of the Sisters of the Blessed Sacrament who steered promising candidates for the religious life to their order.

It would be wrong not to acknowledge there were considerations quite beyond the health of the existing black congregations. The Blessed Sacrament annals, compiled shortly after the fact, give two more reasons.

First, racial feelings in the country would make it impossible to obtain white candidates for the community and the congregation would fail. Young white women might be willing to devote their lives to the Indians and Colored, but to live with them as equals was quite another matter. Also, years of prejudice had made both Indians and Colored sensitive to slights. Would an ordinary rebuke by a superior to a Sister be seen as racial prejudice? This would be disruptive.[26]

Katharine's caution on the matter of admitting non-white candidates to the congregation should not suggest she thought them unfit for religious life. In 1898, Josephite Father Slattery suggested the proper role for Colored women who aspired to the religious life would be through a lay "pious society" without vows that would work with the Sisters. "Why should they not be religious?" Mother Katharine asked Father Slattery, who was the American clergy's foremost advocate for African Americans. "If it be possible — as seems to be the case — that the Colored girl may live in religion, why should she not do so, and enjoy its advantages?"

In addition to her documented support, through money and candidates, for the African-American congregations, there is also evidence of support for black clergy. Augustus Tolton, America's first black priest, was subsidized by Mother Katharine by a total of $30,000 over the course of the years.

Again, it cannot be emphasized too strongly even a century later when racial prejudice still exists, how virulent it was at that time. Earlier in the 19th century, an integrated religious congregation, the Sisters of the Presentation, had been founded in New Orleans, but was suppressed because racial integration violated state law. Katharine's own hometown of Philadelphia had racial prejudices even in the highest places in the Church.

Theresa Maxis, who had mixed parentage, was one of the founding members of the Oblate Sisters of Providence. She had left that congregation and helped found the Sisters, Servants of the Immaculate Heart of Mary in Michigan and Pennsylvania. She quarreled with Peter Lefevre, bishop of Detroit, who in a letter to Philadelphia's Archbishop James F. Wood, asked that she not be allowed to live in a local convent, saying she had "the low cunning of the mulatto." Sister Theresa was banned from both Michigan and Pennsylvania and lived in exile with the Grey Nuns of the Sacred Heart in Canada until Archbishop Wood's death made it possible for her to return to the Immaculate Heart Sisters in Pennsylvania.[27]

Ellen Tarry, an Alabaman and graduate of the Blessed Sacrament Sisters' school in Rock Castle, Virginia, is an African American with white features. In her autobiography, *The Third Door*, she tells how, in the early 20th century, white friends of her father could never stay overnight at the family home because of the prejudice that existed in Alabama.[28] An integrated order working in the Deep South would have been a risky venture, to say the least.

Holy Providence School, which provided a training ground for the Sisters as they prepared for teaching careers in the mission fields, laid the groundwork of a solid education that was generally unavailable to black children. But first and foremost in the Blessed Sacrament mission was the work of evangelization. First fruit of this apostolate was harvested on Holy Saturday in 1893. On that day, fifteen Holy Providence children were received into the Catholic faith through baptism.[29]

"Sisters," Mother Katharine would tell her congregation, "the fields are ready; they are black and red, but beautiful. Let us prepare ourselves for the work to which God has called us, so that we may be ready for the voice of the Beloved."

The time for Sisters to leave their Pennsylvania convent was approaching. In October 1893, Father Stephan asked again that Sisters be sent to St. Catherine's, the Indian school Mother Katharine had built in Santa Fe. Archbishop of Santa Fe Placide Chapelle added his voice to the plea. "Wait another year," said Archbishop Ryan, who thought the Sisters were still too young in both age and religion. Again, Katharine acquiesced. St. Catherine's closed for lack of faculty. The Sisters redoubled their training. Holy Providence added industrial education, with courses for the students in dressmaking, sewing, and shoemaking.[30]

The following March, Archbishop Chapelle wrote once again. He had received a government contract for St. Catherine's. The funding was there, and the pupils were ready. Now if only there were Sisters. Bishop Peter Bourgade, vicar apostolic of Arizona, also wanted Sisters to work among the Navajo and Pueblo Indians of Arizona and New Mexico.

Once more Mother Katharine asked Archbishop Ryan for permission to visit the western missions. The Archbishop consented, but promised nothing. Accompanied by Sister Evangelist, she returned to the West. St. Catherine's, she discovered, was in great need of a house cleaning but was quite serviceable. After visits to other missions, she came home to report to Archbishop Ryan. It was April 29, the feast of St. Catherine of Siena. Her patroness must have been smiling on Katharine, because this time the Archbishop said yes, she could send Sisters to the missions.[31] Sisters Evangelist, Mercedes, Gertrude, Inez, Sebastian, Clare, Francis de Sales, Anthony, and Loretta were chosen.

"We are free when we practice
voluntary poverty.
We fly unimpeded
to God."

SAINT KATHARINE DREXEL

Chapter Eight
Mission Days

On June 13, 1894, the first wave, Sister — now Mother Evangelist — and Sisters Gertrude, Francis de Sales, and Sebastian, said their goodbyes. The convent bell was rung, and Sisters waved handkerchiefs from the windows, a spontaneous gesture that became the traditional farewell to succeeding waves of departing missionaries. Mother Katharine accompanied the Sisters as far as Philadelphia. She saw to their luggage and stopped in Wanamaker's Department Store to purchase an alarm clock and a gong that could be used as a bell. She took the Sisters to Archbishop Ryan for his blessing.

The good Archbishop blessed them and gave each a copy of *The Following of Christ*. This was an emotional moment, and Mother Evangelist wept. "You seem to feel this most deeply," Archbishop Ryan said. He then told them of a similar experience when he was Bishop of St. Louis. Franciscan Sisters had come to him for permission to go to Memphis to nurse victims of a yellow fever epidemic. "I gave them permission," he said, adding, "I knew when they went down the steps they were walking into their graves."

"Consoling it was not," Mother Evangelist later remarked.[1]

With a start made on the Indian missions, Mother Katharine turned her attention to the black apostolate. Louise and Edward Morrell had just purchased "Belmead," a 2,400-acre estate in Virginia near the James River, which had been formerly owned by General Philip St. George Cocke. It was the Morrells' intention to found a training school for boys. This would be very similar to

Elizabeth's St. Francis, but larger. All the student-residents would be black, and it would be named St. Emma, in honor of Louise's mother's patron saint. This estate, part of a 4,600-acre plantation once tended by 800 slaves, would now be the means for many hundreds more black young men to learn the skills necessary to compete as men in a free society.

After seeing her Sisters off to the West, Mother Katharine traveled south to the James River. She, too, purchased property which had been part of General Cocke's plantation. It was a beautiful tract of 600 acres, located in Rock Castle, adjacent to Louise's St. Emma's.[2] In the not-too-distant future, Katharine would build her own school; hers would be for girls and named St. Francis de Sales, in honor of her father's patron. But through its long history, generations of girls and Sisters would call it simply "Rock Castle." There was one key difference between schools for black children and schools for Indian children: No government funding was available for the black schools. Mother Katharine Drexel and Louise Morrell would be on their own.

Back at St. Elizabeth's, the second wave of Sisters packed for their westward journey to St. Catherine's.[3] The irrepressible Sister Mercedes was group leader. They departed on June 24. This time it was Mother Katharine's turn to break down in tears at the leavetaking. The five Sisters encountered no road agents or hostile Indians during their journey west, but it was not uneventful. This was the time of the great Pullman strike. They got as far as La Junta, Colorado, on June 29. There they sat; no trains were running west. Sister Mercedes telegraphed the news to Mother Katharine. It was a violent strike, and the worried superior ordered the Sisters to remain at La Junta if there was any danger.

Quite clearly, Katharine meant, "remain where you are." Sister Mercedes chose to interpret it as "remain on your journey." When, on July 4, a heavily guarded train was scheduled to depart from La Junta in spite of rumors a tunnel would be blown up when the train was in it, Sister Mercedes volunteered her band of five Sisters for the passenger list. The other Sisters suppressed their misgivings, because Sister Mercedes had been designated their leader. After stops and starts, with the Sisters riding hobo-style in a freight car for the final leg of the journey, they arrived in Santa Fe on July 9.

On hearing the news, Mother Katharine telegraphed the glad tidings to the anxious parents of her Sisters, and had a thanksgiving service celebrated at St. Elizabeth's chapel. If she suspected Sister Mercedes had deliberately misinterpreted her instructions, she did not say so. But she gently chided her, "Good gracious, child, did you think your Mother imagined you were staying at La Junta for pleasure? It was because I feared your going despite the danger that I telegraphed."[4]

When September came, Mother Katharine revisited St. Catherine's to be on hand for the opening of the school. Her Sisters had been busy, both preparing the school and visiting the pueblos surrounding Santa Fe. The visitation was important, not only to obtain students for the boarding school, but to fulfill the Blessed Sacrament mandate of outreach to the Indians. While the conduct of schools was, and remains, an important work of the congregation, they were just one part of the apostolate. Visitation to the people, the sick, and the prisoners was every bit as important.

When the Sisters visited the little Indian communities, they were cordially received. The Indians were aware that Mother Katharine had built St. Catherine, just as she funded day schools conducted by lay teachers within the pueblos. This did not immediately translate into students; because the Indians were family oriented and protective of their children they were reluctant to send them off to boarding school, even a free boarding school.

A major difficulty they encountered was that few of the children spoke English, and the Sisters did not speak Pueblo. But along with their native tongue, the children knew a bit of Spanish. The Sisters found it easier to learn Spanish than Pueblo, which made communication easier until each learned more of the other's language. But difficulties were overcome; the children learned to love the Sisters who taught them, and of course, the Sisters loved them back.

When Mother Katharine visited in the fall of 1894, there were just five boys at the school, a disappointing total. She wrote to her Sisters at St. Elizabeth's: "Pray every day that Our Lord will give us 100 souls for Jesus. I shall leave here happy if there be 100 in the school. Yet if it be not God's will I shall be equally happy provided it be His Will. Pray only for this — the Will of the Sacred Heart."[5]

By year end, through the diligent work of the visiting Sisters aided by the priests, if not the 100 children Katharine desired, there were 84 children of both sexes who had been enrolled, some of them traveling more than 100 miles. One major disappointment was the loss of the government contract. Before the century ended, it would be apparent that Katharine must not only build schools for the Indians, she must fund their operation.

While the nine missionaries in Santa Fe were beginning their work at St. Catherine, expansion was under way at Holy Providence. A new laundry room was being built so that older girls could be trained in this occupation. The construction was to be done by the William Dougherty Co. in Philadelphia. Mother Katharine, accompanied by one of her Sisters, went to the company offices to meet with the builder. She approached a young clerk at the counter, and before she could state her mission, he opened a drawer, took out a nickel and threw it across the counter.

"That's all we can give today," he said in a gruff voice. Mother Katharine took the nickel, put it in her pocket, and very sweetly asked to see Mr. Dougherty.

"Mr. Dougherty is too busy to be disturbed," she was told. Unperturbed, Mother Katharine explained who she was. The clerk's face reddened. "I beg your pardon, Mother Katharine," he said, "but we are bothered here so much by the begging nuns, sometimes we cannot do very much." "It's a beautiful work these good religious are doing," Mother Katharine softly replied, "begging for the poor and the outcast."[6]

Actually, most of the older children did not remain at Holy Providence. Through Mother Katharine's financial assistance, the Josephites purchased a 200-acre property near Claymont, Delaware. There, at St. Joseph's School, Holy Providence boys would be sent to learn a trade.[7] Under the contract signed with the Josephites, the school received a $30,000 annual subsidy from the Sisters of the Blessed Sacrament. A similar training school for girls was opened in a renovated mansion in the Germantown section of Philadelphia. At this school, also purchased by Mother Katharine but staffed by Good Shepherd Sisters, the older girls were placed for further training. Again, Mother Katharine subsidized the upkeep of the students.[8] During this period when the congregation was just starting its active apostolate, several other schools were built in Indian territory, but staffed by other congregations. Lump sum donations were given to the Philadelphia Catholic Boys' Protectory and the St. Clement Foundling Asylum with the stipulation that shelter or reformatory treatment be provided for 12 Colored infants or boys at the schools.

At this point, when the Blessed Sacrament Sisters were engaged exclusively in boarding schools, a large dwelling on Pine Street in a black section of Philadelphia was purchased by Mother Katharine and turned over to the Notre Dame Sisters.[9] They conducted a day school for Colored children at this location, until later, when, with Mother Katharine's assistance, nearby St. Peter Claver Parish opened an elementary school.

The year 1895 marked a final milestone in Katharine's religious formation. On January 9, she would make her final profession. On that date, when her first vows would expire, she could simply walk away. If she renewed her vows, it was for life. Of course, it was simply a formality. In her own mind, an irrevocable pact with God had been made years earlier. It was, at her request, a simple ceremony, and there were to be no guests, but Archbishop Ryan invited the Morrells and Walter George Smith. She repeated to the Archbishop the vows she had taken five years earlier. He gave her a plain silver wedding ring, symbolic of her marriage to Christ. The inscription, her own choosing, was "My beloved to me, I to Him."[10]

* * * *

Katharine visited St. Catherine's later in 1895. For all her active life, visits to the mission fields were energizing. But in addition to the physical hardships that were part of travel to the undeveloped West, there was spiritual hardship. Home at St. Elizabeth's, she experienced the joy of daily Mass and Communion. This was not possible when she was on the road. "Happy you who this morning have received Our Lord in Holy Communion," she wrote to her Sisters at St. Elizabeth's. "What in all the whole earth and even in heaven can make up for one Holy Communion. We shall lose three and they are lost forever. Yet the will of God sweetens all, for indeed, were we forever deprived of Holy Communion what could we truly say but Domine! Non sum dignus."[11]

Meanwhile, work at Rock Castle was progressing. Mother Katharine, accompanied by Sister Mercedes (back from New Mexico for treatment for her eyes), visited the site for the July 1895 cornerstone laying. The journey meant changing trains in Richmond. She arrived in the city at 1 a.m. with an eight-hour layover before boarding the train to Rock Castle. It was Mother Katharine's intent that she and Sister Mercedes would spend the night sitting on a bench in the train station waiting room, attend an early Mass, and then eat breakfast. They were taken aback when they discovered the Richmond waiting room was not open at night. Here they were in a strange city in the small hours of the morning with no idea where they could go.

As the two were pondering their predicament, an old-fashioned carriage pulled up. The elderly black man approached, tipped his hat, and asked, "Are you the ladies which the Sisters on Duval Street sent me to meet?" Mother Katharine knew the Franciscans had a convent on Duval Street, but she had made no arrangements to stay there. Perhaps their architect had realized they would need lodgings and made arrangements for them. The Sisters entered the carriage and were driven to St. Joseph's Convent on Duval Street. Their driver deposited their bags by the door, rang the bell, and departed. Mother Katharine and her companion waited some time before repeated ringing of the bell produced a response.

Finally, a Sister roused from her sleep answered the door and admitted them. As it turned out, the Franciscans had not expected them, but welcomed them nonetheless. Their architect had made no arrangements for them either, and Mother Katharine herself could not think of anyone else who would know they were stopping in Richmond. No one knew who their mysterious driver was, but Mother Katharine had a suspicion. In her mind, this was a visitation by St. Joseph. What's interesting is not so much Katharine's childlike faith, but rather her willingness to accept a St. Joseph in so humble a disguise.[12]

The building of St. Francis de Sales, Rock Castle, was accomplished in large part through materials obtained on the property. This was practically a necessity, because some of the materials came by rail to the other side of the river and then were transported across by flat-bottom boat. Clay was fired into bricks, and stone for trim was quarried from native rock. The building, typical of the schools and churches erected by Mother Katharine, was substantial and practical. Attractive, yes, but certainly not lavish. Stone and mortar were poor investments in her view. Her attitude on grandiose churches was encapsulated by an observation made after a visit to New York's St. Patrick's Cathedral. "It was built they say by the donations of the poor. Every five dollars represents a soul lost to the church." In her opinion, money spent on lavish adornment would be much better spent on evangelization.

St. Francis de Sales, Rock Castle, opened in 1899. It had been ready the previous year, but Archbishop Ryan thought it premature for the Sisters to take on a second school. When the first Sisters arrived, they discovered their barn had burned down under suspicious circumstances, but fortunately the main building itself was untouched. Given the hostile reaction the Sisters of the Blessed Sacrament would so often face, Mother Katharine always insured her buildings as soon as possible.[13] In this case, insurance did cover half the cost of replacing the barn. A barn was a necessity, because like similar institutions at the time, much of the food was obtained through farming the property. Mr. Mosby, the first farm manager at Rock Castle, had been born in slavery; this former slave plantation now housed the free children of former slaves, sustained by crops grown by men once enslaved, now free.

The school had a capacity for 250 boarding students. It was envisioned as a high school and normal school, that is, it would train girls who would be equipped to go forth and be teachers themselves. Over the course of time, thousands of African-American girls would be educated at St. Francis de Sales, but oddly enough, the first student resident was Mary Boyd, an Indian girl who was a former pupil at St. Stephen's Mission in Wyoming. Mary was probably the first religious vocation to come out of Blessed Sacrament schools. After she completed her education, she entered the Sisters of St. Francis in Glen Riddle, Pennsylvania, and subsequently served in the Oklahoma missions.[14]

St. Francis de Sales charged no tuition in its earlier years, but the parents or guardians of the girls had to sign an indenture that bound the students to the school until age 21. They did not go home for summer vacations. This system proved to be impractical and was abandoned because most parents were unwilling to sign so strict an indenture.[15]

In one case, when a mother tried to break the indenture and the Sisters thought "Susie" would be returning to a poor home environment, Mother Katharine directed her attorneys to defend the contract in court. They did so at a cost of $400. The Sisters prevailed; the child remained with them. Before long, the mother came to appreciate the education and training her daughter received, and was taking religious instructions at the time of her death.16

Clearly, the governing philosophy at Rock Castle was that the school needed complete control if it was to accomplish its mission of education and evangelization. While from the very beginning most of the students were non-Catholic when they arrived, there was an excellent possibility they would be Catholic when they left, especially if they remained until graduation. But no girl could be received into the faith until she had been at Rock Castle at least two years.

Ellen Tarry, an Alabaman who attended Rock Castle in the 1920s, is a case in point. When she entered the school, she fully expected to be a Congregationalist missionary to Africa after completing her education. As a matter of fact, her father, a deacon in his church, consented to her attending the school only after she made a solemn promise she would not become a Catholic. Tarry took this promise very seriously, especially because her father died shortly after she assured him she would not become a Catholic. Her King James Bible was one of the most important articles she packed for the trip to boarding school. Yet at Rock Castle, which had mandatory chapel and constant reinforcement of the Catholic faith, Tarry's resolve weakened. She loved the Blessed Sacrament Sisters and had come to love the religion they so joyfully professed. Before she graduated she did indeed convert. But Tarry, who went on to a successful writing career, emphasizes that at no time did the Sisters pressure her in any way or suggest she should become a Catholic. Ellen's Catholic baptism could not take place without the consent of her mother. Clearly, example was the most persuasive argument.17

Tarry received her diploma from Mother Katharine herself, and years later, she wrote a biography of the Blessed Sacrament foundress, *Katharine Drexel, Friend of the Neglected.* "Few authors," she wrote in her foreword, "have been privileged to write a book about the person who, in a spiritual sense, has been the source of their greatest gift, the gift of Faith."

Like their other missions, the Sisters at Rock Castle reached out to the surrounding area, in this case mostly to impoverished blacks, whether through home ministry or ministry to prisoners at a nearby work farm. Prison work could be grim because it involved visiting condemned prisoners. One prisoner whom the Sisters visited asked to be baptized and was received into the Catholic Church. The Sisters' chaplain, Father DeMunyk, accompanied the poor man to the gallows and was sick for a week after.

A unique ministry grew out of another train trip by Mother Katharine to Rock Castle. She was on the train journey home, when near Columbia, Virginia, she noticed a cross glittering through the trees. She was unaware of any churches in the area, but out of curiosity, asked Mother Mercedes, who was now the superior at Rock Castle, to investigate.

Mother Mercedes, another Sister, and a student familiar with the area set out for Columbia. The girl, Rebecca Kimbro, knew about the cross. It surmounted a chapel that had been built years earlier by the Wakeham family. Their son was a Sulpician priest who sometimes celebrated Mass there. But this was long ago, and the Wakehams were dead or had departed. The only Catholic in the area was Rebecca's father, Zack Kimbro. It was he who lovingly kept the 200-seat chapel clean and supplied with fresh flowers and altar linens. It was he who polished the gleaming stove in the chapel. Some day, he was certain, that stove would glow once more, as it warmed men, women, and children gathered for holy Mass.[18]

With permission from the Bishop of Richmond, Augustine van De Vyver, the Blessed Sacrament Sisters, aided by some of the older girls from Rock Castle, began a Sunday School at the chapel. Perhaps thirty people were attending on a regular basis. These were people who well remembered the bad old days of slavery. Sometimes, they told the Sisters, they had to work to 1 or 2 a.m. and were still expected to rise for more work at 4 a.m. They also remembered people who had a finger cut off for some infraction of plantation discipline. Others, who had kinder masters, actually learned to read and write.[19]

There was no Mass at first, but Mother Mercedes would read the Epistle and Gospel of the week and give a short instruction. In her first week, she spoke of how God had created the human race in His own image. "You may find it hard to believe," she said, "when all have such different faces, but the image is in the soul." In those decidedly pre-Vatican II days, this bothered her a bit; was she usurping the role of a priest? Bishop Van de Vyver assured her that what she did was fine, and eventually with his help, Josephite priests were secured for a monthly Mass for the little black congregation. In time it grew and prospered and became a full-fledged parish, all through Zack Kimbro's stubborn faith and Mother Katharine's glancing out the train window at just the right moment.

Katharine would have wished more hands-on missionary service for herself, but administrative duties rendered this impossible. Not that she would not, at times, try. Early in the western apostolate, an epidemic broke out at San Domingo, one of the pueblos near Santa Fe. Katharine asked for permission from Archbishop Ryan to send two Sisters to nurse the gravely ill Indians. When permission was granted, much to the consternation of the congregation, she and Mother Evangelist, the superior at St. Catherine's, volunteered themselves. The two set out for the pueblo, while the other Sisters fervently prayed for their safety. When Mothers Katharine and Evangelist arrived at San Domingo, the Indians would not grant them entry. They could do nothing but return to St. Catherine's and pray for the Indians whom they wished to serve.

While the Sisters were clearly worried about their Reverend Mother's safety when she left for the pueblo to nurse people with an infectious, life-threatening illness, there was something else their superior should have considered. At this point, the Blessed Sacrament Sisters had little outside income, tuition or otherwise. The congregation was entirely dependent upon Mother Katharine's trust fund.

Msgr. Stephan, writing in 1899, laid out the problem very clearly. Her order ministers exclusively to Indians and Negroes but cannot receive postulants from these groups. Other orders, too, obtain revenue through teaching and nursing and obtain donations from the public. But because of the extreme prejudice against Negroes and Indians, Katharine could expect no such donations. It didn't matter while she was alive. "What would happen if you were called away in the near future?" the veteran missionary asked. Should this happen, he suggested, the Sisters of the Blessed Sacrament could fail.

The Blessed Sacrament Sisters, following the common model of the day, had at the time two classes of Sisters. Most were choir Sisters who would be trained as teachers or for other professional or administrative duties. Others were lay Sisters who, because of their lack of previous education, were assigned to the more domestic duties. Lay Sisters would not rise to position of superior or participate in convent elections. Choir candidates were expected to bring with them $50; lay Sisters $25. This money was to be invested for their future upkeep. Even in that uninflated currency, it was hardly sufficient to the need, and Mother Katharine often waived the requirement for a poor but promising candidate. Also, should a Sister leave, her dowry was returned to her. Clearly, the congregation was dependent on its superior for physical sustenance.

From the very beginning, Bishop O'Connor had advocated that Mother Katharine lay aside an endowment for the future support of the Sisters of her congregation. His suggestion was $50,000 a year, until such time when the investments were sufficient for the need.

"Consider your Sisters first in your almsgiving," Father Stephan wrote, "because they are your spiritual children for whom you must first take care, so that when you are gone and sleep the sleep of the just, the evil spirits may have no power over them...."[20] Katharine resisted. In her mind an endowment was strictly against the spirit of poverty she wished for the Sisters of the Blessed Sacrament. "The dominant end of our vocation," she told her Sisters, "is not to acquire something, but rather to spend ourselves and be spent in a special service to Our Lord in the Blessed Sacrament." In the same vein, she wrote, "May you all become as great saints as our Lord desires you to be. All for His glory, nothing for self."[21]

That was all well and good, but as it stood, the congregation would clearly be in jeopardy should Katharine die. Her trust fund would die with her. Was there to be no provision for older Sisters, who after a life of giving in the mission fields, must be supported in their declining years?

Finally, common sense prevailed. In 1897, upon the advice of the Sisters of her Council and with the consent of Archbishop Ryan, Katharine took out several life insurance policies. They totaled $500,000, and most of them would mature in 20 years, at which time they would revert to the congregation. In time, money was added to the little endowment fund, but probably never at a rate that could really support the congregation on anything but a very basic level. Later, when the Sisters of the Blessed Sacrament sought approval from Rome, the endowment would take on added significance. The ability of the congregation to support itself was one of the factors that would be considered.22

In the meantime, Katharine continued to place mission before her own health and well-being. Four of the Sisters were sick with Rocky Mountain spotted fever when she visited St. Catherine's in 1897. Clearly, more hands were needed. She willingly pitched in, spending the day in the school laundry. There were no washing machines or other automatic equipment. It was simply hard, monotonous work. At the end of the day, the Sisters noted she looked tired but refused to admit fatigue.23 Archbishop Ryan did what he could to keep her out of harm's way. One year, as she was preparing for a visit out West, he ordered her to visit St. Catherine's last, knowing there was a diphtheria epidemic in that area. Better for her to wait until it was over.

The danger to health was very real in the missions. In 1901, the people of Pena Blanca pueblo were stricken with malaria, and the Blessed Sacrament Sisters nursed the sick and dying. "Funerals are an everyday occurrence," Sister Perpetua wrote in a letter to St. Elizabeth's.24

Katharine herself came down with symptoms of malaria two years later, probably as a result of these western visitations. A worried Archbishop Ryan ordered her to see a New York specialist. The treatment was apparently successful. Archbishop Ryan wrote after her visit to the physician: "I was afraid to tell you how much stronger you looked the day you called than you did on my last visit to St. Elizabeth's. I say afraid because it might furnish you with temptation to disobedience. But you have done great in going, in relieving the anxiety of your friends...." This was quite typical of Katharine who throughout her long life would push herself to the limit. Only through the kind intervention of the Archbishop, her family, and her congregation could she be persuaded to take due consideration of her own health.

Arizona was the next mission of the Sisters, this time, St. Michael, in the heart of Navajo country. While the school did not open until 1902, the groundwork was laid in 1895, when Father Stephan wrote to Mother Katharine of the

Francis Anthony Drexel (1824-1885), father of St. Katharine Drexel.

Emma Bouvier Drexel (1833-1883), mother of Louise Drexel and stepmother, biologically speaking, to Elizabeth and Katharine, but a true, loving mother in every other sense of the word.

Hannah Jane Langstroth Drexel (1826-1858), mother of Elizabeth and Katharine. She died of a fever caused by complications at Katharine's birth.

Katharine (left), Louise (center) and Elizabeth, photographed when Katharine was age seven.

(All photos in this section are provided courtesy of the Sisters of the Blessed Sacrament unless otherwise noted.)

Bishop James O'Connor, spiritual director to Katharine from childhood until her entry into religious life.

Assumption of the Blessed Virgin Mary Church, Philadelphia, where Katharine was baptized on December 29, 1860.

(Robert S. Halvey)

Bedroom of Elizabeth and Katharine at 1503 Walnut Street (left); family oratory in the same townhouse.

Undated photograph of St. Michel Sunday School at the Drexel family summer home in the Torresdale section of Philadelphia, where the young sisters taught catechism to children in the neighborhood. The photograph was probably taken before school closed for the season. The children are holding practical gifts (including tools) given to them by the Drexels. Also note in the upper right a small group of African-American children, a rarity in schooling during that racially prejudiced era.

Portrait of Katharine, probably at age 16.

The three women are believed to be the Drexel sisters in a photograph taken at Pen Ryn, the estate of cousins not far from St. Michel. Katharine is listed as the figure with garden hat and book.

A photograph taken during an 1888 visit by the Drexel sisters to White Earth Indian Reservation, Red Lake, Minnesota. Three children were sponsored in baptism by the sisters and given their names.

Bottom: Another visit to Red Lake, the Thompson Ranch in 1889. Katharine with large feather in her hat (far left); Elizabeth is shown in the middle with feather in her hat. Bishop O'Connor is seated; Msgr. Joseph Stephan is the cleric with a white beard.

General Edward Morrell, husband to Louise Morrell, on horseback. Walter George Smith, husband to Elizabeth.

Johanna Ryan, faithful nurse and beloved servant to the Drexel family.

Mother Katharine Drexel, 1891, shortly after her profession into religious life.

St. Elizabeth Convent, motherhouse of the Sisters of the Blessed Sacrament; named by St. Katharine in memory of her older sister.

(Charles F. Sibre)

Mother Katharine Drexel
with children during a 1927
visit to Beaumont, Texas.

Mother M. Francis Xavier and Mother Katharine (right) during a visit to the Indian missions that same year. Also shown, Native-American silversmiths and Franciscan Father Jerome Hesse.

Mother Katharine Drexel; undated photograph at Kiddies' Day, Xavier University in New Orleans, Louisiana.

Mother Katharine with her sister Louise Morrell, at a graduation ceremony at St. Emma's Industrial and Agricultural Institute, Belmead, Virginia.

Mother Katharine with children; Kiddies' Day, Xavier University, New Orleans, Louisiana.

St. Michael's Shrine of the True Cross at St. Michel. It served as a mission center, retreat house and chapel. Louise hoped Katharine and other family members would be entombed in the chapel crypt. The property was eventually sold to Frankford Hospital.

St. Martinsville School —
one of the schools for
African-American children
built by Mother Katharine
in rural Louisiana.

Native
Americans and
dignitaries at
50th anniver-
sary celebration
of the Blessed
Sacrament
Sisters in
Cornwells
Heights,
Pennsylvania,
in 1941.
Cardinal
Dennis
Dougherty of
Philadelphia is
second from
left.

(Catholic Standard and Times)

Undated photograph
of the Council
General of the
Blessed Sacrament
Sisters, early 1930s.
Rear (from left to
right): Mother M.
Philip Neri, Mother
M. Jerome. Front
(from left to right):
Mother M. Agatha,
Mother M. Katharine
Drexel, Mother Mary
of the Visitation.

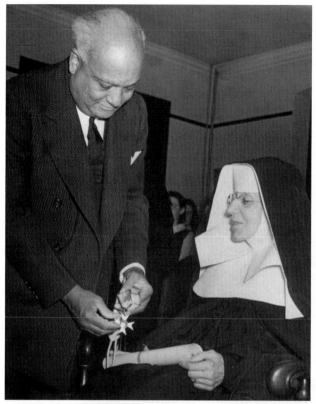

Elie Lescot, president of Haiti, visited St. Elizabeth Convent in 1942 to present Mother Katharine with a medal honoring her for her service to the Negro race.

Robert Gutherman, recipient of the miracle needed for Mother Katharine's beatification, at her tomb in Bensalem, Pennsylvania, in 1988.

(Charles F. Sibre)

(Robert S. Halvey)

Philadelphia celebration of Mother Katharine Drexel's beatification at the Cathedral Basilica of SS. Peter and Paul; Archbishop (later Cardinal) Anthony Bevilacqua presiding.

(Joseph Louderback)

(Robert S. Halvey)

Amy Wall (left) who received the gift of hearing through the intercession of St. Katharine Drexel, is shown with her parents, Connie and John Wall at the January 27, 2000 news conference where Cardinal Anthony Bevilacqua announced the Vatican had accepted her cure as the miracle needed for canonization.

Mother Katharine Drexel and a montage of people associated with her in ministry or educated by her Sisters of the Blessed Sacrament. It was executed by Blessed Sacrament Sister Lurana Neely for her 1988 beatification.

need for Catholic missionaries in the area. She was in no position to do more than purchase land and help the Cincinnati Province Franciscan Fathers establish a mission. The Franciscans observed strict poverty and therefore owned nothing. Katharine built and completely furnished the mission. The dream was the establishment of a coeducational boarding school, but it was not so easily accomplished. Because the Navajo Indians were resistant to academic education, a program had to be formulated that included a great deal of vocational training. Another complication was the Navajo language. No adequate Navajo-English dictionary had ever been compiled, and unlike many other tribes, the Navajo spoke no other tongue. Fortunately, one of the Franciscans, Father Berard Haile, had compiled a good, practical dictionary by the time the Sisters arrived. He did so with the help of a mail order catalog. Father Berard would point to an object in a picture; the Indian children would give the Navajo name for the object, and so the dictionary grew.

The vast Navajo reservation was located in a truly desolate area, a reality Mother Katharine's Sisters would discover in the company of their superior as they traveled to their mission station. It was a five-hour drive by buckboard from Gallup, New Mexico. Sister Agatha wrote of the trip:

> We started our long ride to the Navajos. Mother Katharine, Sister M. Angela and myself in the back seat of the uncovered buckboard. Mother Evangelist and Father (Berard) in the front... During the long ride we saw four crows, two wagons and a few Indians. I think we enjoyed it very much as there was a great deal of laughing done, making up prayers in between times. We were almost pure white with dust, at least our shawls and veils were, and the sun poured down on us, but we were not the least troubled, because we were on the way to the Navajo.[25]

St. Michael was at least modestly successful in its first year. The variety of vocational programs — blacksmithing, farming, carpentry, homemaking — coupled with the good will the Franciscan Fathers had generated, afforded the school an enrollment of 47 children. The Navajo were extremely protective, and some of the parents stayed for weeks, camping on the grounds, watching carefully to see that promises were kept and the children were not mistreated.

The school opening was not accomplished without some pain. The first winter was unusually cruel, with temperatures dipping well below zero. The discomfort worsened because the buildings were still somewhat under construction — no pews in the chapel, fireplaces that would not draw, and a well that often lacked water. Laundry was done by the Sisters in a nearby stream.

On at least two of her trips to the western outposts, Mother Katharine brought her cousin Josephine along as her companion on the way. Josephine, the crossbearer at Katharine's reception, was now a young woman who had expressed an interest in seeing the West. Mother Katharine was quite aware this could be misinterpreted within the congregation, perhaps seen as being "too close" to natural family. She took great pains to explain her motives to the Sisters.

"I think it is in the greater glory of God to interest her in the Indians," Katharine told her congregation. "She will be tolerably rich and influential one of these days, and I think it would be well that the Indians should, if possible, have a friend in her. Besides, I am sure it is Our Lord who has put it into the head of this young girl to wish to visit the Indians."[26]

In any event, Josephine must have had her share of Drexel spunk. It was a rough journey with few amenities. Of course, Katharine, ever on the watch for religious vocations, secretly hoped her young cousin would enter the religious life. She writes of this to her Sisters: "I remember in my girlhood I felt no attraction to the call. Will it be so with this dear girl who is by my side?"[27]

Their luggage had not arrived in their rail car, and Josephine mentioned to Mother Katharine that she did not have the copy of Rosseau's poems she had intended to read. Katharine smiled inwardly, but as casually as possible, she suggested, "Jo, if you care to read the life of St. Teresa in French, here it is."

Josephine read the book throughout the first day, but to Katharine's disappointment, put it aside the second.

"I confess," she wrote, "the vocation of this dear soul may depend on our begging, and it is such a lovely soul, too good, too pure for any creature. I want it for God, to belong to God and that it may be a little instrument to save souls for God."[28] Either God or Josephine or both had other thoughts. She did not enter religious life, but later, as Mrs. Josephine Seton-Henry, she remained an ardent supporter of the Sisters of the Blessed Sacrament and all their works. Her mother, Mrs. Joseph Drexel, had recently purchased Pen Ryn, an estate not far from St. Elizabeth's. She also supported Mother Katharine's work among the Indians. But she would make donations only for Indian day schools, not boarding schools. She regarded separation of children from their parents as unnatural.[29]

Another young person served as Mother Katharine's traveling companion during one of these western visits. This time it was a little Indian boy who accompanied her home to Cornwells Heights. The little fellow became the darling of the Holy Family School because the black children had never seen an Indian child. But his parents missed him, so he had to be sent home.[30]

Father Stephan (Msgr. Stephan by this time) did not live to see St. Michael

School. The grand old champion of the Native Americans died in 1901. Katharine Drexel had been his greatest supporter in life, and her support continued in death. Msgr. Stephan's remains were brought back to St. Elizabeth's, where he lies buried at the edge of the convent cemetery where so many of Mother Katharine's own missionaries rest in their final sleep. He was succeeded at the Bureau of Catholic Indian Missions by Msgr. William A. Ketcham. Msgr. Ketcham, a convert himself, was an experienced missionary. Just as she had aided Msgr. Stephan, Katharine provided financial aid to Msgr. Ketcham, but ever so quietly. She requested that no publicity be given to her donations, and whatever support she gave to individual missions or schools through the bureau simply be listed as aid given directly by the bureau.

One of Katharine's disappointments during her western visits was the scarcity of full-blooded Indians. Not that she objected to their intermarrying with whites; she wanted to see them become Catholic first. A 1902 visit to St. Elizabeth School in Purcell, in Indian Territory, was especially discouraging. This school had been founded 14 years earlier largely through her money, but was conducted by the Sisters of St. Francis of Philadelphia. She was shocked to find that not one of the 55 girls in the school had Indian features. Yet every one of them claimed to be part Indian — Chickasaw, Creek, Choctaw, whatever.

If Indians were held in low esteem, why were so many whites so anxious to claim Indian blood? The answer has more to do with greed than sentiment. A law that had recently been passed entitled every Indian to 360 acres of land. Each of these children had that entitlement as did the parent from whom they claimed Indian descent.[31]

Full-blooded Indians quite naturally resented what they considered stealing of land that was intended for them. Katharine was unhappy about this too, but she philosophized that since these children would grow up to be people of influence, it was better to give them Christian training. Future generations, she said, "may not be able to discern differences in nationality, but that mingled into one nation all may serve God on earth and praise Him eternally in heaven." A visit to the Cherokee Nation confirmed this apparent assimilation of the tribes. She discovered there were 28,000 Indians of one-quarter blood or less and only 7,000 full-blood Cherokee.[32]

There were many good things to ponder, too, during these visits. On one visit to Arizona she counseled, "See Jesus and Mary in your Sisters when you speak to each of them or serve them. Love one another as Jesus has loved you. It pleased me so much to see your cheerfulness at the recreation. Continue this holy cheerfulness. Let there be no 'Sister Vinegars' at St. Michael's."

On many of these trips to the West, Katharine, as a courteous goodwill gesture, would attend various Indian ceremonies. One of the more interesting rituals she attended during this particular visit was an eating of the sacred mescal button (peyote). "It is a ceremony which in some ways is typical of the Blessed Eucharist," she told her Sisters. "The ceremony lasts five or six hours!" She and her party "tasted a wee bit of one. It was very bitter," she reported.[33]

During the years of the "Peace Policy," the Catholic Indian school conducted by various congregations had received a cumulative $4 million in operating expenses. After this source of income was withdrawn, Mother Katharine Drexel was their chief means of support. She was a woman of wealth who could support many projects, but she was only one person — her funds were not unlimited. At this point, she was donating about $70,000 annually to the Bureau of Catholic Indian Missions, the bishops' outreach to the Indian missions. This was more than half its annual operating budget, according to a 1906 report filed by Msgr. Ketcham. This did not include, by his estimate, the $1,000,000 she had expended for buildings. But as her own congregation grew, the needs of its own missions would place increasing demands on her purse. She well knew more was needed, and for this reason, advocated the foundation of The Society for the Preservation of the Faith Among Indians. Through this society, she and the bishops who supported it envisioned a national collection. If just 400,000 Catholics gave 25 cents a year, that would be $100,000.

The collection, held on the first Sunday of Advent each year, proved disappointing. At no time did it come close to raising its goal. In 1903, $39,434.41 was raised; two years later, this was down to $14,957.21. While prejudice against the Indians may have accounted for part of the shortfall, another factor was a lack of support from bishops who already felt overburdened by national appeals. A case in point is Santa Fe, New Mexico, where Mother Katharine conducted and fully supported St. Catherine's School. In 1904, Mother Katharine wrote to Archbishop Peter Bourgade, who was the ordinary. She asked that the collection be taken up in Santa Fe, pointing to its necessity for the support of schools such as St. Catherine's. The Archbishop's reply was less than courteous:

> Mother, I am well neigh sick at heart of endless requests, calls, reproaches heaped on me for money collections in my diocese for the Holy Father, the Propagation of the Faith, the schools in the East, the Indians, the Catholic Universities and what not, while our people and myself are a sore object of charity. In the name of justice, how can I call upon my destitute Mexicans to help build and keep schools for the Indians: The Indians are better off than themselves in every sense of the word. The Indians have fine free boarding and day schools, while our Mexicans have no free Catholic schools. Was there any money to

be had from the Mexicans I would invest it in parochial schools for their own children.

For pity sake! When you can no longer provide them support for St. Catherine's or the other Indian schools let them be closed, Mother; but don't ask us to place burdens on our poor Mexicans in order to keep them up.[34]

Archbishop Bourgade, before his advancement to Santa Fe, had been Bishop of Tucson, and was one of the first to request Mother Katharine send Sisters to his diocese. That was in 1894 when he was seeking missionaries for the Navajo and Pueblo Indians. The Blessed Sacrament Sisters were a very young religious order and not able to send Sisters at the time.

* * * *

As poorly as the Indians were treated in America, discrimination against blacks at the turn of the century was far worse. It would have taken a great deal more than 360 acres of land for a white man in the Deep South — or anywhere in America for that matter — to claim his child was one-quarter black.

Mother Katharine had been very quietly aiding many missions for the black apostolate throughout the country. In 1904 alone, not including her support for Rock Castle, she distributed more than $100,000 to various missions throughout the South. In many instances, this was not for exclusively black churches or missions, for the simple reason that there was neither the personnel nor sufficient local support for a widespread Catholic outreach to the black community. Typically, Katharine would give a donation toward a new church on the condition that a specified number of pews be set aside for black worshipers. This was a necessity because neither Jim Crow laws nor the underlying prejudice would permit the mingling of the two races in the pews. In most churches, black Catholics were relegated to an upper gallery; that was not good enough for Katharine. When she made a donation, she would always insist the pews reserved for blacks were to be as good as those reserved for whites. In itself, this did not create full equality. There were other practices she could not control. For example, blacks could not be given the Eucharist until every white had received. It is a small wonder that in this unwelcoming atmosphere, there were few black congregants.

Katharine saw this during a visit to St. Peter Church in Charlotte, North Carolina. One side had 20-25 pews reserved for blacks. That side, to her great satisfaction, had stained glass windows representing St. Francis of Assisi and St. Patrick. "I am glad the saints are on the Colored side," she wrote in a letter to St. Elizabeth's. But the black pews had only six congregants. "The church is well-filled, except for the pews occupied by the precious six," she wrote.[35]

The same held true in St. Augustine, Florida, where "whites will not sit with the Colored," Katharine found.

Sadder yet was Montgomery, Alabama. Here, "there is not a single Catholic Colored school," Katharine wrote." Bishop Allen says the white Catholics "are so opposed and prejudiced to the blacks that Sisters who would dare to teach at one would have uphill work indeed."[36] Bishop Allen may have overstated the case. A decade later, working with the Josephite Fathers, Mother Katharine funded the construction of St. John the Baptist Church in Montgomery. Not long after, Sisters of the Blessed Sacrament staffed the parish school, but only after overcoming the prejudices of the white community and the black community, which had no prior experience with Catholic Sisters. Relations with their community, both white and black and largely Protestant, became so good that when the convent was threatened by a fire at a nearby Protestant school, the neighbors pitched in to remove all portable items and helped with the cleanup afterward.

New Orleans, Louisiana, had a large black population that, because of the city's Spanish and French origins, included many Catholics. Protestant influence increased after Louisiana was purchased by the United States, and by the 1890s there had been a tremendous loss of Catholics among the blacks. While this may not have disturbed many white congregations, it did disturb Archbishop Francis Janssens, who was one of the most progressive members of the hierarchy in matters of race.

"There is nothing in my administration of the diocese that worries me more than our Colored people," the Archbishop wrote in a 1893 letter to Katharine. "I cannot find the means to counteract those who capture them. They look for the conversion of the colored people and I have to look out against perversions. I often feel discouraged."

In 1895, when New Orleans' St. Joseph's Parish needed a new church because of an expanding congregation, the Archbishop saw the opportunity to create the first black parish in his archdiocese. This was not done as a means of imposing segregation — blacks, if they chose, could remain members of a territorial parish. Rather, it was hoped the new parish, with all the lay societies and offices controlled by black congregants, would encourage faith rather than destroy it, as segregated churches so often seemed to do. Mother Katharine donated the $5,000 needed to refurbish the church for its new congregation, and in gratitude, it was renamed St. Katharine's. But it was a complex issue. While some black Catholics saw it as a means of taking charge of their own spiritual lives, others saw it as simply a new segregation and opted to remain in their neighborhood parish. This was especially true among the large, racially mixed population of New Orleans, a city that had an intricate caste system based upon one's degree of whiteness or blackness. During a 1904 visit to St. Katharine's, Mother Katharine counted only 75 people at the 10 a.m. Sunday Mass. But she was told that many who normally attended other churches would come to St. Katharine's for the monthly Sodality Sunday.

In this period of crucial foundations for Katharine's congregation, Louise Morrell was quite ill. She seems to have suffered a breakdown. There had been some manifestations of this at the time of Elizabeth's death, but by 1898 she was seriously ill and under the care of physicians. While she kept up some contact, most of the affairs of her charitable interests were handled by Edward. Even though her recovery would be complete, Katharine did not have the benefit of her usually sensible advice during this particular period. Much of Louise's time was spent with Edward in the solitude of their Maine retreat, although she would muster the strength to spend Christmases with the children at her beloved St. Emma's in Virginia. Louise's health was such that, in 1902, when Mary Cassidy died, the news was withheld from her for several months. The following year, she visited Lourdes seeking a cure, an indication in itself that her health was improving. While in Europe, Louise visited the Father General of the Holy Ghost Fathers to seek more priests for the missions. The Holy Ghost superior visited St. Elizabeth's Convent the following year.[37] A report to Rome by Holy Ghost Father D.J. Fitzgibbons estimated there were, at the time, 10 million blacks in the United States, "perhaps 150,000 nominal Catholics and certainly not more than 50,000 practical ones. The harvest here is more than ripe," he wrote.[38]

Another Southern diocese that was graced with a progressive bishop was Nashville, Tennessee. Bishop Thomas S. Byrne headed a diocese that included about 500,000 blacks, but very few were Catholic. Katharine had been aiding missions at Dayton, Memphis, and Nashville since the early 1890s. In 1904, while he was visiting the West for his health and she was visiting her missions, the bishop persuaded Katharine to open a school for black girls in Nashville. Bishop Byrne knew of a four-acre property, the former residence of the Ewing family, that was for sale. It was not far from a black parish, the Church of the Holy Family.

The proposed school, while it would offer courses in the domestic sciences, would be primarily academic. This was because Nashville was now considering abolishing academic high school education for blacks in public schools. Mother Katharine's school would fill the void such a measure would create if it passed. Probably for the same reason, the proposed school would be a day school, a departure from Mother Katharine's prior policy of boarding schools. Bishop Byrne suggested enrollment be limited to Catholic students, but Katharine and her Council would not agree to his recommendation.

"Our congregation is consecrated to God for the conversion of the Negro and Indian races," she wrote in a letter to Bishop Byrne. "A missionary congregation should not make this distinction."

Through an intermediary, a 60-day option was taken on the property, with a purchase price of $25,000. Subsequent events proved the strategy of working through a third party to be wise. Had the sellers known the real buyer, there would have been no sale.

There was, for Nashville, an unusually heavy snowstorm on the January day when Mother Katharine, accompanied by Mother Mercedes, came to inspect the property. She and Bishop Byrne circled the grounds in a closed carriage. They did not enter the large residence on the property, but peering through the half-closed blinds of the carriage, they could see a large, somewhat shabby house in the middle of a spacious lawn. It was obviously in need of repairs. In spite of this, they decided the property was probably a good buy, considering the difficulty in obtaining property for black schools.

But Katharine was not one to buy at the asking price. Through Thomas J. Tyne, her agent, she offered $18,000. The owner, Samuel Keith, would not budge. Finally, Katharine raised her bid to $24,000 and wouldn't go further. Bishop Byrne, rather than see the purchase fall through, said he would pay the other $1,000. To this, Mother Katharine would not consent. In the end, she paid the entire $25,000. On Feb. 2, 1905, Tyne purchased the property in his own name and the same day conveyed it to the Sisters of the Blessed Sacrament.

Katharine returned to Cornwells Heights, where a few days later she received a message from Bishop Byrne. The cat was out of the bag; Keith had learned who the true buyer was and became quite upset. The bishop advised that she insure the property at once, which she did.

The newspaper report in the *Nashville Banner* was straightforward; the purpose of the proposed school would be for the education of Negro girls 8 to 18 years of age. "The school," the newspaper said, "will be conducted by capable teachers who are well qualified in the work. The students will be taught all lines of industrial work and will be given a primary education."

Keith wrote a letter of protest to Bishop Byrne. "...Had I known the purpose for which it was purchased, I should not have made the sale at any price. The place has been the residence of myself and my family for nearly 25 years, and I would not have been willing to sell it for any purpose that would be either offensive to the sentiments of my neighbors or damaging to their property."

He further said he had heard the property was being purchased by the Little Sisters of the Poor as an old people's home, and he would not object to it being used for that purpose. If the Little Sisters of the Poor would purchase the property, he would provide easy mortgage terms and donate $2,500 to help the work.

Keith wrote a similar letter to Mother Katharine, who, in her reply, expressed "regret that you or your neighbors should feel as you do concerning the property." The Sisters of the Blessed Sacrament, she said, "are Religious who are of the same race as yourself, and we shall always endeavor in every way to be neighborly to any white neighbors in the vicinity, and we have every reason to hope we may receive from our white neighbors the cordial courtesy for which the Southern people are so justly noted.

"It is true we intend to open an industrial school and academy for Colored girls, but the girls who come there will be only day scholars and in coming to the academy and returning to their homes, I am confident they will be orderly and cause no annoyance."

Mother Katharine also noted the "proximity of numerous homes occupied by Colored families," and "even were the property to be the residence of Colored teachers, which it is not, I think no just exception could be taken to the locality selected."

Another letter was written to Mother Katharine signed by some of the white ladies in the neighborhood, asking that the property be put to another use.

In her reply to them, Mother Katharine said:

> I think I can fully realize how you feel about your old and revered home, around which are so many attachments to the past — the sweet relations of home life hover. I feel the same with regard to mine, and confess that some time ago, when passing it in the trolley cars, when I saw a bill of sale on it, a whole crowd of fond recollections of mother and father and sisters, etc. came vividly to my imagination. Then I more than ever realized how all things temporal pass away, and that there is but one home, strictly speaking that eternal home where all hope to meet our own, and where there will be separation no more.

Keith had all the correspondence published in the Nashville papers as a paid ad — they would not run Mother Katharine's letters any other way without her prior consent. It is doubtful he expected that publishing the letters would help his cause, considering the gentility of her replies. Most likely, his real intent was simply to emphasize to all that he had not knowingly sold the property for use as a school for black girls.[39]

There was a movement to have a city street run through the property at this point, but nothing came of it.[40] In the end, Immaculate Mother Academy opened for the 1905 fall term. When Bishop Byrne blessed the building, Mrs. Keith and her daughter were in attendance. Even a concerted effort by black Protestant clergy to block enrollment had little effect. The school opened with 29 scholars, and shortly after, grew to 55. Immaculate Mother very soon became a respected Nashville institution, and, as always, the Blessed Sacrament Sisters did not confine their outreach to teaching.

In 1908 during an outbreak of typhoid fever, several of the Sisters who had been engaged in hospital ministry sickened, as did one of the lay teachers. Sister Mary of the Assumption died of the illness, a martyr to her vocation. The school that grew to a four-year high school closed in 1954.

Schools, of course, remained only a means toward the real mission of the congregation. Writing home during a 1905 visit to St. Michael's, Mother Katharine could report 46 baptisms among the Navajo children during the school's first three years. "It reminds me of the first ages of Christianity," she said, "and indeed, it is the first age for them."

At dinner they ate string beans, cabbage, cucumbers, and potatoes grown on St. Michael's farm — "even one watermelon," and milk from their cow. "Best of all," Mother Katharine reported, "is the crop of souls. Father Anselm says he has little doubt we shall have 50 more pupils than last year."

In Tennessee, one of the converts was a parent. Mr. Crosswaithe was a prominent attorney in the black community. "It has long been a conviction of mine," he wrote Mother Katharine, "that the Colored people's salvation must come through the holy Catholic Church. The various sects that are assuming the spiritual guardianship of that people are doing little else than keeping alive the name of God in the people's mind."[41]

Katharine's support for the Indian apostolate continued. Msgr. Ketcham, who was director of the Catholic Indian Bureau, noted that Mother Katharine was contributing more to the Indian missions than all the other Catholics in the United States put together.[43] Msgr. Ketcham was possibly less confrontational in his call for Catholic Indian rights than Msgr. Stephan, but he was every bit as effective. In a 1908 letter to President-elect William Howard Taft, President Theodore Roosevelt wrote, "He (Msgr. Ketcham) has always been a high-minded zealous and reasonable friend of the Indians. He has sought in every way the rights of the Indians in his church and the representatives of his church who are dealing with the Indians... and what is very unusual, on the occasion when I have been obliged to differ with him in my views of government policy, he has not held the difference to indicate a criminal nature on my part."[44]

Chapter Nine
Go to Rome Yourself?

From the time the Blessed Sacrament Sisters were founded, it was a goal of Mother Katharine's that the congregation should obtain official Vatican sanction through the approval of its rule, an important consideration for a congregation that would be established in many different dioceses. In the beginning, the Sisters adopted the rule of the Religious Sisters of Mercy, the congregation from whom Katharine and her band of pioneers received their formation.[1] But the Mercy Sisters, although they had many apostolates, were not a missionary order. A rule was needed that would address the Blessed Sacrament Sisters' vision of missionary and social outreach while giving due recognition to their focus on the Eucharist.[2]

At the suggestion of Archbishop Ryan, Katharine wrote to a number of different congregations, asking for a copy of their rule. Among those that appealed to her were the rules of the Holy Ghost Fathers and the Jesuits, but neither could be taken as whole cloth and adapted to the new institute.

After prayer and reflection, Mother Katharine came to the conclusion that the Mercy rule, after all, with its combination of the spiritual and corporal works of mercy and deep, interior spirit of prayer, was really best suited for the Sisters of the Blessed Sacrament, with few alterations. Father (later Bishop) John O'Gorman, novice master for the Holy Ghost Fathers, helped with the preparation, as did several other canon lawyers. When Katharine and her council put together a rule, which they believed conformed to both their vision but within Rome standards, they thought it was merely a matter of having it translated into

Latin and sending it off to the Vatican. It would prove to be a much more complicated and time-consuming venture. A first step was to receive the "decretum laudis," the "decree of praise," which was recognition by Rome that the Sisters of the Blessed Sacrament existed and were engaged in noble work.

Cardinal Francesco Satolli, who was the apostolic delegate to the United States in the 1890s, had come in contact with the fledgling congregation on several occasions. He had visited St. Catherine's Indian School in Santa Fe in both 1895 and 1896, and while a guest of Walter George Smith, the cardinal had visited St. Elizabeth's Convent. At St. Elizabeth's, he remarked about how much the Sisters had already done for the Indians and Colored people and assured them Pope Leo would be pleased when he reported to him the work the Blessed Sacrament Sisters had accomplished.[3]

It was not long after Cardinal Satolli returned to Rome that the Sisters received, through the Propaganda Fide (Congregation for the Propagation of the Faith), notification that their decree of praise had been issued. The next step was approval of their rule — a rule that covered everything in their lives — governance, spiritual life, nature of vows, and mission. It was a slow, painstaking process, and it wasn't until 1905 that the rule was formally presented for consideration by Propaganda Fide's Commission to Review the Rules of Religious Institutes.

Cardinal Satolli was the chairman of the commission, but this did not assure automatic approval. Ultimately, the critique which had been prepared by the commission staff praised the Blessed Sacrament Sisters on all counts except one — the rule. The commission's expert argued the rule, as submitted, did not conform to the Normae, the established norms for such congregations. This is understandable. The Normae were even then under revision, and the rule Mother Katharine imitated — that of the Mercy Sisters — predated the most recent norms.

This was frustrating news for Katharine and her congregation. Once again, Archbishop Ryan came to their assistance. He directed Father Henry Heuser, a respected canon lawyer at St. Charles Borromeo Seminary, to take on the task of recasting the rule in a form that would be acceptable to Rome.

While Father Heuser was working on the technical end of the rule, a distinguished visitor to St. Elizabeth's Convent gave Katharine some very practical advice. It was Mother Frances Cabrini, foundress of the Missionary Sisters of the Sacred Heart. Mother Cabrini, who would eventually become the first U.S.-citizen saint, knew something about Roman bureaucracy.[4]

At this first meeting, the two Reverend Mothers were chatting like old friends when Katharine brought up the problem of the rule and asked if Mother Cabrini could suggest any way to speed the process.

"Go to Rome yourself," was Mother Cabrini's advice. The problem was that there was a high volume of mail and many matters to be considered. When a letter was received, no matter how important, there was a tendency to simply shelve it. However, if someone were there in person, the matter was not so easily ignored.

Katharine was taken aback. She didn't think Archbishop Ryan would approve. "Ask him," Mother Cabrini advised. And Mother Katharine was wrong. The Archbishop thought it a very sensible idea and so did Father Heuser. She would go to Rome.

Katharine booked passage for herself and Mother James on the *Konigin Luise*, sailing date May 11, 1907. She purchased second-class tickets, but this suited neither Archbishop Ryan nor Louise. The Archbishop ordered her to travel first class. "Mother James is not strong," he blandly explained. Louise paid for the upgrade so that Katharine could not plead that it was a burden on the congregation.

The voyage, by secular standards, was indeed first class, but in Katharine's eyes, it could have just as well have been steerage. Because there was no priest on board, there was neither Mass nor the Blessed Sacrament. One of the first land sightings was the isle of Faial in the Azores. In the distance, Katharine beheld a church spire. Because the island was a Portuguese possession, this was probably the spire of a Catholic church.

She wrote home to the Sisters at St. Elizabeth's:

> "Oh! Near the Blessed Sacrament once more. You have not been away from the sacramental presence as we have for six days. I kneel in spirit before the lonely tabernacle of that little village church and beg Our Lord to come to me and bless all my dear daughters who dwell with Him in the land not far behind us, beyond the reach of eye."[5]

Then, too, there was the African coast. Katharine was on the opposite side of the ship when landfall was sighted. She quickly crossed over and strained to see the shoreline. "There live 200 million of those for the salvation of whom our congregation is instituted," she wrote home. "...the sight of it brings into my heart questions — shall I ever live on that continent? Shall you?"[6]

In Rome, the two American nuns stayed with the Sisters of the Cenacle; there was time for sightseeing, but for Katharine, sightseeing meant church visiting. "There are 500 churches in Rome," Mother James wrote to the Sisters at St. Elizabeth. "This morning we went to Mass at the Cenacle, heard two more at St. Claudia; one Mass at St. Sylvester where we went to confession, one Mass and benediction at the Gesu, and got home for dinner." Katharine took a special liking to St. Claudia, which was under the charge of the Blessed Sacrament Fathers, because this church had perpetual adoration of the Blessed Sacrament. "It is the nearest place to heaven in Rome," she remarked to Mother James. Mother James had a different take — too many fleas. "I did not expect to find fleas in heaven," she replied.[7]

On the feast of Corpus Christi, Mothers Katharine and James attended many Masses at St. Claudia and prayed before the Blessed Sacrament. Mother Katharine prayed over the constitutions, that the Lord would make every word according to His will. She firmly believed that God does answer intercessory prayers. As she prayed, she remembered her own vocational discernment process, when she would pray to the Lord, "I do not wish to be a religious unless you wish it." Only once had she openly asked God to grant her a religious vocation. At her next confession her confessor astounded her by suggesting, "Why don't you become a religious?"[8]

Katharine's path to the Vatican had been smoothed by advance letters from Archbishop Ryan to Cardinal Satolli and Msgr. Thomas Kennedy, rector of the North American College in Rome. Msgr. Kennedy's first interview with the two nuns was disappointing. The priest whom he had chosen to do the necessary translations of the rule had died; Kennedy himself had just returned from the United States and had a backlog of work. Everything would take time. Katharine was visibly crestfallen. "You pray," he advised Katharine. In the meantime, he would try to find a priest qualified to do the necessary translation and revision of the rule.

Katharine prayed. She visited the Minerva, the church where St. Catherine of Siena is entombed, and there she asked her patron saint for someone who could help with the rule.[9] Two days later, Msgr. Kennedy wrote to tell her that he had found the priest she needed. He was Father Joseph Schwarz, a Philadelphia-born Redemptorist who was serving in Rome as councilor general for his congregation. He had just completed a translation of the rule for the Sisters of St. Francis of Philadelphia, and, out of gratitude for the support the Drexel family had given the Redemptorist churches in Philadelphia, he was more than willing to take on this new task.

Through the good offices of Msgr. Kennedy, an audience was obtained with the Pope, by this time Pius X, a pontiff who shared Katharine's great love for the Eucharist. Had he been pope when she was a little girl, it probably would not have been necessary to delay her reception of the sacrament until she was older.

The Pope blessed Mother Katharine and Mother James. "I bless your constitutions," the Pontiff told her. "I bless them and hope they will very soon be approved." With Msgr. Kennedy as interpreter, she asked that he bless all the

Sisters, their families, and all the Indians and Colored people. "I bless their families and I bless each and every one of the Indians and Colored," the kindly Pope said, "all — all — all." He blessed the tray of medals and religious articles Mother James presented, too.[10]

Of course, blessing the constitutions was not the same as approving them. While the final approval would come from Pope Pius, Katharine fully understood this would not happen until they had come to his desk with proper approval through the Propaganda Fide's Commission to Review the Rules of Religious Institutions. Father Schwarz was completing his work of revision and translation. Cardinal Satolli, the head of the Commission, had already seen informal drafts of the document and was pleased, especially of the American thoroughness in detailing the financial reports that were required.

"Fifteen days after you present your constitutions you will have approval," Cardinal Satolli promised. "If you wait you can take it home with you."

On the Fourth of July Mother Katharine and Mother James, dressed in their very best habits, (but their shoes were somewhat shabby from trudging the streets of Rome), accompanied Msgr. Kennedy and another priest from the North American College to the Propaganda Fide, where they called upon Cardinal Girolimo Gotti, the congregation's prefect.

When the two Sisters were admitted to the Cardinal's presence, he permitted them to kiss his ring, then ignored them. He struck the Sisters as somewhat haughty, but this may have been due to his not speaking English and their very limited Italian. All the questions were addressed to Msgr. Kennedy, who relayed them to Mother Katharine.

Cardinal Gotti asked if she had testimonials from the bishops of the dioceses where her Sisters were missioned. "Yes," she answered; these had been gathered and sent when the rule was first submitted.

"Has the congregation entered any other dioceses since then?" Gotti asked.

"Yes," Katharine replied. "Nashville and Harrisburg." Harrisburg was most recent; Sisters were working among the students at the government-operated Carlisle Indian School.

"You will have to get letters from these bishops," Gotti said dryly.

Katharine's head swam. It would take at least a month to get such letters. It would be too late for this session of the committee, and they would not meet again until November.

"Cardinal Satolli has promised that the constitutions would be approved shortly," Msgr. Kennedy told the Cardinal.

Katharine, who did not understand the conversation, turned to Kennedy and said, "Tell him both Bishop Byrne of Nashville and Bishop Shanahan of Harrisburg heartily approve of the order's work."

Kennedy, without changing facial expression, said, "Leave the matter alone; he seems to have passed over the difficulty since he knows that Cardinal Satolli has promised to approve the constitutions soon."11

Katharine took the hint and kept quiet. The meeting proceeded without further difficulty.

After leaving Cardinal Gotti, the party visited Cardinal Satolli. "The cardinals will meet on your constitution on July 6, between 10:30 and 12:00," he told her. "You pray. I think you will soon be able to cablegram to your Most Reverend Archbishop that your constitutions and the congregation of the Sisters of the Blessed Sacrament are approved."12

At the appointed hour, Katharine had a Mass celebrated at the Minerva, at St. Catherine of Siena's tomb. Neither she nor Mother James was there. They were storming heaven with prayers at St. Peter's Basilica. "We heard Mass at 9:30, at 10:00, at 10:30 at 11:00 and 11:30," she told her Sisters, "and also a high Mass and two other Masses which were going on whilst we were hearing the above Masses."

It wasn't long after that Cardinal Satolli told Mother Katharine the constitutions were indeed approved, and within hours of receiving the report, the Pope gave his consent, too.

This was a conditional approval for the first five years. After that the process would be reviewed before final approval was given, but that was for another day.

Mother Katharine and Mother James sailed for America on July 18. The steamer they chose was Italian, the *Re d'Italia*. It was not nearly as luxurious as the *Konigin Luise*, but it advertised a chapel. The chapel was outdoors and consisted of a box placed on the first-class deck; the 800 or so passengers in steerage had to look up to the deck. The important thing was the Divine Liturgy as far as Katharine was concerned. Whether celebrated in a box or a cathedral, Mass was the high point of her day.

Home in Philadelphia, one of the first orders of business was the convening of a chapter to formally elect a Superior General and a Council. There were no surprises at this November election. Mother Katharine was elected to the newly named office of Superior General, and all the other councillors who had been previously appointed by the Archbishop were officially elected.13 The congregation was truly on its own. The only real change was that Sister Juliana was appointed to the office of Novice Mistress. While this relieved Katharine of a heavy responsibility, it deprived future novices of the close contact with and formation by Katharine that many of them might have wanted.

This does not mean the Sisters were bereft of the wisdom and counsel of their foundress. Formal and informal exhortations would flow from her pen for the rest of her active life. Shortly after her return from Rome, she told her Sisters:

> The primary object which the Sisters of the congregation propose to themselves is personal sanctification, our vocation is to bring the souls of the Indians and Colored to a worthy reception of the holy Communion, so that the ardent desire of Our Lord in the Blessed Sacrament to give Himself to them may be fulfilled.[14]

Katharine wasn't the only Drexel scouting for souls. Louise, laboring in a somewhat different vineyard, could report her own successes. Ned's now twice-widowed mother, Ida Powell Morrell, this child of Philadelphia's Protestant aristocracy, had converted to Catholicism in 1907. Louise wrote:

> She is very lonely and has no one but the nurses. On Sunday last, after Mass (which was at seven) Father Lessard brought holy Communion to Mrs. Johnson. It was the first time I had been with her when the dear Lord came into her heart, and it made me grateful and happy to have the opportunity of being in her room at such a juncture.[15]

Louise's health was still not quite what it should be. Somewhat later, when the Morrells were in vacation at Banff for her health, she could report on Ned's progress from convert to model Catholic. The little chapel had no altar server. Ned not only served the Mass, he took up the collection.[16]

* * * *

Meanwhile, in the mission fields, Katharine's goal remained much more focused on the evangelization of the children rather than their acculturation. This is clear in a 1909 letter to the Sisters at St. Michael's, Arizona:

> And so the little Navajos are learning to crochet baby caps and baby sacks and dressing their dolls in European costume. When in the days in the far future, you as old ladies in Religion, have the Navajos who are still at St. Michael's bring their children's children to see you, will they wear the European or the Navajo costume? May their souls be clothed in the beautiful white baptismal robe, and then what matters it as to the covering used for this mortal frame, provided it be neat and clean.[17]

As the first decade of the 20th century came to a close, another chapter was ending in Mother Katharine's life. Archbishop Ryan had guided the little congregation from birth through its official acceptance by Rome. Now that the Sisters of the Blessed Sacrament could stand independently, his role was reduced to trusted adviser and honored presider over congregation ceremonies. He was approaching 80, and his health was failing.

"I can't see a gray hair on your head," Katharine assured him. "Pray for me," the Archbishop said.[18] The aging prelate was in his final illness in late January 1911 when Mother Katharine and other heads of religious congregations were called to his bedside. The group of mothers superior was waiting in an ante chamber when they were called to the sick room.

Everyone hesitated. Finally, two turned to Mother Katharine and urged, "You go first because the Archbishop is so interested in your community."

Katharine shrunk back. "No," she insisted, "we should go last because we are the least." Katharine entered the room last and stayed in the background.

The next day she was granted another visit. She kissed Archbishop Ryan's ring. "Most Reverend Father," she said, "You have been so good to us. You have been a real father to our little congregation."

"I was always interested in your work," he responded.

"You are the founder of our community, because if it was not for your interest I could not have gone on," she told him. "Do you remember after Bishop O'Connor's death when I was at St. Xavier's with the Sisters of Mercy — just a novice, and I told you I could not go on. I felt that I could not go on, I could not keep up the work; and you said to me, Most Reverend Father, 'Well, if I help you now can you go on?'"

Suddenly, in her humility, thinking of what little consequence the incident must have been in his eyes no matter how great it appeared to her, Katharine said, "But of course, Most Reverend Father, you do not remember."

The Archbishop's breath was labored; between gasps he said, "I do remember, my child, I do indeed." He looked at her lovingly and said, "I remember something else you told me that time, too."

Whatever Archbishop Ryan was alluding to remains a secret. While Mother Katharine told her Sisters of this last encounter with the dying Archbishop, she would not reveal what he had meant. "That day I told him something that only God and I know," she said.[19]

Louise Morrell was also summoned to the Archbishop's residence. During this farewell meeting, Archbishop Ryan mentioned a beautiful emerald episcopal ring Louise had purchased for him in Paris in 1889 while on her honeymoon. Would Louise mind if he gave this to Archbishop Glennon of St. Louis? "The ring is yours, Your Grace," Louise replied. "Do with it as you wish."

Archbishop Ryan died Feb. 11, 1911. He had been a respected and well-beloved bishop for Philadelphia. If his entire diocese mourned his passing, none mourned it more than Katharine's Sisters of the Blessed Sacrament. He had been a true friend and insightful guide throughout the two decades of its young existence. For the next year, at the request of Katharine, every Blessed Sacrament Sister offered 15 decades of the rosary for the repose of the soul of the Archbishop in addition to the five decades they were already required to pray. His death had come on the feast of Our Lady of Lourdes. A new parish she was funding in Atlanta, Georgia, was named "Our Lady of Lourdes" in his memory.

"The heavens are mine,
the earth is mine, and the
nations are mine; mine are
the just and the sinners
are mine; mine are the angels
and the Mother of God;
all things are mine, God Himself
is mine and for me,
because Christ is mine
and all for me."

SAINT KATHARINE DREXEL

Chapter 10
Firm Faith
Confident Hope
Ardent Charity

During the second decade of the 20th century, America began a migratory phenomenon that would last at least a half century and forever alter the character of its great cities. African Americans, drawn by the promise of better wages and a better life, left their Southern rural communities for the industrial North. The influx from the South accelerated with the onset of World War I — many hands, no matter what the color, were needed in the factories. The better wage was true enough; the better life was more problematic. The new arrivals were not, as a rule, welcomed by their new northern neighbors, either as fellow residents or fellow congregants in the churches.

Except for her school on the motherhouse grounds, Katharine's work among blacks had been in the officially segregated South. Now she turned her attention to the unofficially segregated northern ghettos. Sisters began teaching at St. Peter Claver and Our Lady of the Blessed Sacrament Schools in Philadelphia in 1908 and 1909. Unlike most of the previous schools, these were day schools connected with parishes Katharine had helped found or fund. South Philadelphia's St. Peter Claver really predated the Blessed Sacrament Sisters; the school had initially been conducted by the Oblate Sisters of Providence and afterward, the Notre Dame Sisters. Katharine, as a laywoman, had purchased the school building, and it was through the efforts of the Drexel sisters that Holy Ghost Fathers were persuaded to institute a formal parish. Now Blessed Sacrament Sisters would staff the boys' school, while Notre Dame Sisters continued to oversee the girls' school.

Also, in North Philadelphia the African-American population was on the rise, and the Catholics among them were ministered to by the clergy of St. Elizabeth Parish. Mother Katharine purchased a property on North Broad Street for a chapel and obtained the services of a former Jesuit missionary to Jamaica, Father Abraham J. Emerick. Our Lady of the Blessed Sacrament Parish quickly outgrew these quarters, and Katharine contributed $65,000 toward the purchase of a former Presbyterian church. When the Jesuits withdrew, ministry was taken over by the Holy Ghost Fathers. The Blessed Sacrament Sisters staffed the school, and, as was their custom, engaged in extensive visitation to the area homes, hospitals, and prisons.

When St. Mark's was founded in Harlem, New York, in 1912, Katharine built the parish school and convent and her Blessed Sacrament Sisters staffed the school. Before the first term ended, the parish could count 19 student baptisms, with a corresponding number of confirmations and first Communions. This was in addition to the numerous adult converts and children's Sunday School participants.[1]

The Blessed Sacrament Sisters were more than teachers; they were a living presence in the densely populated Harlem ghetto. If their first convent was outwardly just another rented house on a block of many houses, in a spiritual sense it was much more. The woman who lived in an adjacent house told the Sisters how much their little convent, with the Blessed Sacrament reposing in the tabernacle, meant to the neighborhood. The rooms nearest the convent had suddenly become the easiest to rent. From here the people could listen as the Sisters in chapel recited the beautiful night prayers.[2]

In Columbus, Ohio, Bishop James J. Hartley asked Mother Katharine to open a school. He estimated there were 30,000 Colored in his diocese, not a single one of whom was Catholic. Katharine responded by sending Sisters and by funding the cost of a convent for the new St. Cyprian Parish.[3] It was an uphill struggle to obtain students for the school because of suspicions and prejudices in both the white and black communities. St. Cyprian was never large, and it was eventually consolidated with other parishes. But it did serve its purpose; as one newspaper article suggested: The school "tried to teach the Negro to be proud of his race, and (to) implant the ambition to do individual work, instead of trying to imitate the white race."

St. Cyprian and the Blessed Sacrament Sisters had an effect on the white community, too. Within a few short years of its foundation, two Columbus candidates joined the congregation — Sister Agnes Murphy and Sister Cyprian Nightwine.

In Chicago, St. Monica School was established, but not without controversy. Because the mission of the Blessed Sacrament Sisters was to labor exclusively among Indians and Colored People, their institutions were, for all intents and purposes, segregated. But of course, the reason for this was quite opposite to the segregation found in the South. The purpose was not to exclude minorities from white schools, but to give the children of the disadvantaged races the same opportunities white children enjoyed.

Within the American Catholic Church, European minority groups actively sought their own parishes and schools, seeing these institutions as a means of preserving their traditional culture. Among blacks, it was quite different. While some African Americans accepted the black Catholic parishes and schools as a means of advancement and empowerment, others thought they were a further imposition of Jim Crow segregation, something they had come north to escape.

So it was in Chicago; there was an initial distrust and a misunderstanding of the intentions of Katharine and other pioneering religious, who sought only to serve, not to segregate. An article in the *Chicago Defender*, a black newspaper, attacked the new school, saying, "The segregation of the race at the little Catholic school at 37th Street and Wabash Avenue is an opening wedge to start segregation in the public schools in Chicago." Another article was more vitriolic: "Romanism," the writer said, "is in harmony with white slavery, thieving, robbing, prostitution, segregation of colors in schools, debauchery, ignorance and all that weakens people."

The bigotry evidenced in the press moved L.C. Vale, a Chicago black Catholic, to write in a letter published by the *Catholic World*: "The Catholic Church has never closed its school doors on the Negro. This fight that has been making its rounds among the Colored people of Chicago of the past months is from poisoned minds, persons who have selfish motives, rather than the welfare of the race."[4]

In the end, misunderstandings were smoothed over in Chicago and elsewhere, but quite aside from community controversies, Katharine's hands-on approach to her apostolate was wearing on her health. As each of these new schools opened, she would participate fully in the preparation process. In some instances, this meant joining the Sisters in the thorough cleaning and rehabilitation of run-down properties in slum neighborhoods, too often the only buildings available to the Sisters. Coupled with this physical labor by Katharine in sometimes less-than-sanitary conditions was a grueling self-imposed schedule of annual visitations to the various houses of the congregation.

By September 1912, the new schools had opened, and Katharine prepared for a visitation to the West. Her councillors noticed she did not look well at all, and they tried to persuade her to forgo the journey. After all, final approval of the rule was due for consideration, which meant another European trip in a few months. Katharine insisted that she was fine, and accompanied by Mother

Loyola, she set out for the West. By the time she arrived in St. Michael's, Arizona, she was definitely sick, but decided to continue on to St. Catherine's, Santa Fe. By this time, the illness, which she took to be a cold, was serious enough to require medical treatment. The doctors diagnosed incipient pneumonia and urged her to go to another climate — the high altitude of Santa Fe was not good for respiratory infections.

Mother Loyola accompanied her to a hospital in Albuquerque and it was here, after her condition worsened, that she finally allowed the Sisters to notify her councillors in Pennsylvania, but still forbade them to come to her. By now the councillors were thoroughly alarmed, especially when they learned the illness could actually be typhoid fever. The typhoid, it was guessed, may have been contracted during her visit to New York when she assisted the Sisters who were cleaning out a germ-infested building for use as a convent/school.

The councilors were in a quandary. They did not wish to go against Mother Katharine, their superior, but she would not come home and insisted they not come to her. Philadelphia's new archbishop, Edmond Prendergast, broke the impasse. Rather than send Sisters out West after Mother Katharine had ordered them not to come to her, he asked Edward Morrell to go and gave him plenipotentiary powers to act in his name.

When Morrell arrived, Katharine was slightly better but not yet out of danger. As soon as her condition permitted, he brought her home on a private rail car hired from the Santa Fe Railroad. Not taking any chances by traveling the direct route over the mountains with thin air, the train took a southern route, which was a longer journey but with more level terrain.[5]

After the fact, Archbishop Prendergast wrote in a letter to Katharine:

> I am deeply indebted to Mr. Morrell and I hope that your Sisters will never forget how much they owe him. I had the greatest confidence in his good judgment and I was not mistaken. Therefore I did not hesitate about directing you to conform to his arrangements. I appreciate your humility and your unquestioning obedience to me as your spiritual superior. That is the true spirit of a religious.[6]

Katharine accepted her illness with good grace. "Well," she said, "I feel perfect peace on an occasion like this. As it is certainly not according to my plans and it must be God's will."

In addition to what was definitely typhoid, Katharine had developed a slight heart irregularity and was showing signs of a possible nervous breakdown if she did not slow her pace. Under physicians' orders, she relinquished most of her responsibilities to the capable hands of Mothers James and Mercedes.[7] One of their first duties was to fill in for their ailing superior in a visit to Boston's Cardinal William O'Connell who wished to have Blessed Sacrament Sisters for his diocese.

Mother Mercedes, in her disarming fashion, wrote of the meeting:

> We reached Boston in trepidation of spirit because we had heard from many sources that His Eminence, the Cardinal, was not a very approachable man and was a stickler for the etiquette of the Roman Curia.
>
> We took up our abode the night before with the good Grey Nuns who had a home for working girls near the cathedral. The mother superior, wishing to help us all she could by her kindly advice, which by the way we asked, told us we must be on time, just on the minute or the Cardinal would regard it as a mark of disrespect. Then we were to be very meek and not make any suggestions unless His Eminence asked for them, and then make them in a way that we were ready to take his better informed advice on the case. She cautioned us to be brief and if the Cardinal told us to sit down we were to sit down, and if he told us to stand up we were to stand up, and in the meantime while we were gone she would burn two candles before the tabernacle and say the rosary that we would do the right thing.[8]

Actually, the meeting (on the stroke of ten) went very well. Mother Mercedes reported:

> The Cardinal was charming and cordial, even if his questions were piercing. He seemed to be a man zealous for the things of God, and had we not heard so many things about him we would have thought he was one of the meekest and humblest of the Church's prelates. He personally escorted us to the door and asked us if there was anything possible that he could do for us to make our stay in Boston pleasant.

There would be another meeting with Boston's formidable Cardinal the following year; this time Mother Katharine went in person, accompanied by Mother Mercedes.

As was their habit, the two Sisters carried food for their journey to and from Boston. Railroad dining car prices were an extravagance. Mother Mercedes was carrying the home-crafted cloth lunchbag as the two awaited the Cardinal in his parlor. Not knowing what else to do with it, she tucked it under her chair. Cardinal O'Connell, when he entered, was accompanied by his pet bull terrier.

The dog, naturally, sniffed out the bag and spilled it on the carpet. Katharine could not suppress a laugh, but Mother Mercedes was totally embarrassed.

"Now see what you got for your vanity," Katharine said after they left the Cardinal's residence. "Wouldn't it have been much better to hold it under your scapular?" Mother Mercedes agreed with her superior, but privately thought it would have been better to spend the dime to check the bag at the railroad station.[9]

Through these meetings and subsequent negotiations, the Blessed Sacrament Sisters were able to open a Boston foundation the following year. Blessed Sacrament Mission Center was unique at the time for the Sisters. There was no school; the primary focus for many years was visitation to hospitals, prisons and homes. As with all of the Blessed Sacrament works, the mission and its succeeding foundations in Boston would be the basis for a number of conversions to the Catholic faith, both among children and adults.

While prison visitation could put the Sisters in the company of the most hardened criminals, just as often the inmates were the real victims — victims of a culture that spurned the poor, especially if their skin had a darker cast. One of the Boston Blessed Sacrament visitors, Sister Eugenia Knightly, told of meeting a man who had been jailed for stealing $4.50 to feed his children.[10]

Katharine's trip to Rome, to present the rule for final approval, had been scheduled for November 1912, but because of her illness, Father Schwarz had obtained a delay until April 1913. This time Mother Katharine elected to travel on the *Ivernia*. This steamer was chosen because Bishop Joseph Schrembs of Toledo was combining his *ad limina*, the visit made every five years by bishops to Rome, with a pilgrimage. The pilgrims would sail from New York on the Ivernia; there would be 14 priests on board and consequently many Masses.

Mother James was left in charge of the congregation during the Superior General's absence; Mother Mercedes traveled as Katharine's "prudent companion." Katharine was seasick for part of the voyage, but "her knees must be the charmed part of Mother's anatomy," Mother Mercedes wrote, "for she must have knelt five hours today" in the temporary ship chapel. When one priest warned Katharine she could develop rheumatism from the cold, hard floor, Katharine made one concession — she used her shawl as a kneeling pad. On Sunday at sea she attended five Masses — two very early Masses, then a 7 a.m. High Mass and two additional Masses later that day.[11]

Mother Mercedes heard only 4 1/4 Masses. "My deficiency was caused by my usual trouble," she explained, "failure to get down very promptly in the morning."

When Katharine wasn't praying she was trawling, at least in a manner of speaking. She would strike up conversations with young single Catholic ladies.

"I spent most of this morning in trying to fish for what you pray for every night," she wrote to the Sisters at home, "good subjects for the congregation."[12]

In Rome, further assistance with a final polishing of the rule was given by an American priest, Passionist Father Elliot Ross. He wrote to Mother Katharine:

> Certainly, as a Southerner whose forbears held slaves for generations (but did not rob and exterminate the Indians as the Yankees), I feel a special responsibility towards the Negroes, and so, if I can ever do anything for you in the future, I want you to be sure to give me that pleasure.

When in Rome Mothers Katharine and Mercedes were often escorted by Lucy Dahlgren, a very pious young relative of Katharine. Lucy, a graduate of Eden Hall, wished to become a Carmelite, but because her mother was not yet Catholic, she remained at home to care for the religious instruction of her younger brothers and sisters. She would eventually join the Blessed Sacrament Sisters but had to return to the lay state when her constitution proved too fragile for convent life.

Lucy's mother invited the two Sisters to stay in a wing of the Barbelin Palace, the magnificent residence the family had leased. Mother Katharine regretfully declined. Even though this would save money for the congregation, accepting hospitality from a relative would be a bad example for the rest of the Sisters.[13]

The final approval of the rule was without incident, and perhaps Katharine's sole regret during this visit was that she had not been able to visit the Pope, who was ill. There were other compensations, of course. On the final night in Rome they revisited St. Catherine's tomb at the Minerva and St. Peter's Basilica. On their way they passed the famous Fountain of Trevi. If one throws a coin in the fountain, legend says, one will return to Rome. Mother Katharine gave Mother Mercedes a penny to toss into the fountain.[14]

The two Sisters did not return directly to the United States; Mother Katharine was still fishing. Their travels took them through Germany, Holland, Ireland, and England in search of young women with a religious vocation. Ireland especially, everyone knew, was the place to go for religious vocations. That in itself presented a problem. Katharine wrote:

> It is a blessing to get lodgings in a convent in Ireland. They are so overrun with travelling nuns, seeking as we, vocations in Ireland that many dioceses have an edict from the bishop forbidding the convents to give them hospitality.

Fortunately for the two Blessed Sacrament Sisters, they had a friend in Ireland. It was Holy Ghost Father John T. Murphy (later a bishop for Mauritania) who had been stationed in Philadelphia when the Drexel sisters helped fund St. Peter Claver Parish. With Father Murphy's help, entry was obtained to a number of Catholic schools.

By Katharine's account, there was a set routine. The Sisters would either go from classroom to classroom, or in some cases, address a school assembly. Father Murphy would give an introductory speech, telling the young ladies how Mothers Katharine and Mercedes were just coming from Rome where they had received the final approval for their congregation. He would tell them it was the Pope himself (Leo XIII) who had suggested the founding of a religious order for Indians and Colored in the United States. They were passing through Ireland in the hopes of finding some zealous maidens who would wish to give themselves to the salvation of these souls.[15]

"And now young ladies," he would end, "the Reverend Mother wishes you to gather around her and you yourselves can ask her any questions you wish about the congregation and its works."

Katharine would field questions, if any, and hope for the best. She wrote:

> It was hard on the nuns we visited, their classes, of course, were suspended whilst the Reverend Father addressed the pupils. Then also they invariably offered us tea and thin bread and butter, for they were all lovely to us. The schools were very simple, sometimes all grades in one room, even with separate teachers. There were few blackboards or even desks.

In Waterford, the party visited schools conducted by Sisters of Mercy, Sisters of Charity, Presentation Sisters, and Sacred Heart of Mary Sisters. In Lismore — Archbishop Prendergast's hometown — they visited a school where his sister, a Presentation nun, was superior.

Katharine found the entire school visitation experience a terrible ordeal. She confessed:

> We got to counting the number of days before sailing that we had to go through this process. I hope it will bring good vocations, if so the pain is worth the gain. But if they are not good I don't want any. It is not the quantity, it is the quality. One fervent religious can do more good for God than one thousand tepid, halfhearted souls.[16]

Katharine did not realize the profound effect she had upon some of the young girls visited.

Augusta O'Brien was 15 and a student at the Presentation School in Lismore. If the teachers found visiting nuns an irksome intrusion on the school day, the students did not. They were used to visitors pleading for missionaries to America or South America or Australia or Africa. Listening to the missionaries was easier than their lessons.

This visit, at least for Augusta, was different. As Mother Katharine spoke, she thought her message was of one of the most Christ-centered, needy works for the glory of God she had ever heard. But when the question was raised, "Who would think of going with Mother Katharine to America?" Augusta was silent. The Presentation Sisters knew their pupils well. Sensing Augusta's interest, they arranged for a private interview with Mother Katharine.

When Augusta went to Katharine, the American nun was seated alone in the garden, looking out upon the verdant Irish landscape. "Isn't it a lovely view!" Mother Katharine exclaimed.

Augusta dearly loved her native land, too, but paradoxically, this simple gesture melted her heart and firmed her resolve. She would forsake the soft beauty of her beloved countryside for the harsher grandeur of the American West or perhaps the gritty slums of those great cities beyond the sea. In later life, Augusta, as Sister Brendan, could recall nothing of the subsequent conversation, only her resolve.

But Augusta was then only 15, too young to give valid consent. She could do nothing without her mother's approval. This would not be obtained easily. It is one thing to have one's child enter religious life; it is quite another, when in doing so, they travel such a distance that they may never see their family again this side of the grave.

Mrs. O'Brien was cool to this request by Augusta, the eldest of her five children. But she agreed to meet with Mother Katharine. She did so the following evening. When she returned, she told Augusta, "She is a saintly mother. It is myself who would be going with her if it were not for the five of ye."[17]

In all, Katharine gained four vocations during this trip. In addition to Augusta (Sister Brendan), Bridget Rogers (Sister Incarnata) came from Ireland; Germany yielded Elizabeth Schmitt (Sister Cecily) and Marie Windecker (Sister Hildegard). None of the new candidates accompanied the Mothers back to Pennsylvania; the Irish candidates came in September; the German girls were held up temporarily by the terrible war that was impending.

The Irish schools would prove to be especially fertile grounds for vocations. During the 1930s, almost 100 young women would come from Ireland to Cornwells Heights. Mothers Mercedes and Francis Xavier were especially active on the annual recruitment trips to Ireland which would end only with the onset of World War II, when trans-Atlantic travel became virtually impossible.

After their Irish recruitment drive, Mothers Katharine and Mercedes returned to America by way of England. There was a stopover in London, where they visited the usual sights. At Westminster Abbey, Mother Mercedes was enthralled by the loveliness of the Abbey choir. Katharine could think of nothing but how the Abbey, once Catholic, was now Anglican. "It made one feel sad," she said, "to see still the traces of the Benedictines in the cloisters outside, in the infirmary on the first floor near the Confessor's Chapel with the small door leading into the central nave where the sick could at ease hear Holy Mass, and to think it has all passed away."18

Westminster Abbey was not alone in its lack of Catholic Mass. The two American Sisters booked passage on the *Cedric*, a ship that could usually be counted upon to have one or two priests as passengers. Mother Katharine even brought along a portable altar loaned to her by Louise, and some altar breads. But on this trip there was no priest aboard.

"We must needs bless Our Lord for all the Masses he has let us hear in the past," she reflected, "and I want the deprivation to be a penance — though nothing less than the Sacred Blood can take this away — for all my faults in life in hearing Mass."19

By August 1913, Katharine was on the road again — a visit to her western missions. Louise thought this ill advised, considering her recent breakdown in health. In typical fashion, she tried to enlist Archbishop Prendergast. To accomplish this, she wrote to the three doctors who had treated Katharine in Santa Fe, asking that they write to the Archbishop informing him that Katharine's health would be endangered by the journey. To her chagrin, Dr. J.A. Reidy wrote for the three and said, "After careful consideration we are of the opinion that there will be no ill effects following her contemplated visit" provided "she takes proper care of herself and avoids unnecessary exposure and hardships." Katharine went.20

At St. Catherine's, she was so overcome by emotion in witnessing the heroic work of her daughters in religion that she tried to kiss their feet. They would not permit it.

Afterward, she explained:

> It was no real joke, my trying to kiss your feet — privileged feet indeed of the Sisters of the Blessed Sacrament who walk in distant parts from the dear motherhouse and away from parents and friends to bring the glad tidings of the redemption. You who have left all things to follow Jesus, Jesus Himself is and will be your reward in the eternal motherhouse where each Sister of the Blessed Sacrament has her throne awaiting her.

It was indeed a strange, dangerous, and exotic path that the western missionaries trod. It wasn't long after this visit that Mother Loyola wrote home from St. Michael's, reporting on a terrible flood that had devastated their region. Cecilia, a 7-year-old pupil at the school, was drowned, as was her 15-year-old sister, who had tried to save her.

The Indians had a great superstition about dead bodies, and it fell upon the Sisters, in spite of their own grief, to wash and dress the two bodies for burial. It was a great sadness to them that neither child had been baptized. Mother Loyola reasoned that perhaps the little one had baptism by desire, "for she wanted to be baptized, and just two days before the flood, when her mother brought her down she blessed herself and said her prayers most beautifully when asked to do it."

Cecilia's grandmother asked that the little girl be dressed as she was in school, and the Sisters dressed her in the clothing she had worn at a recent pageant.

The grandmother grieved over her older grandchild, but little Cecilia was too much for her. Overcoming her ingrained dread of the dead, the old woman took the child, cradled her to her bosom, spoke to her softly in her native tongue, and cried bitterly.[21]

* * * *

If the eternal vision of God was the goal of the Sisters of the Blessed Sacrament, both for themselves and for the souls to whom they ministered, that was in the future. In the here and now, the great throne was in the convent chapel where their Lord reposed in the tabernacle. It was in 1914 that Archbishop Prendergast, while visiting for the profession ceremony, granted the Sisters the privilege of daily exposition of the Host. The exposition was after the first Mass of the day until 6 p.m. During this period, at least two Sisters would be in prayer before the Blessed Sacrament at all times. The Archbishop would have granted nocturnal adoration, too; but Katharine realized the convent community was too small to provide the needed Sisters 24 hours a day.[22] She would wish for perpetual adoration, but would not see the great privilege taken lightly. For Katharine herself, the scheduled adoration was a high point of the day. Pressing convent business could wait. "I have another appointment," she would tell the Sisters, before she would put aside the task at hand for her precious time with God.

Prayer was an integral part of community life. The Sisters were asked to pray for a variety of intentions, including, but not limited to, the intentions of the Pope and the Archbishop, sanctification of the congregation, the conversion of the Indian and Colored races for missions and missionaries, and for the propagation of the faith. Earlier, Katharine had recommended 10 intentions for which the Sisters could pray during their daily Mass.

- A most firm faith
- Confident hope
- Ardent charity
- True contrition for their sins
- Grace never to commit a grievous sin
- To die rather than commit a mortal sin
- The perfect accomplishment of the Holy Constitution
- That no soul be lost through the fault of a Sister of the Blessed Sacrament
- A tender devotion to the Passion
- Final perseverance and a plenary indulgence at the hour of death.[23]

Katharine Drexel funded the Archbishop Ryan Memorial School at Our Lady of Lourdes Parish in Atlanta, Georgia, in 1912, and this was followed by St. Peter Claver School in Macon, Georgia. These institutions faced bitter opposition in their early years. A concrete example is a bill introduced into the Georgia Senate in 1915, the year St. Peter Claver opened. It would prohibit "the teaching by any white teacher, in any school for colored pupils in this State, or the teaching by a colored teacher in any school for white pupils in this state, whether the said school be or not be a part of or belonging to the public schools of this state. Any person guilty of violating this act shall be guilty of a misdemeanor."

Such a law, if enacted, would make it impossible for congregations such as the Blessed Sacrament Sisters to operate in Georgia. "Is the motive plain bigotry against the Church, or is racial prejudice the source of it?" Archbishop Prendergast asked. Edward Morrell was sufficiently disturbed by the bill that he wrote to U.S. Chief Justice Edward Douglass White, requesting an opinion on the constitutionality of a law of this nature. Fortunately, the bill, which passed first reading, was killed before second reading.[24]

This incident in Georgia tells something about the level of racial bigotry that existed in parts of the South and the extremes diehard bigots would go to assure that black men and women would never rise from the state-sanctioned peonage that had replaced slavery.

On the other hand, a different dynamic was working in New Orleans, and it was because of this that the Blessed Sacrament Sisters made a bold leap that same year — 1915 — into higher education. The new thrust was dictated by the unusual situation in Louisiana, a state with a past history of racial mixing. In most other areas of the United States, African Americans were for the most part culturally Protestant, either churched or unchurched. This was because the slave owners had been Protestant, and the slaves followed their master's religions. Louisiana, formerly under Spanish and French rule, had a long Catholic history. The challenge to the Church was not in gaining black converts, but rather holding onto black and mulatto Catholics in a society that was becoming increasingly Protestant-dominated. Sadly, racial bigotry had increased in Louisiana in direct proportion to its Americanization.

Prior to this Katharine had given monetary support but had not sent Sisters to New Orleans because she did not wish to undercut in any way the Sisters of the Holy Family, the black congregation headquartered in New Orleans.[25] But needs were changing. In 1915, the black Catholic population was estimated at 55,000 and falling — at least 40,000 had already been lost. Louisiana actually had four colleges for blacks or at least institutions that were called colleges. Three were conducted by Protestant denominations; the fourth, Southern University, was originally denominational but now a state school.

While this educational system suggests Louisiana (or at least New Orleans) was more tolerant of blacks than other Southern states, there were limits. Southern University, located near New Orleans, was in a neighborhood that had experienced an influx of white residents. The whites successfully lobbied to have the college relocated to a site near Baton Rouge. This was especially difficult for black Catholic parents, because although Southern had a Baptist flavor, it was a state school, and as such, did not have compulsory Protestant religious services. The loss of Southern to New Orleans left no other college that black Catholics could attend with a minimum risk of prosyletization. The colleges were actually contributing to the loss of black Catholics, especially of potential black community leaders.

Meanwhile, Southern University's buildings were empty and the property was up for sale. The Josephite Fathers, the African-American Catholic community, and New Orleans Archbishop Joseph Blenk saw this as a golden opportunity and persuaded Mother Katharine to purchase the entire facility.[26] Such a school could aid the Sisters in their own mission. One of Katharine's great challenges was the lack of personnel within her own congregation to staff all the schools where they were needed. While some of the graduates of Rock Castle went on to obtain teaching certificates, what was needed was a normal school that would turn out graduates qualified to teach in the six parishes Archbishop Blenk was planning to open for black Catholics.[27]

Mothers Katharine and Mercedes visited New Orleans in April 1915, and inspected the property. The main building had an auditorium that could seat 500 for worship services, eight classrooms and room for a convent on the top floor. There was another building that could serve as a rectory for a priest, and finally, a building — former slave quarters — that could be converted into shops and a science laboratory.

The Sisters prayed on the day of the auction; a prominent Catholic community leader did the actual bidding. Mother Katharine purchased the property for $18,000; it was a steal, well under the price she would have been willing to pay.[28]

Old Southern reopened that September, and like Rock Castle, it was under the patronage of a St. Francis — in this case Francis Xavier — but in time the name was shortened to Xavier University. Frank Drexel would have been proud of how his daughter chose to honor him as she spent his money on charity. Interestingly, while Katharine often chose to name schools or other foundations for the patrons saints of family members — and several charities assisted by her named schools for her patron — there was no desire for personal aggrandizement. When her new college was dedicated she chose to sit anonymously in the balcony. Katharine also forbade any mention of her name during the ceremony.

The school reopened in 1915 with Sister M. Frances as director of studies. While it had more students — and the Sisters found them to be well-qualified — than its small faculty could handle, it was hardly a university in the modern sense. That first year saw classes in the upper elementary years and three years of high school, but this was actually more than the Sisters had expected. It opened with grades seven through eleven, and the Sisters planned to add one grade each year in the future.

But it was only a few years before Xavier began offering true college courses, at first on a level comparable to a modern community college, and finally bachelor's degrees and graduate degrees. By 1932, it had grown to such an extent that Mother Katharine relocated the college on a new, larger campus, with the high school level retaining the first campus.

From the very beginning, Xavier was unique. It was the first and only black Catholic college in the United States. It was, from its foundation, coeducational, an important step that most Catholic colleges and universities, large or small, would not undertake until after World War II at the earliest. And just as significant, it was an integrated faculty, with black and white men and women working side by side with the Blessed Sacrament Sisters.

A brochure issued at the time the college reopened used the name "Old Southern." The mission of the school was explained:

> By placing before the student truth in its various aspects — as revealed through religion, literature, history, science and art, the Sisters shall aim to bring the pupils into personal relations with wider worlds and

larger life. 'Old Southern' shall continue to welcome to its advantages pupils of every denomination and anything like an attempt to force religious convictions on non-Catholics shall be scrupulously avoided. For the sake of uniformity and the preservation of discipline, all pupils are required to be present at the public religious exercises and the catechetical instructions, but non-Catholic students may be exempted. All Catholic and non-Catholic students shall be taught to appreciate religious principals and moral worth.[29]

The college would face many challenges and crises over the years, but by and large it would be the crown jewel of the Sisters' achievements.

Xavier would be the training ground for many black teachers in Louisiana. The Blessed Sacrament Sisters opened normal schools in Lake Iberia and Lake Charles, and Katharine made good use of many of them.[30] Now that she had an assured supply of qualified teachers, she eventually built a series of rural schools — 24 in all — in the backwoods and bayou hamlets of Louisiana. Within a few years, these schools, in such places as Abbeville, Reserve, Point-a-la-Hache and St. Martinville, were built by Katharine at a cost of $2,000-$4,000 apiece. They were very small but adequate for the need; each was staffed by two Xavier graduates whose salaries were paid by the Blessed Sacrament Sisters. Some of these schools would become the nucleus for future parishes and larger schools. All served a critical need by providing quality education to poor black communities up until the time of *Brown v. Board of Education of Topeka, Kansas*, in 1954 which mandated public school integration and ushered in better education regardless of race.

A 1921 visit by Mother Katharine to one of the rural schools tells something of both their triumphs and the challenges. Father Van Baast, a Josephite, was her guide. To reach the school they had to cross the Mississippi in what seemed to be a questionable boat. After climbing the riverbank, they reached a little church that had a school staffed by two Xavier graduates who had just completed high school and a certification program.

"There are about 100 children here," Mother Katharine wrote. "The children here are very bright; I was surprised at this as they are back in the woods. They are very nice and they would have had more schooling here, but that smallpox broke out in February."

Father Van Baast had attempted to buy a different property for a school near a location where a Lutheran school was converting Catholic children. The cost of the property was $800, and the priest went to the local bank to borrow the money. The banker, quite naturally, asked for what purpose the loan was being made, and when he learned how the money would be used, he told the priest he would "not lend money for a nigger school." The banker went further. He bought the property himself just to make certain Father Van Baast could not purchase it.[31]

If progress was made on one front at Xavier in 1925 when a four-year liberal arts college program opened with a two-year pre-medical course, ground was lost the next year. The ground literally was land for a ball field. When Katharine tried to buy it for the school, the owners would not sell because it would be used by blacks.[32] This was a secondary reason the college was moved to another location. The primary reason was increased enrollment. The relocation would not be accomplished until the end of the decade.

As negotiations for the new property were in progress, Katharine wrote to her Cornwells Heights community about a visit to the Archbishop of New Orleans:

> We told him it was facing a big, broad street on one side and was sufficiently large for football and baseball activities. I am not mentioning to you where, because at present it is a dead secret, for we have not yet paid for the property nor do we have title to it. And on two other occasions when we got thus far we were frustrated in our designs by protests because it was for a 'nigger school.' We will not reveal its locality until it is in our possession.[33]

With a ball field there came sports teams, and sports teams travel. When Katharine visited Xavier she would ride the streetcar. Yet the athletic team had a $13,000 bus given by her, according to Victor Labat, a Xavier graduate and teacher who testified for her cause for canonization.[34]

If Katharine deliberately took a back seat during the dedication of Xavier, this was very much in keeping with her style, according to Sister Mary Florence Kuhn, who taught in New Orleans for many years. "When bishops or others would call, she would ask one of the other council members to meet them," she said. "She preferred to stay at adoration... she was not anxious to be in the limelight at all."[35]

As the college grew, the curriculum expanded and more and more courses were offered. But accreditation was not easily obtained. While the Sisters believed this was mostly due to prejudice on the part of the accrediting agency known as the Association of Southern Colleges, there were other factors that had to be addressed. For instance, the Association desired more degreed teachers and a separate endowment fund for the college. The academic requirements were met, but Katharine balked at the $40,000 annual contribution to an endowment that the association requested. While the association felt an endowment was necessary to assure the school's continuity, Katharine was not easily convinced. But an endowment made sense; if Xavier's diploma was to be worth the paper it was printed on, the school needed guaranteed continuity. Certainly, Katharine could support the college during her lifetime, but what would happen after she died if there were no endowment?

Finally, Katharine, accompanied by Mother Agatha Ryan, president of Xavier, called upon Thomas S. Gates, the president of the University of Pennsylvania. Gates, who had been a business associate of Francis and Anthony Drexel, convinced her that the college should be endowed.[36]

The school was also required to upgrade certain facilities, including its library. The $146,000 needed for the improvements were met partly through a $53,000 Rockefeller Educational Board grant and a $20,000 grant from the American bishops, and in 1938, the college received Class A accreditation. It remains a force in education to this day.

Before entering the Oblate Sisters of Providence, Sister Pierre Gardiner had been a telephone operator at Xavier. Her local Catholic church had three back pews for blacks. When they approached the Communion rail, the priest would bypass them until all whites had received. She contrasted this to Mother Katharine: "When she was coming everybody would get ready for her as if for a queen or a princess. Yet when Mother Katharine spoke, it wasn't 'You are Negroes and you are white.' She just acted as if we were all her children."[37]

If Xavier had great impact in black education through its graduates, it also affected the education of the Sisters themselves. With a college to oversee, there was a greater need for degreed Sisters, and indeed, even on the elementary and high school levels the various states were tightening their requirements for teacher education.

A few years earlier, Mother Katharine had hired a "teachers' teacher," Miss Byrne, to help train the young Sisters at St. Elizabeth's Convent. The salary was very good for the time — $2,000 per annum less room and board, the same amount Miss Byrne earned in public education. It was Katharine's hope that Miss Byrne would join the congregation. Apparently, she did not do so.

Miss Byrne was not the first lay teacher hired to train the Sisters. Katherine Gorman Akin was hired in a similar capacity in 1896 and served until 1901. Because she lived at St. Elizabeth's Convent with the Sisters, she gained an intimate knowledge of the congregation that few outsiders could ever obtain. Of Mother Katharine, she would later say, "The day I went there and she hired me, I said, 'She's a saint if I ever saw one.' And I never changed my opinion."[38]

In addition to the presence of professional teachers at St. Elizabeth, more and more Sisters were taking courses at the various Catholic colleges in the Philadelphia area. Mother Katharine was beginning to see the wisdom of Bishop O'Connor's earlier suggestion of a longer training period for the Sisters.

One of the pleasant motherhouse traditions in those early years was an annual picnic for the novices at St. Michel. After the old home ceased being a novitiate, Louise had maintained the property, with Johanna Ryan in charge. It was quite possibly a way to keep Johanna from crossing swords with Ned, who did not always appreciate the old servant's blunt mannerisms. It was good-hearted Johanna who began the annual picnics. At the first picnic, Johanna supplied chicken. "These are too much," Katharine said. "There are only two or three," Johanna assured her. One of the novices looked at the many drumsticks. "Johanna's chickens must be centipedes," she said.[39]

Whatever Katharine might have thought, Johanna had the full backing of Louise, who would continue the picnic long after her servant's death. Johanna — "Peggy" to Louise — was much more than a servant to her mistress. It was a familial affection. When Johanna became old and feeble, it was Louise's turn to care for her. When she died, Louise kept the final vigil. "I want to be alone with Peggy, this is my last visit," she said. At her request, Johanna Ryan, who in youth wished to be a nun, was buried in St. Elizabeth's convent cemetery. Her tombstone reads, 'Well done thou good and faithful servant. Enter into the joy of thy Lord."

In May 1917, Katharine accompanied the novices at St. Elizabeth to the St. Michel picnic. It rained. The novices didn't mind, because they were young and healthy and it was a break in routine. Katharine, on the other hand, caught a severe cold, but ignored it. She had already arranged to travel to Virginia for commencement exercises at Belmead, and she would not break her word. In Virginia, Katharine's cold turned to bronchitis. When she returned to St. Elizabeth's, her physician ordered her to bed and there she stayed, bedridden from June to mid-August. The convent infirmary was on the upper floor adjacent to the chapel. So near, and yet far. Katharine was denied the consolation of her visits to her Lord.[40]

She accepted this new cross and wrote:

A person may say, 'Dear Lord, I do not deserve ever to be in Thy presence!' And that is the truth, but all the same the heart, while it says, 'Cast me not away from Thy Face, and take not Thy Holy Spirit from me,' feels the great privation of not being in the presence of Our Lord in the Blessed Sacrament, nor assisting at Mass. Of course, I grant we are spoiled children, for how many there are who do not have the privilege of hearing Mass even once a year because of living far from a church.[41]

Edward Morrell saw a practical solution. He sent workmen to the convent who constructed a little oratory in the infirmary. It was like a bay window over-looking the chapel altar. Here, Katharine — or other sick sisters — could pray to their heart's content. "Sleepy Hollow" was the name Mother Francis Xavier gave it, because of its quietude and seeming remoteness from bustling convent activities.[42]

Many Sisters would have recourse to the infirmary over the years, and one, Sister Lucy, had a special gratitude for Mother Katharine. Sister Lucy had in-flammatory rheumatism that was so agonizing she could not sleep. Even the touch of the blankets was painful, so much so she lay with her arms upraised. One evening Katharine came to her and prayed. Then she said, "Sister Lucy, you will sleep all night." She took the sick nun's hands and gently placed them under the covers. Sister Lucy did indeed sleep. And after the fact, declared, "I have never had pain, swelling or rheumatism since."

Sister Lucy's account of her affliction was recorded by Mother Mercedes in 1925. She clearly had the thought a cause for canonization for Katharine would some day be a very real possibility.[43]

It was at this same time that Mother Mercedes wrote to all the convents, requesting that each Sister preserve any letters from Katharine, even if they were confidential. These would be sealed and forwarded to the motherhouse to be opened only after Mother Katharine and the Sister were dead. "Mother's writings should be kept and not destroyed," Mother Mercedes wrote, "because they will be of great use to the community in the future."

Canonization is just a stamp of approval; so far as Katharine was concerned everyone was a saint, or at least a potential saint. "We are all called to be saints," she said during a 1926 retreat talk. "Don't forget that, and here is the way to become a saint. Our Lord says, 'Take up thy cross and follow Me.' The cross is mortification of ourselves, the denying of ourselves so that we may grow like Christ."

In a letter to her Sisters in the Indian missions, she wrote:

> One day, and it is not too far off for the youngest of us — will be the day of eternity. There forever you will rejoice and God Himself as He wipes the tears from the eye will show you a crowd of happy souls and call them your souls, clad in white garments and singing the praises of your Lord. 'Who are they,' you will say. 'Amen,' the King will say, 'they are your and My souls among the Sioux — see their children's children. These too are yours and Mine.'

Further on, she advised, "Don't deprive the children of bread and meat so as to weaken them. Keep the children happy. If they love the school and all the

Sisters, you will have done much towards winning them to the Church."[44]

She also noted the Sisters had purchased a record player for the children and asked which type it is, so that she could buy them some records.

* * * *

The chapel oratory was Ned Morrell's final kindness to the Sisters. He died September 1, 1917. His obituary could list a string of accomplishments: a distinguished member of the bar and a member of the 56th to the 60th Congresses; a former member of the Philadelphia School Board and former Judge Advocate General and Inspector General of the Pennsylvania National Guard; and a rumored candidate for Mayor of Philadelphia in 1912.

It would not be polite for them to mention, from a monetary standpoint, that he had married extremely well. But for Edward, his marriage to Louise had been beneficial in a less tangible fashion. His cousin, Mary Powell, observed in a letter to Katharine, "It was Ned's marriage with that high minded, holy-hearted young girl that has been the full making of his life."[45]

Katharine experienced another death in the family two months later. This was in her spiritual family, fully as important, if not more so, than a family of blood and marriages.

Mother Mary James (Nora Ottis) died at the age of 51 in November 1917, after a long illness. She had been one of the Mercy Convent pioneers. She was born in Omaha, and as in the case of Mother Katharine, Bishop O'Connor had been her spiritual director. It was he who steered her to the newly forming Sisters of the Blessed Sacrament. Mother James was first counselor, second in authority to Mother Katharine from 1895 until her death. Her passing must have been especially difficult for Katharine. She personally chose the grave site for her assistant and requested that the adjoining plot be reserved for herself. That would be many years in the future, and the congregation would have different plans.[46]

Mother James had been superior at Rock Castle, and under her guidance it became the solid institution its name implied — forming battalions of young women who would occupy positions of influence in the black community.

Chapter 11
Bigotry and Blessings

War was coming in 1917, and the Sisters at Xavier, caught up in the national mood, wondered if it would be proper to purchase Liberty Bonds. "The deficit of the schools makes the idea preposterous," Katharine replied. There was another concern. Two of the Sisters at the college had contracted influenza. "If you have to close the school, let the Sisters visit the sick, even nursing them if necessary, using all precautions, however," she wrote. Katharine could not know this influenza strain, born in the American West, would circle the globe as one of the great pandemics of modern history.[1]

Philadelphia-born Nan Connor, in religion Mother M. Philip, had entered the congregation at the turn of the century with visions of service in the mission fields. A light-hearted, happy woman who hated to discipline children, she had never left St. Elizabeth's. By 1918, she was the Blessed Sacrament Sisters' treasurer, an office she filled well but only in a spirit of obedience, because her heart was in the mission fields. Every day, Mother Philip prayed 15 decades of the rosary for the conversion of the Indians. "You have souls," she remarked with sadness to one of the Sisters. "God did not deem me worthy, so He gave me figures." She was delighted when Katharine asked her to be her companion during the annual visitation to the Indian schools. Mother Philip had a cold when the two left Cornwells Heights, but she wasn't about to pass up this visit to Indian country. Her cold turned out to be influenza; she died within two days of her arrival at St. Michael's. Mother Philip was buried at St. Michael's in the heart of the Indian mission, a field that had claimed her own heart so many years earlier.2

The epidemic was worsening. Mother Mercedes saw between 40 and 50 coffins being loaded into a train at Trenton, New Jersey. They were meant for young soldiers who had died at Fort Dix.3

Between September and November 1918, 13,000 died in Philadelphia. During the emergency, the city's new Archbishop (later Cardinal), Dennis Dougherty, ordered nuns in all affected areas to nurse the sick. The Blessed Sacrament Sisters served at the municipal hospital, and members of their Germantown convent visited the sick in the black and Italian communities. St. Peter Claver School became a temporary hospital that served patients of all races and creeds. Katharine, in keeping with the Blessed Sacrament constitutions, had wished the Philadelphia Sisters to work exclusively among the city's black population. Archbishop Dougherty, in view of the emergency, ordered otherwise.

"I am a little disappointed that we cannot give ourselves exclusively to the Colored," she told her Sisters, "and hope since His Grace says there will be no discrimination at a time like this, there will be none later in the schools and hospitals. This will be a strong point for argument in the future, which we may find it good to use."4

This was the worst of the epidemic; but even though it abated, there would be outbreaks in the mission fields for several years thereafter. Such was the case in 1921 in the Fort Defiance and Chin Lee areas, near St. Michael's Indian School. "Our Lord is sick in these Indians and we are consecrated to serve them," Katharine wrote. "Visitation of sick Colored and Indians is one of the special works assigned to us by the Church in our approved rule."

Katharine herself had become ill again in 1920 and was confined to the infirmary for six weeks. Nevertheless, she was determined to make the annual visitation to the South. Cardinal Dougherty, like his predecessor, insisted she travel by Pullman rather than the more economical day coach. As before, Louise paid the bill.

This luxury really bothered Katharine, and when she and her companion, Mother Francis Xavier, reached Montgomery, Alabama, Katharine attempted to get around Cardinal Dougherty's order by deliberately choosing a train without a Pullman section. She should obey the Cardinal, Mother Francis remonstrated, otherwise "God won't bless us," she warned. Mother Katharine gave in, which turned out to be a good thing — the train she had picked was wrecked.5

On the other hand, traveling with Mother Katharine had its advantages for her companion. Sister Evangelist Gillespie recalled a trip on a night train when she was just a young novice. In the old Pullman cars, the lower berth was to be desired; climbing into the upper could be an athletic challenge. Even though Mother Katharine was in her 60s, "She strongly insisted I take the lower berth,"

Sister Evangelist said. "When I demurred, she said, with the sweet smile always habitual of her, 'obedience.' When traveling she would usually give her companion the window seat."

Another visitation was to Washington, D.C., to a property at 2100 H St., N.W., which Katharine purchased for the Indian Bureau. Mothers Katharine and Mercedes helped with the cleaning. They started with an "amicable quarrel" over a broom as to who would sweep the third floor; when Mother Mercedes won out, Katharine fumigated the second floor. The next day all pitched in to scrub the future chapel.

With the Washington property in order, they traveled on to Cincinnati, Chicago, and Winnebago, and then St. Michael's and the Navajo "where 12 days seem as one," Katharine wrote. There were 200 children, 50 more than expected, and the corn crop was excellent. The children tended the sheep while the men cut and stacked the corn.

A diversion was a baseball game between the St. Michael's employees and employees of the Fort Defiance government school.

"Can you imagine me taking an interest in baseball?" Katharine wrote. Most of the nuns watched the game, but Sisters Michael and Honora went to the chapel to pray for the home team. "Prayer won the game," said Katharine. The next stop was St. Catherine's where 250 children were in school, mostly from the Pueblo tribe. Many more had applied, but there simply was no room.[7]

Returning East, there were visits to schools in St. Louis, Cincinnati again, and Columbus.

These trips, while outwardly invigorating, were taxing on Katharine's health. In late 1923, the year she turned 65, what would be a normal retirement age today, she developed a severe cold while visiting Chicago. Again, the congregation was sufficiently worried to ask Cardinal Dougherty to intervene by directing Mother Katharine to return home and rest.

The Cardinal's response is interesting. He told the Sisters he really did not have the authority to intervene, and he was correct. When the congregation received official status from Rome, the authority of the local bishops over them was severely curtailed, except in matters that directly affected their diocese. Katharine herself had recognized this, when, on one occasion, she politely declined to accede to a request by one of the bishops for internal financial data of the Blessed Sacrament Sisters.

While Archbishops Ryan, Prendergast, and Dougherty himself had directed Katharine when they were concerned for her well-being, it was at this point merely persuasion without direct authority. The Council itself, under the Blessed Sacrament constitutions, did have the power to order Katharine home for her own good, but was reluctant to command its beloved superior to do anything.

While Cardinal Dougherty would not order Katharine home, he did send a telegram that accomplished the purpose:

"Please pardon liberty I take in urgently requesting that on account of having contracted a cold you return immediately to Cornwells for rest and recuperation finishing visitation later on."[8]

Katharine seems to have sensed the Council had appealed to the Cardinal, because she wired home asking if it was their wish that she should return. It was their unanimous opinion, they wired back. Katharine returned; her cold fortunately cleared, but an important precedent of Council authority had been asserted.

Over the years, Cardinal Dougherty would be a frequent visitor to Cornwells Heights. Naturally, this was a major event for the Sisters, and frequently the carefully primed children would present a little pageant for His Eminence. During one such visit, the Cardinal and Msgr. Ketcham were presented with a program that reflected both the Indian and Colored apostolates.

Because of its location, virtually all the children at the convent's Holy Providence School were black, but one little Choctaw boy memorized a short oration in his native tongue. At the last minute the child had stage fright and absolutely refused to give the speech. The resourceful Sisters dressed a light-skinned black child in Indian costume and gave her the address to read. She read it flawlessly as Msgr. Ketcham translated for the beaming Cardinal.

The ruse worked — up to a point. "What part of the West are you from?" Cardinal Dougherty asked. "Lombard Street, Philadelphia," she answered.[9]

* * * *

During her visitations to the missions, Katharine would witness visible progress, but often against very great odds. "All men are created equal" may have been self-evident to the founding fathers, but their descendants did not seem to always understand this truth.

The 1920s were a time of particular prejudice against the Church, certainly, but most especially, against African Americans. Josephite Father Alexis LaPlante had, with Katharine's financial help, founded Blessed Sacrament Parish in Beaumont, Texas, in 1915. It was a port city where the burgeoning oil industry was causing an influx of workers, including black Catholics from Louisiana. Within a few years of the parish foundation, there was a Blessed Sacrament Sisters' school headed by Mother Mary of the Visitation.

In Beaumont (as elsewhere), 1921 was a banner year for the Ku Klux Klan, and part of the problem was that some of their members or sympathizers were the so-called officers of the law. Blessed Sacrament was a special target because this was the church where a number of black professionals worshiped.

In March, one parishioner, Mr. Richardson, whose daughter was a Holy Family Sister, was flogged by the Klan. A white judge who opposed the KKK was tarred and feathered. On March 21, a sign was posted on Blessed Sacrament Church: "To the pastor of this church: We want an end to services here. We will not stand with any priest consorting with Nigger wenches in the face of our families. We give you one week to suppress it or a flogging and tar and feathering will follow." Another note warned parishioners the building would be dynamited if they continued coming.

Mother Mary of the Visitation compared community reaction to the parable of the Good Samaritan. Priests from the area white parish, St. Anthony, looked the other way when they passed Blessed Sacrament. However, the local rabbi came to Father LaPlante's defense. "Let them blow up our places. We'll collect the insurance and sue them and soak them," he told the priest.

It would be wrong to suggest all whites in Beaumont were bigots. When the Klan held a parade it was quickly broken up by a gunshot in their direction. White members of the local Knights of Columbus Council came to guard the rectory. And while the Beaumont police couldn't be trusted, Mother Mary of the Visitation noticed a car with three men, probably federal agents, parked by the convent. Mother Katharine offered to send a paid guard, but Father LaPlante declined.

God, at least in the minds of the Sisters and Father LaPlante, intervened at this point. On March 25, a violent rain and electrical storm visited Beaumont and destroyed several buildings, all rumored to have Klan connections. There were many injuries and two deaths, including, according to reports, the father of the police chief, a reputed Klan member.[10]

Glencoe, Louisiana, where Mother Katharine had built a rural school for black children, did not have a separate church for black Catholics. During a 1925 visit to the community, she recorded recent incidents of prejudice almost beyond belief at the church, supposedly a house of worship for the God of all people. On Easter Sunday, a fight broke out after a black student brushed against a white man. When a black man rose to go to the altar rail at the same time as whites, white men in the congregation rose from their seats and ejected him from the church. The year before there had been another fight when a white man deemed himself insulted because a black youth dipped his fingers into the holy water font before he did. Even one of the benefactors of the school took offense when a black child received Communion at the same time as his child. "Would you allow a nigger to go to Communion at the same time as your daughter and not resent it?" he asked. The pastor could do nothing. His predecessor had been forced out of the parish for the mortal sin of burying a black woman near white graves.[11]

In his 1981 testimony for Katharine's cause, Bishop Harold R. Perry, Auxiliary Bishop of New Orleans, addressed this idea of the obstacles Katharine and her Sisters had to overcome. Bishop Perry had been educated by the Blessed Sacrament Sisters in Lake Charles, Louisiana, in the 1920s.

> I think the young people saw in her a leader who would dare to do something that nobody else would dare to do, try to convert Indians and blacks to the Church. For her, in her time, to have that courage was a great inspiration to young women who would give their lives to God through the leadership of such a person. Now, they were well aware that they would receive some abuses along the way because they were trying to do something for people who cannot be taught religion, people who are uncultured and almost savages and recently freed slaves. It is true that Mother Katharine and the Sisters had to accept some reprimands and occasionally some abuses from whites who thought that they had gone just a little bit too far as nuns. It was all right to pray for the blacks in the convents, but not to go out and live among them and educate them. I know personally the Sisters did receive evidences of prejudice towards them and abuses towards them for what they were trying to do for God's work. But it was her example that really inspired them to go on.[12]

Mary Rose Moore was educated at one of the Louisiana schools conducted by the Blessed Sacrament Sisters. Katharine would visit and Moore was struck by her absolute sincerity.

> You have to be black and a Southern black, in a prejudiced community here, and have been born and reared in a prejudiced community to understand that. It isn't anything anybody can explain and tell you. It is just something you know, that a person isn't putting on a front. There was still something left over from slavery; that a Negro was next to an animal. I think (of) the human pride she always made us feel, that because of our soul we were worth God's crucifixion. He would have gone through that for blacks only. And that's a great pride.[13]

In Prince Anne County, Virginia, where Josephite Father Warren received aid from Mother Katharine, a band he had helped form was giving a concert in a black settlement. Fifty to 60 automobiles surrounded the house where he was. The priest was seized, questioned closely about his work, then driven 30 miles to the edge of a swamp and released with the warning, "We don't want Negroes educated down here."[14]

Incidents like these explain why Katharine and others like her preferred to provide separate facilities, even churches, for blacks. Given the prejudice of the times, it was only among themselves that black students or congregants could worship or study in the atmosphere of dignity that was their right.

In some instances, not only was there no black Catholic church, but blacks were not permitted to attend Sunday Mass at the local Catholic church. Such was the case in Rayne, Louisiana, the site of another of Katharine's rural schools. Sister Eucharia, accompanied by Lafayette's Bishop Jules Jeanmard, visited the pastor. The priest offered to celebrate Mass for the children of the school on Thursdays; his people did not want them at the Sunday liturgy. He could not understand why this solution satisfied neither Sister Eucharia nor his bishop. Bishop Jeanmard, one of the staunchest champions for African Americans among the hierarchy, ordered the priest to admit blacks to the Sunday Mass. Finally, the Josephite Fathers established Our Mother of Mercy Parish for the black families of Rayne. A full-fledged parochial school was established by the Blessed Sacrament Sisters after World War II. This has since been consolidated with the white parochial school.[15]

One did not need to visit the Deep South to encounter racial prejudice or ignorance. Sister Mary Florence Kuhn, who taught at Xavier, discovered this while taking a course at Cornell University. Another nun, of a different congregation, asked her if she really thought "these people usually called in this day, 'niggers,' have souls."

"Sister, I am shocked. Of course they have souls," Sister Mary Florence replied.[16]

St. Elizabeth Convent itself was touched by the prevailing prejudices in 1926.

The Ku Klux Klan held a huge rally near St. Francis School, Eddington, Pennsylvania, on June 23. A cross was burned in the neighborhood. Not long after, the outdoor shrine to the Little Flower at neighboring St. Thomas Aquinas Church, Croydon, was torched.

But while the Klan was probably responsible for the burning, in a figurative sense it was a Catholic priest who lit the torch. It happened earlier in the month, on June 6, at the dedication of a new school for St. Charles Borromeo, directly across Bristol Pike from St. Elizabeth's Convent. The parish tried to cultivate good relations with its Protestant neighbors. As a gesture to the community, Father Francis J. Flood, who was both rector at St. Charles Parish and chaplain to the Blessed Sacrament Sisters, invited members of the community, Catholic and Protestant, to the school dedication. The speaker was to be Dr. Corrigan, rector of St. Charles Seminary. Because of a scheduling conflict, he was replaced at the last minute by Father John Mellon, pastor of a West Philadelphia parish, St. Agatha.

Father Mellon was a fiery speaker, and he uncorked an oration that touched upon every injury, real or imagined, that had ever been inflicted upon Catholics by Protestants. The guests were insulted and Father Flood was mortified. It is no wonder that the neighborhood was visited by anti-Catholic demonstrations in the weeks that followed.[17]

One might argue that while the Ku Klux Klan members were bigots, so was Father Mellon in his own parish in a way that would gladden the hearts of the Klan. St. Agatha's was located in a "changing neighborhood" by the 1940s — white families were moving out while black families were moving in. Should any black worshipers come to his church, they would be very quickly directed to St. Ignatius, the neighboring black parish that Katharine Drexel helped fund. Further, Mellon was one of a number of Philadelphia pastors who tried to stem white flight from the parish by the simple expedient of buying up houses for sale along the main routes to his church. These were rented only to white families. St. Agatha's was a huge and proud church; its block-long campus closed in 1965 when the parish merged with nearby St. James. The church itself was converted into apartments, leased by African-American tenants.[18]

One bright spot was Cleveland, Ohio, where Katharine funded Our Lady of the Blessed Sacrament Parish in 1921. While the people wanted a black parish, they were less interested in a black school. Part of the reason was nearby St. Agnes Parish where "the Sisters of St. Joseph are wonderfully kind in receiving Colored," Katharine wrote. The same held true at the hospital conducted by the Sisters of Charity which Katharine had aided. They "take such an interest in the Colored people and they refuse no Colored person," she wrote. "They actually thanked me and the Sisters (of the Blessed Sacrament) for helping them in their work."

Care for black patients was more of a problem in Katharine's Philadelphia. In 1926, Katharine and Louise, knowing their own mortality, wrote a joint letter to St. Joseph's Hospital, an institution that would be an ultimate beneficiary of the Francis Drexel estate some time in the future, when they were both dead. The sum to be received by the hospital would be approximately $450,000, quite a bit of money for the times.

Katharine and Louise asked that St. Joseph's use the money to provide free beds in a ward for the Colored people of Philadelphia. It wasn't until some months later the reply came back. The hospital refused to honor their request.[19]

In another instance of their joint advocacy for social justice, Louise and Katharine challenged the manager of the Associated Press in New York in 1927 regarding the treatment of blacks in the reporting of news. Often, if not always, attention was drawn to the race of the perpetrator when a crime was committed by a black person. "It embitters the poor Colored people and because of the possible bad conduct of a few lawless ones, the whole race is stigmatized," they protested. Katharine followed up the meeting with a letter to all her convents, asking Sisters to scan their local papers, and when they found instances of prejudice, to write to the editors.20

"Colored were the last hired and the first fired," Mother Katharine and Louise Morrell wrote in a 1930 letter to Secretary of Labor Frances Perkins. They petitioned on behalf of the parents of the Negro school children and Negro workers in general that there be no discrimination against Negroes in the government unemployment relief program.21

There were positive examples of role models for blacks, Katharine was convinced. She was one of 11 influential signatories to a petition to the American bishops to have the feast of St. Peter Claver observed in all dioceses, as well as the feast of the Ugandan martyrs.22

* * * *

While more of the Blessed Sacrament Sisters were missioned in the black community, where the dearth of priests and sisters was the greatest, her support for Indian missions continued. These missions were mostly conducted by other congregations, but her support wasn't just a matter of sending a check and moving on.

In 1925, Katharine was saddened to learn that St. Elizabeth's Indian School in Purcell, Oklahoma, had been destroyed by fire. She had built the school years earlier, and it was named in honor of the patron of her dead sister. Fortunately, no lives were lost in the fire and she was able to tell the Franciscans who conducted the school that it was insured. She had been carrying insurance on the building for 35 years. Between the insurance and local generosity, a new and bigger St. Elizabeth's rose from the ashes.23

Bigotry on the part of white Catholics is clearer against Negroes than against the Indians, but it certainly existed against the first Americans, too. A letter from Msgr. Ketcham, the director of the Bureau of Catholic Indian Missions, addressed the issue. Msgr. Ketcham, as a convert, understood prejudice because he had been abandoned by many of his friends and most of his family when he became Catholic. Of anti-Indian prejudice, he said:

> When I became a priest and saw the neglect of the Indians here and the hatred (for that is the word) of the priests here for them, my soul was revolted at the outrage. I saw the money you were giving squandered and misused and heard yourself and your congregation ridiculed. I rec-

ognized the injustice and infamy of it all and tried to do something to stop the outrageous waste.24

The network of parishes and schools Katharine founded or funded until this point had been accomplished almost entirely through dependence on her trust fund. Partly due to inflation and the ever-expanding apostolate, her inheritance was becoming insufficient for the needs. Adding to the shortfall was the introduction of income taxes, which meant a slice of her annual income went right to the government. As early as 1919, it was suggested that influential members of Congress could be contacted with the hope of obtaining tax relief. The Council prayed upon it and decided to leave the matter to God's providence.

The issue came up again in 1921 when it was estimated 50 percent of Katharine's income was going for taxes. Francis Drexel had written a "spendthrift will" to protect his daughters, but now it was coming back to haunt them. Direct inheritance would have been subject to a much lower inheritance tax rate; trust fund income was treated as ordinary income for tax purposes. The Sisters appealed for a ruling on the matter, and as Walter George Smith predicted, the ruling went against them. The only avenue for tax relief was through legislative means.25

Edward Stotesbury, one of the Drexel estate trustees, mentioned the problem to Pennsylvania Senator George Wharton Pepper who came up with an ingenious plan. He introduced a bill in Congress in 1924 that would exempt from income tax anyone who had given at least 90 percent of their income to charity in the 10 preceding years.26 The bill, which passed, was so narrowly crafted that it was believed Katharine Drexel was the only person in the entire United States who qualified at the time for the exemption.27

Tax relief did not solve all problems. The Great Depression would cause an estimated 35 percent drop in income for Mother Katharine, and probably a corresponding drop in principal. It was estimated that Katharine had paid a total of $800,000 in federal income tax before the law was passed that effectively exempted her. Thomas Gates, president of the University of Pennsylvania, had succeeded Walter George Smith as attorney for Katharine after the 1924 death of Elizabeth's husband. Gates, who also worked without fee, approached Senator Pepper once again, but Pepper could not find sufficient congressional support for the refund. "Let the matter drop," he advised. The Sisters did, but the basic tax exemption remained in effect for the rest of Katharine's life.

If expenses were beginning to outrun income, it was not because of an extravagant lifestyle on the part of Katharine or her Sisters. Others might waste the resources she gave them, but Katharine did not.

Some of her economies might seem absurd, but one must remember the purpose. These acts of self-denial provided more money for the missions, and at least as important, were tools for achieving the perfection Katharine sought for herself and her daughters.

Katharine always used the inside of envelopes or the backs of letters for note paper and urged her Sisters to do the same. Louise Morrell, who did not wish to see her personal letters so used, would scribble curlicues over any blank spots on the paper before sending letters to her beloved sister.

As late as 1921, St. Catherine Indian School, Santa Fe, had no telephone. Father Bernard Espelarge wrote to Mother Katharine, urging her to permit one to be installed. It was a necessity, he maintained, because the school was located out of town. If there were a fire, how could the fire department be notified?

May Williams, a former student at Philadelphia's Our Lady of the Blessed Sacrament School, couldn't help but notice the frugality practiced by the Sisters. Out of kindness she sent them $1.50 for train fare so they might go to St. Elizabeth's for a "free day." The Sisters wrote to Mother Katharine, asking if it was permissible to accept the gift.

"I admire the spirit of gratitude in May and every part of her kind act," Mother Katharine replied, then chided the Sisters for even considering accepting such a gift for an act of pleasure, not necessity. It was, in her mind, a violation of the congregation's spirit of poverty.[28]

Mother Amabalis of the Religious of the Good Shepherd recalled a visit to her order's convent by Katharine in the early 1920s. "Slight, of medium height, pleasant, intensely observant, our revered visitor was all that we hoped for, a simple, dignified, courteous Religious." She left to visit the Magdalenes in their cloister, leaving her shawl and prayer book on a chair. The shawl was shabby, the book well thumbed. "Did you see Mother's veil?" one whispered. "It was shiny and green!"[29]

This ideal of possessing nothing was demonstrated for the novices and postulants when Sister Juliana, the novice mistress, was transferred to Rock Castle. The senior novice asked Mother Katharine if they could give Sister Juliana a book as a going-away gift.

"Sister Juliana is in religion, and what will she do with a book after she gets it?" Mother Katharine gently asked. She looked in her desk for a suitable memento. "Look at what the Lord has put here!" she exclaimed. It was a little picture card, Mary holding the Child Jesus with three crosses in the background. "This card is just what we want," she said. "You see it is the Child and His Mother. You in the novitiate have always represented the Infant Jesus to Sister Juliana." All the novices signed the card and Mother Katharine gave Sister

Juliana permission to keep it in her office book.30

Sister Mary Louis Nestler was Katharine's companion on one visitation when they inadvertently took the wrong train. Katharine, loath to waste money that rightfully belonged to the congregation (but really her inheritance) because of her mistake, begged train fare from other passengers.

To be a Sister of the Blessed Sacrament meant to embrace not only holy poverty, but to eschew worldliness in all its manifestations. That included motion pictures, as Katharine explained in a 1926 talk to Sisters home for summer classes:

> There is a great risk in these moving pictures. I don't like them. They might be all right if you read your meditation before going to bed, but I think it should be for us, as Religious, to go very seldom. How can we have our minds recollected when these things of the world are running through them? Some souls might pray for these things that happen in the world and beg Our Lord to have mercy on them. Ah, the spirit of the world will enter very much through these moving pictures, I fear. For our children who have to go out into the world they may be all right, and of course, a Sister will have to be with the children, but she should read her meditation before she goes to bed.31

Yet, for all of this, Katharine was a happy person. In later years, Mother Agatha Ryan, one of her councillors, testified to her spontaneous joy: her exclamation, "Holy Angels," if something amused her. She remembered, too, how Katharine could walk away from pressing business whenever the chapel bell rang. How a look of joy would transform her as she entered the chapel and her total familiarity with her God. "Now listen, Lord," she would say. "You have to listen to these petitions," and then she would start the office.32

Having a familiar relationship with God did not affect Katharine's own humility. A salesman told of visiting St. Elizabeth's. A Sister in a gingham apron was sweeping the front porch. He asked if he could see Mother Katharine. Pleasantly and courteously she said she thought so. The Sister entered the convent and re-emerged a few minutes later and said, "You wished to see Mother? I am she."33

The American Church experienced a wealth of religious vocations in Katharine's day, and while her congregation grew it could not begin to keep up with the needs of its chosen apostolate. In one vocation talk, she conceded the mission of the Blessed Sacrament Sisters was "a work which prejudice sometimes hinders otherwise generous souls who would be glad to do anything for God or otherwise give Him the best service in their powers."

Meanwhile Katharine continued to help the black congregations. In 1928, Mother Theodore, foundress of the Handmaids of Mary, asked Mother Katharine to train a novice mistress for the congregation. Sister Dorothy came to St. Elizabeth's for the special training she would need to form future Sisters. It was a successful and satisfying venture for both congregations. Although she was not a Blessed Sacrament Sister, Sister Dorothy was the first black religious to live at St. Elizabeth's for an extended period of time.

Katharine's own congregation had a constant need for new candidates. Louise Morrell, a woman of singular foresight, saw a possible remedy to the vocation shortage. During a visit of her own to the mission fields, she wrote to her sister:

I am more than ever convinced that we have come to the age of the lay apostolate. Up to now the lay people have held back, leaving the field to priests and Sisters. These are no longer able to meet all the pressing mission needs in detail, but are not the Sisters particularly, especially filled by their training to act as teachers and leaders and guides to those of good will?[34]

Louise further proposed that St. Michel be used as a base for a lay apostolate. She mentioned having come in contact with Father Thomas Judge's Trinitarians, who wore semi-secular clothing and took year-to-year vows. She suggested Katharine sponsor a similar congregation for black girls, perhaps using Xavier graduates.

"What I feel is required for the missions is not so much branching out in every direction in the desire to save souls," she wrote, "but rather to do so intensively, bringing to bear on the work efficient methods guided by trained, clear minds. "I suppose," Louise concluded, "you think I am crazy. If I am, show me, as the slang puts it."[35]

Louise's plans for St. Michel went further than a base for a lay apostolate. She built St. Michael's Shrine of the True Cross upon the property. This was a large edifice that became a chapel of convenience for Catholics in the Torresdale section of Philadelphia as well as a temporary house of worship for Polish Catholics of the area. It also became a center for retreats and days of recollections directed by the Blessed Sacrament Sisters. At first the Council was cautious about this new enterprise. Even though there was a heavy emphasis on adoration of the Blessed Sacrament, it was a departure from their stated mission — to work exclusively among African and Native Americans. But through St. Michael's Mission Center, the apostolate was probably well served — many Catholics, especially potential candidates for the congregation, received their first knowledge of the work of Katharine Drexel through retreats in Torresdale.

Both Katharine and Louise deeded their interest in the property to the Sisters of the Blessed Sacrament; Louise leased it back for $1 a year.[36] The Drexels had already built a crypt beneath the Lady Chapel at Eden Hall; now Louise built a much larger crypt beneath St. Michael's. All the Catholic Drexel dead (along with Edward Morrell and Walter George Smith) were brought here. Louise established a perpetual Mass fund for the family, funded through the sale of her mother's diamond earrings and a diamond necklace Edward gave her at the time of their wedding.

* * * *

The Blessed Sacrament Sisters, who had once eschewed the political scene, were much more active now. In 1928, when Al Smith, a Democrat, became the first Catholic to gain the presidential nomination of a major political party, Cardinal Dougherty of Philadelphia wrote to all religious congregations in his Archdiocese, urging them to vote. He did not say how they should cast their ballots, of course, but there was a certain presumption. At Cornwells Heights, 55 Sisters registered to vote. Katharine wrote to all her convents informing them, "The Council General desires that the Sisters vote this year in the presidential election." She further authorized payment of up to $4 in poll tax, and stipulated Sisters should register only if their local ordinary approved. While it is probable a majority of the Sisters voted for Smith, according to convent tradition, most of the Sisters at the time were Republican.[37]

Certainly, Catholicity could come into play in the community's votes. In 1930, when Gifford Pinchot, a Republican, ran for governor of Pennsylvania, the Sisters apparently voted against him. Pinchot was a pioneer on forestry and conservation issues, but, unfortunately, he was also by reputation anti-Catholic.

"In spite of all our voting against him, he was elected governor last Tuesday," Katharine wrote in a letter to Mothers Mercedes and Francis Xavier who were on a vocation recruitment trip to Ireland. "Western Pennsylvania gained the day for him." But she could report one small victory to her traveling Sisters: "We just heard the returns of the Boston-Villanova game — victory for Villanova, 7-1."[38]

If the quest for vocations was not yet successful, "I don't give up hope," Katharine would write. "The best wine was served last, you know." The congregation was praying for their success and "these aspirations must pierce the Heart of Our Lord and cause Him to put you in the way of souls that perhaps He is holding back," she said. As a practical measure, Katharine directed that some of the younger candidates be placed in an Irish boarding school conducted by the Sisters of Mercy before coming to America.[39]

Religious vocations from abroad, particularly Ireland, contributed greatly to the health of the congregation. But there were American-born candidates, too. Some of these young ladies had met Katharine before their arrival; others had not.

When Freda Goerschner arrived from New Jersey in 1926, Katharine was out. Because it was Reverend Mother's custom to welcome each new candidate personally, Freda was asked to wait on the porch. Her mental picture of the foundress was of a tall, dignified woman, a stately nun. Freda was somewhat taken aback when tiny, vivacious Mother Katharine arrived. "Oh, a new postulant. Goody, goody, goody," she exclaimed. If reality was different than expectation, Freda took it in stride. As Sister Ancilla, she had a long and happy vocation with the Blessed Sacrament Sisters.[40]

Sister Edith Pardee, who was professed in 1911, came from New York. She was not only a converted Episcopalian, she had been Superior General of the Anglican Sisterhood of St. Mary's in Peekskill. Her decision to become a Roman Catholic was made only after a long period of inner soul-searching. When she did so, Archbishop Ryan asked Mother Katharine to provide a temporary home for her at St. Elizabeth's. The Reverend Mother and the former Superior General became instant friends, and Mother Edith applied for formal membership into the Sisters of the Blessed Sacrament, a request that was joyfully granted.[41]

Sister Francesca McCusker, who was professed in 1918, was one of Katharine's earliest biographers. For her the attraction to the vocation of a Blessed Sacrament Sister was an intuitive reaction at her first meeting with the Reverend Foundress. She, along with several other girls, visited Our Lady of the Blessed Sacrament Convent in Philadelphia. After the spiritual exercises, Mother Katharine entered the room. "Her very presence inspired me with a feeling that she was a holy person," Sister Francesca said. "Then and there I wanted to be a Sister of the Blessed Sacrament. In all the years that I knew Mother Katharine I never lost this feeling of reverence for her when I encountered her; in fact, it grew in intensity."[42]

Virginia Young was a homegrown Philadelphia girl who had a cousin in the Sisters of the Blessed Sacrament. But her main contact with the congregation was through volunteer work at St. Michael's Shrine of the True Cross. This was in 1922, and Miss Young also volunteered as a catechist among Italian children in South Philadelphia.

Mother Katharine, when she learned this, remarked that she probably had to go through a large Colored section to get there. When Miss Young said yes, Mother Katharine suggested she say a little prayer every time she saw a Colored person.

It seemed to be a wonderful idea and Virginia agreed to do it. Then she found her trolley was passing so many Colored people that she couldn't possibly keep up.

"I had to close my eyes," she told Mother Katharine.

Katharine laughed. "Well, just do the best you can, but keep them in mind. They need your prayers," she counseled.

The two had many discussions about Miss Young's vocation — either as a Blessed Sacrament Sister or in another congregation, but Katharine never pressured her. "Make sure it is where God wants you to be," she advised.

After she entered the congregation in 1927 as Sister Mary David, their relationship was, by necessity of convent discipline, more formal. But Sister David was always struck by Katharine's solicitude — she never failed to ask about members of her family during their chance meetings.

The congregation still had two classes of Sisters, and Sister David entered as a choir Sister, that is, she would probably be a teacher. But during her novitiate she considered changing to house Sister. Her reasoning was that house Sisters, although their tasks were humbler, had more opportunity for prayer time and possibly a greater influence on the children in their care because of a more relaxed relationship with them.

Katharine counseled her not to change. She had entered as a choir Sister with the ability to be a teacher, and there was a great need for teachers. Sister David took her advice and remained in choir status. Over the years she filled many important offices for the congregation, eventually becoming Superior General. It would almost certainly have never happened had she chose to become a house Sister.[43]

* * * *

The Depression was beginning to be felt everywhere. Katharine noted that the Salvation Army was giving food to people in need in Philadelphia's Our Lady of the Blessed Sacrament Parish. A closed Baldwin Locomotive plant had been fitted with beds for the homeless. On the first night, 1,000 men came — 600 white and 400 Colored.

"We are buried in snow," Katharine writes during a Depression winter. "...I grieve that it will make the poor Colored suffer who so warmheartedly attend the Mass and receive Holy Communion. May no one break their limbs or take cold, Dear Lord, through the merits of Jesus Christ, Amen."[44]

On matters of racial justice, Katharine supported mainstream organizations that fought prejudice, for instance, the National Association for the Advancement of Colored People (NAACP). During the 1930s, the organization's president, Walter White, wrote to thank her for her support of anti-lynching legislation, and again to thank her for a donation made to support the NAACP's fight against lynching.[45]

The great loyalty to the Sisters by their employees, especially people of color, is perhaps the greatest testament to their work. These men and women were insiders; they would know insincerity if it existed. Their actions show the opposite to be true. In 1930, Jacob Stokes, a black employee of the Sisters and a convert, willed his estate of two building lots and $693 to the Sisters of the Blessed Sacrament.[46]

As Katharine saw her investment income shrink and the needs of the poor increase, Cardinal Dougherty did what he could to help. She had been the great bulwark of the Bureau of the Catholic Indian Mission. Now it was the bureau's turn to aid the Sisters. Even though the annual collection had diminished and appropriations to the various missions had to be cut 10 percent, the Cardinal, as chairman of Indian Mission board, could assure Katharine in 1932 that the Blessed Sacrament Sisters would receive their full appropriation — $25,000.[47]

"Only the Providence of God can tide us over our present difficulties," Cardinal Dougherty wrote in 1934. "I am confident that Our Lord will not permit the labors and sufferings of so many holy priests and Sisters, who have given all for the Indians and Negroes, to perish."

In future years, the appropriation would be cut to $10,000 — the money simply was not there. But Cardinal Dougherty pursued another avenue. In 1941, a letter was sent to all his parishes that informed them the Sisters of the Blessed Sacrament had his permission to solicit money at archdiocesan churches, "because of the financial crash that took place 10 or 11 years ago which utterly destroyed some investments and lessened the income from others." Mother Katharine, he told the priests, "has been obliged to close some of her institutions for lack of funds; there is a danger of her being obliged to close others for the same reason."[48]

Institutions of Cardinal Dougherty's archdiocese would be the principal beneficiaries of the Francis Drexel estate after Katharine's death. The fund had remained static, showing no increase over the years, primarily because the investment emphasis was income, not growth. The Cardinal's own financial advisers urged him to have an archdiocesan representative named as an estate trustee. This he refused to do. Even though Mother Katharine was aging, so was he. The Cardinal would take no action that could work against her congregation in the event he predeceased her, for example, if the trustees changed the investment strategy to increase the future value at the expense of her income.

It was quite clear to Mother Katharine and Louise Morrell by 1928 that their fortunes, while considerable by ordinary standards, were inadequate for their work among Indians and blacks. Nor was it simply a matter of money. No single religious congregation had the numbers needed for the education and religious conversion of the minority races.

One possible solution was the formation of a lay auxiliary society for the Sisters of the Blessed Sacrament, one that would provide both the treasure and talent needed for the work. It was Katharine's fond hope that such a society would attract millions of American Catholics to the cause. Through the good offices of Cardinal Dougherty, even Pope Pius XI was enlisted for the campaign.

In 1932, the Cardinal delivered a letter written by Katharine and Louise to the Holy Father. In their letter, the two sisters pointed to the needs of the unchurched Negroes of America — 6,000,000 out of a 12,000,000 population, by their estimate — as well as the plight of the unchurched among America's 334,000 Indians. They asked the Pope to write a letter of commendation "which may be used by us to further this campaign of propaganda for informing and educating the white Catholics of the United States concerning the spiritual needs of the two aforementioned races." They further asked for an apostolic blessing for the Society of Auxiliaries of the Sisters of the Blessed Sacrament for Indians and Colored People.[49]

It was clear from the Pope's response that he well understood the work of Katharine — the response came directly from himself, not, as is the ordinary case, through his secretary of state:

> ...It was particularly pleasing to us to learn from your letter that, under the inspiration of divine grace and fraternal charity, you have associated others in your good work of spreading the Catholic Faith among the Indians and Negroes of the United States. We are well aware of the zeal and devotion with which you have labored for so long a time in the propagation of the Kingdom of God among the natives of America and We realize that you and your associates have spared neither labor nor expense in thus promoting the Glory of God and the salvation of souls. Your present project is so excellent, so replete with Christian charity, that not only do We heartily approve of it but We deem it worthy of Our highest praise.
>
> ...We are most desirous that the greatest possible number of Catholics of your Country, with the support of the Episcopate and of the entire body of the clergy, may be induced to favor your projects and become associated in all your works.[50]

The auxiliary did have some modest successes, but despite papal approval and blessing, it never achieved the numbers Katharine had hoped for. American

Catholics, as a whole, did not have the zeal and sense of justice needed for so arduous a task.

* * * *

There are surprisingly few photographs of Mother Katharine, when one considers her prominence and her long life. This is typical of nuns of her generation. Photographs were frowned upon. In 1913, Katharine and her council went so far as to forbid Sisters in temporary vows to have their portrait taken. Prior to this, as soon as a Sister professed and was in habit, she had been allowed to have a photograph taken of herself that could be given to her family.

Katharine's personal physician, Dr. Max Herrman, was not Catholic, but nevertheless was a great admirer of his distinguished patient. It was he who finally coaxed her to sit for a formal portrait — to be paid for by himself; Katharine would have never agreed to an extravagance of this kind. As might be expected she initially declined the honor; it was only after Dr. Herrman asked Cardinal Dougherty to persuade her to sit for the portrait that she consented. The artist was Lazar Raditz, and the painting was formally unveiled in January, 1935. The painting is of a mature woman — as it should be, because she was 76. If there is just a hint of a smile, there is also a piercing gaze, a suggestion of caring about the person to whom she is look-ing. Nevertheless, "The artist did not get the delicate expression in the face and could not reproduce the wonderful light in the eyes," an anonymous critic recorded in the Blessed Sacrament annals.[51]

In any case, after the unveiling ceremony in the community room, Mother Katharine ordered the picture removed for storage in the convent archives, where it remained until it was resurrected after her death. It is still the most commonly reproduced likeness of St. Katharine Drexel.

"How can we ever thank God for our religious vocation!... people think out in the world you are doing something great in giving yourself to God. And that is not the case at all. It is God who is great in giving us a chance to be His spouse."

SAINT KATHARINE DREXEL

Chapter 12
Please Dear Lord, Spare Her

Katharine had been leading her congregation for 44 years. It had been demanding work when she was younger; now it was more so. She had suffered a slight heart attack in 1934, and the Sisters were understandably concerned when their Superior, accompanied by Mother Mary of the Visitation, departed for her Western tour in the fall of 1935. There were stops at Columbus, Cincinnati, and Chicago, then on to Marty, Winnebago, and St. Michael's. At every stop on the way, the Sisters noted how worn and haggard Katharine looked, but they hoped the Western air would be a tonic and a relief from the daily grind at St. Elizabeth's.[1]

Katharine, for her part, was more concerned about the Sisters she was visiting. During a stop at Houck, Arizona, she was shocked to find how sick Sister Stanislaus was. She brought her to a hospital in Gallup and continued her visitation. At St. Michael's, while dictating a letter to Mother Mary of the Visitation, she suffered a dizzy spell and fell to the floor. A doctor who examined her diagnosed hardening of the arteries, and recommended she not continue her visitation.

Katharine shrugged off his advice and continued on to St. Catherine's, then took the still ailing Sister Stanislaus to Chicago for a more thorough diagnosis. The next stop was Marty, where Katharine suffered another attack, but forbade the Sister who was present to mention it to anyone.

During this trip she also visited a congregation being formed by Benedictine Father Sylvester Eisenmann specifically for Native Americans — The Oblate

Sisters of the Blessed Sacrament. This new order was located in Marty, South Dakota, where the Blessed Sacrament Sisters had staffed St. Paul's Mission since 1922. Katharine agreed to supply a novice mistress — Mother Mary of Lourdes — who would help train the young Sisters. Just as their Sisters had been nurtured by the Sister of Mercy, the Blessed Sacrament Sisters would nurture this new congregation during its formative years.

On her return to Chicago, Katharine was advised that Sister Stanislaus really needed specialized care. She took the sick woman to St. Vincent's Sanitarium in St. Louis, and it was here that Katharine suffered a heart attack of such intensity that Mother Mary of the Visitation felt compelled to notify the Council at St. Elizabeth's. She wired home that she believed Reverend Mother was extremely ill. A telegram came back swiftly, calling for Katharine to return home immediately.

"Did you do that?" Mother Katharine asked Mother Mary of the Visitation.

"Yes, I did," the younger nun replied. "I felt it was my duty, for if anything happened to you I could never go back to the motherhouse and face the community. I could never face them."

"I don't think you would do that, where would you go?" Katharine asked.

"Well, I guess I would go out to St. Michael's and bury myself in the rocks," Mother Mary of the Visitation told her.2

Sister Anne, a nursing sister from St. Vincent's, accompanied Mother Katharine on the trip home. She was not optimistic. Given the gravity of Katharine's condition, she warned the Sisters they should be prepared for the worst.

At Cornwells Heights, she was examined by Dr. Herrman, and Sister Anne advised that she also be seen by a heart specialist, Dr. Arthur Stephens. He was quite emphatic in his diagnosis — if Katharine wished to live, she would have to cut back on her work and her travel. He told her she "owed to her community and to humanity at large to prolong her life on account of her work."

"Nobody is necessary for God's work, as God can do the work without any of His creatures," she replied.

"Certainly, Mother, I agree with you," Stephens said, "but ordinarily He does not."3

During her illness, Katharine received visits from many churchmen, including Cardinal Dougherty. There were letters from the great and humble.

One of the most telling, because it touched directly upon her work, was from Al Jones, a black man who was ill himself. Jones, the child of a couple who had been employed by the Drexel family, composed a prayer for Katharine, which read in part:

Dear Lord, I am a living witness to the fact that she was a mother to the motherless, father to the fatherless, a home for the homeless for thousands of Thy dark-skinned children here in Thy vineyard; working night and day to convert them to love Thee, to follow Thee and to serve Thee, and to educate them that they too have a God to serve and a soul to save; and please dear Lord spare her to look over the fruits of her labor for a few more years. Thou will send down a legion of angels to bear her loving soul to the foot of Thy throne, and grant I pray that when she arrives she may find her dear mother and father and my mother and father waiting her arrival to present her to the throne.[4]

Katharine did cut back her schedule, but she did not retire. There was a relapse in April 1936 and another in the summer, and again in September. At Christmas she was well, but the inexorable effects of age could not be stayed forever.

Meanwhile, times were changing. Radio was another modern innovation that had gradually crept into convent life. At first it was used for very specific purposes — for instance, in 1932 for the Pope's annual Orbi et Urbi message. But by 1936, Mother Katharine, writing to the convents, suggests that Sisters who intend to vote should listen to the radio addresses given by the different candidates and their supporters so that they would "be in a position to form good judgments on policies as well as candidates."

In 1937, the Blessed Sacrament Sisters were facing an election closer to home.[5] Katharine's term as Superior General had been renewed for 12 years at a 1931 chapter. In the same year, the constitutions were amended so that superiors would be elected every six years. It was not clear whether her term should extend to 1943 or end in 1937. In any case, Katharine cited her health as insufficient to the task, given her age — 79 — and her recurring heart problems. The Sisters, she said, should elect a new Superior General.

The election was held on August 14, and Mother Mercedes O'Connor, who had been vicar general, was elected superior general. Mother Katharine was elected to the council as vicar general. By a special vote of the chapter, Katharine retained the honorific title, "Reverend Mother." As a further mark of respect for Katharine, Mother Mercedes pointedly refused to occupy the Superior General's stall in the chapel. This would be reserved for the foundress so long as she was able to occupy it.

Mother Mercedes wrote to the convents, "I am merely a substitute and a poor one." As foundress, she said, "Reverend Mother's place is unique and can never be duplicated.... We want to preserve Reverend Mother's life as long as God wills, as the longer she remains with us the more grace and blessings we shall receive."[6] Katharine would disagree. She had once remarked, "I am not the foundress. Our Lord is the founder."

As vicar general, Katharine would be Mother Mercedes' second-in-command and closest adviser. While she continued to take an active interest in the affairs of the congregation and the world, she was clearly on the decline, and there were many periods when she was confined to her room. In 1939, Pope Pius XI died, and this was the first time many Catholics around the world would have instant access to the papal election through the marvel of radio. Miss Super, the private duty nurse Louise had hired for Katharine, brought her own radio to her aging patient's room. "Let it be Pacelli," Katharine prayed. Her prayer was answered. Eugenio Pacelli was elected Pope — Pope Pius XII. Cardinal Pacelli, when he was the Vatican's Secretary of State, had been greeted by Blessed Sacrament Sisters from Laguna, New Mexico, when visiting the Western United States.[7] "The Sisters of the Blessed Sacrament were founded by Reverend Mother M. Katharine Drexel, the most noted woman in America today," Bishop Francis Spellman, then auxiliary bishop of Boston, had told the future Pope.

* * * *

In 1939, too, we find a letter to Louise in which she tells her sister that Mother Anselm reported that when a Catholic University professor visited New Orleans he stayed at the home of one of the black students. "That is when I fainted again," Katharine wrote, "To think that he dared do such a thing in New Orleans."

Katharine's letter is warm and personal, with flashes of wit. But some sentences are incomplete; this was a subtle suggestion of waning capacities. Her handwriting, never elegant but at least clear, had become less so.[8]

Cardinal Dougherty may have been not so subtly referring to this as early as 1936:

> Your last letter, written by your own hand, has been received, but I wonder that you go to the trouble of composing, and even writing in your own hand, a letter to me, when it would have been quite sufficient to get one of the Sisters to write me what you had to say. In view of your present condition I feel that you should take a complete rest, so that, as soon as possible, you may be back to your former self.[9]

Also in 1939, as part of the university's Golden Jubilee Convocation, The Catholic University of America tendered an honorary degree to Katharine. It truly was an honor, because the university had never given such a degree to a woman before this.

"The motivation of your citation will be the unique place you hold in the history of Catholicity in these United States and your splendidly Catholic contribution to the Nation through your untiring devotion to the two races whom you and your Sisters serve," Bishop Joseph Corrigan, the university rector, wrote in his letter of notification. Katharine accepted, but under the condition she need not be present. Her health simply was not good enough for a journey to Washington.[10]

Mother Mercedes had relieved Katharine of the burden of governance; it was a burden she herself was destined to carry but a short while. In early 1940 she too became ill. It was quickly diagnosed as cancer. By March her condition had advanced to such a point she was confined to her room. Katharine was deeply moved by Mother Mercedes' illness. She had been with her from the beginning. She had always been a lively, quick-witted, loyal bundle of energy. Now she was dying.

One day Katharine, who was confined to a wheelchair, entered the sickroom. She did so as quietly as possible so as not to disturb Mother Mercedes. She simply wanted to pray.

When Mother Mercedes noticed her, she said, "Mother, please go back to your room."

Mother Katharine pleaded, "Please let me stay, I want to pray for you, I want to help you."

Mother Mercedes told her, "Mother, the community does not need me, but it needs you. Please go back to your room." Obediently, Mother Katharine left.

Toward the end, Katharine visited once more.

"When my own mother was dying I asked her if she would pray for me when she went to heaven," Katharine said. "She looked at me with such tender affection and said in tones of tenderest love, 'I will pray for you and pray for you and never cease praying for you until you come there too.'" Then Mother Katharine told her former Sister, now her superior, "You are not like my mother who had only three children to think of, but you have so many — four hundred or more, and will you promise to pray for each one of them as my mother promised to pray for me, won't you?"[11]

"Yes, I'll promise to do that," Mother Mercedes assured her.

Mother Mercedes died on April 9, 1940; as vicar general, Mother Katharine succeeded her as head of the congregation until a general chapter could meet to elect a new Superior General.

When a chapter was held, with Cardinal Dougherty presiding, Mother Mary of the Visitation was elected Superior General. Katharine was elected vicar general for Mother Visitation's first term.[12] Even after that she remained actively interested in convent affairs.[12]

Mother Mercedes' last official acts as superior had been the planning of a new Holy Providence School building on the grounds of St. Elizabeth Convent. After her death, this building would be named Mercedes Hall; its dedication was the last time Mother Katharine ventured outside the convent proper.

The honorary degree from Catholic University was the first of many honors during this period. Most notably, 1941 was a year of Jubilee — it was 50 years since Katharine had taken her vows at Mercy Convent, and in so doing, created a congregation. As far as she was concerned, the anniversary should pass unnoticed. Cardinal Dougherty thought otherwise. He convinced her a jubilee was a thing of joy that must be celebrated. Mother Katharine consented to a celebration, provided it did not center around herself, but rather the work of the congregation.

Although the actual birthday of the Blessed Sacrament Sisters was Feb. 12, the celebration was set for April 18-20 to accommodate the Cardinal's schedule. But the Sisters had a private celebration on the actual anniversary date.

It was a simple program, and the Sisters were pleased that Katharine could come down to address those assembled in the parlor. Mother Francis Xavier, who had been one of the pioneer novices at Mercy Convent, spoke of those days and of her own honor of being the cross bearer at Katharine's profession ceremony. Then the revered foundress spoke to her spiritual daughters:

> I thank God I am a child of the Church. I thank God it was my privilege to meet many of the great missionaries of the Church and to have had the prayers of those great missionaries like Msgr. Stephan and Bishop Marty.... I saw them in their agony, those great souls! I thank God He gave me the grace to see their lives. They are a part of the Church of God, and I thank God like the great St. Theresa that I, too, am a child of the Church.

The public celebration was a grand affair. Bishops and priests and nuns representing the dioceses and religious congregations helped by Mother Katharine converged on St. Elizabeth's convent for the three-day celebration, as did lay men and women from all walks of life. Cardinal Dougherty celebrated the closing Mass. Entertainment ranged from intricate Indian dances to presentations from glee clubs of the many Blessed Sacrament Schools. The Xavier University music department presented scenes from "Carmen."

Katharine had said she did not want the celebration to center upon herself, but of course, it did. It must have been rather like viewing one's own funeral. Bishop Corrigan, who preached at the final Mass, spoke of the liturgy as "the living sacrifice of the Victim of Calvary, of the Body once spent on the Cross for all men, in thanksgiving for her who in fifty years of loving labor, finds her own frail body spent but her soul gloriously young with the youth of eternal life."

In the foreword for the Jubilee book, Cardinal Dougherty spoke of Katharine's own personal sacrifice when she embraced her great mission.

He wrote:

> Humanly speaking, the sacrifice was heroic. She did not give up nets and other fishing apparatus as the first Apostles; she did not leave poverty and drudgery; she turned her back on wealth, social prominence, enjoyment of all that money can buy in order, even in her early youth, with its bright prospects, to dedicate her life to the outcast, downtrodden despised Indians and Negroes of the United States.
>
> If she had never done anything else but set such an example for a frivolous, self-seeking world, she should be regarded as a benefactress of the human race.
>
> ...Whilst others persecute and revile Indians and Negroes as if they are mere hewers of wood and drawers of water, rather than God's children for whom our Savior's blood was shed, she, the refined lady of culture, takes them to her heart and makes their cause her cause.

Bishop (later Cardinal) Richard Cushing wrote: "Her greatest contribution was herself, stripped of self, to become part and parcel of God's plan to relieve the Negro and Indian of the United States."

Pius XII also sent a message. "...We gladly avail ourselves on this most happy occasion to renew the expression of our interest in your mission and to call upon our American children to give you and your community the encouraging support which this great work so justly merits."[13]

Katharine's response to the Pope was delayed several months by her ill health, because she was determined to write the letter herself. She simply lacked the strength to compose an entire letter at one time.

"Your words, Most Holy Father," she wrote, "are indeed a source of consolation and spiritual gratification. As I meditate on them they awaken in my soul thoughts of all that God has done for our Congregation, and my utter incapacity of rendering Him sufficient praise for His goodness."

These plaudits, of course, were from the mighty Churchmen. More important was praise received from the little people, those whom Katharine had pledged to serve. Perhaps there is no greater testament to Katharine than the intense loyalty of the African- and Native-American men, women, and children who knew her in everyday life during her years of ministry.

One Native American, Joseph Padilla, a former student at St. Catherine's Indian School, gave his testimony:

> Everything that is beautiful was in the life of Reverend Mother M. Katharine. Hers was a flaming desire to dream lofty dreams, an ideal of what you and I could be. After fifty years of lofty dreaming, dazzling realities were unveiled at the Motherhouse of the Sisters of the Blessed Sacrament, so dazzling that neither poet nor painter, sculptor nor scientist could sound them all, nor fittingly record their complete inspiration.... We are glad we came from the far West to see this realization of Reverend Mother Katharine's dream. God-like Charity, God-inspired Faith, God-sustained Hope inspired her dream and brought it to this never to be forgotten fulfillment.[14]

There were many accounts of the grand jubilee and all imply Mother Katharine's presence, but none actually state so. While there are many photographs in the Blessed Sacrament files of the celebration, these are of prelates in procession, Indians dancing, choristers singing, black Sisters of Providence, smiling Sisters of the Blessed Sacrament and ordinary people, white, black, and Indian, dressed in Sunday best. Yet there is not a single picture of the Reverend Foundress herself. In all likelihood, Katharine's view of the celebration was from her quiet tribune window overlooking the chapel.

More honorary degrees would follow — Duquesne University, Pittsburgh; Emmanuel College, Boston; St. Joseph's College, Philadelphia (which also honored Louise). Katharine accepted the awards for the good of the congregation, but of course, she could not attend the ceremonies.

Another award came in 1942 when Elie Lescot, president of Haiti, visited to present Katharine with a medal from his government. The picture taken that day in the convent parlor shows Katharine, the president, Louise and members of the congregation in what is the last picture of the two sisters together.[15]

"Her smile was very sweet and pleasant," the Blessed Sacrament annalist noted, "but she was so quiet, as if there was little strength to be any more than just there in person."

It was as if God had granted Katharine's wish from half a century earlier. She was a contemplative now. Health permitting, she would sit at the little window overlooking the chapel and pray. Because she was often too ill to go to the oratory overlooking the chapel, the little altar before which she and her sisters had received their childhood sacraments was now brought to her room. Cardinal Dougherty, during a 1943 visit, granted permission for Mass to be celebrated in her room each weekday.

Katharine's prayers were often turned toward the far-flung missions she would never again visit. Daily she could be seen in her ritual of blessing, her little hand moving up and down with holy water in the form of a cross, first one mission then another, and always remembering the Holy Father. Lower and lower droops her head, as if bowing down before the throne of God.

Mother Mary of the Visitation writes to tell the Sisters: "Reverend Mother spends most of her time now with the Lord in the Blessed Sacrament, and she never goes alone, but carries with her every one of her dearly loved daughters."

When possible she is brought to the chapel.[16] More often, Katharine was confined to her room. Postulants or novices would be assigned to bring her meals. Sister Thomasita Daley recalled this pleasant chore. One day Mother Katharine looked at her tray. "Oh, strawberries," she exclaimed. "Are the Sisters having strawberries with dinner?"

"No, Reverend Mother," Sister Thomasita replied. "Well, I'll not have strawberries either," Mother Katharine said.[17]

It was also at this time that many of her private meditations were written. If some of them reflect upon her own aging condition, it is understandable.

> Alas, the springtime of my life is gone. From this old stump, watered by the grace of the Blood shed on Calvary, may there shoot forth sprouts like from those big trees in Virginia which were cut down, like my past life. Behold the ground beneath them springs forth little green branches, which in time become trees.[18]

Branches there were indeed. By 1940, more than 400 Sisters of the Blessed Sacrament had left Cornwells Heights for the far-flung missions — St. John the Baptist in Alabama; St. Michael and St. Catherine Tegawitha in Arizona; Our Lady of Lourdes and St. Peter Claver in Georgia; St. Monica, St. Elizabeth, and St. Anselm in Illinois; St. Francis Xavier, Holy Ghost, St. Edward, Blessed Sacrament, Corpus Christi, St. Peter Claver, Sacred Heart, Xavier University, and St. Monica in Louisiana; Blessed Sacrament Mission in Massachusetts; Our Mother of Sorrows and St. Theresa in Mississippi; St. Augustine and St. Nicholas in Missouri; St. Augustine in Nebraska; St. Catherine in Houck, New Mexico; St. Mark, St. Benedict the Moor, St. Peter Claver, St. Charles, and Little Flower in New York; St. Cyprian, St. Ann, Our Lady of Blessed Sacrament. Holy Trinity and Madonna House in Ohio; Holy Providence, St. Peter Claver, Our Lady of the Blessed Sacrament, St. Catherine, St. Michael, Holy Savior, and St. Ignatius in Pennsylvania; St. Paul in South Dakota; Immaculate Mother in Tennessee; Blessed Sacrament and Sacred Heart in Texas; St. Francis de Sales in Virginia; and Tekakwitha House in Washington, D.C.

While Katharine's first love had been the Indian apostolate, it is interesting to note that most of her personnel were missioned to the black community. This is deceiving; the records clearly show expenditures were evenly divided between the two apostolates. The difference was that most of the money spent for Indian missions was channeled through the Bureau of Catholic Indian Missions or directly to missions of other congregations working among Native Americans. There was a much greater need for teaching Sisters among African Americans, a field that had generated less interest from other religious orders.

These were years of war, and the troubles of the world are often on Katharine's mind in her private meditations. For instance, she wrote this meditation in 1944:

> To heal the sick, to comfort the dying — the sad, to console the distressed, to defend the weak, to honor the poor — such were the words dreariest to the compassionate heart of Jesus. Dear Jesus, defend my weakness in yielding to impatience. Thou dost heal the sick, how much greater in Thy eyes are the sicknesses of soul than the sickness of the body. With regard to every one of our soldiers now engaged in a war in which the blood of human beings is being poured out as in a river, bring forth Thy pity, Thy mercy, Thy compassion such as moved Thee to restore the son of the poor widow's tears, the cry of the wayside beggar that was blind.

The following is another meditation she wrote in 1944:

> The altar of the Sacred Heart is in this room whereon Jesus, both Priest and Victim, offers Himself up six times a week and is really offered as upon the Cross of Calvary. There on the Cross He sees beneath the Cross all over this world wide war only souls to save. I have the immense privilege of having the priest offer it up for all our valiant soldiers, their salvation, their chaplains and for all those who die now by being bombed, for all the Germans, and even Hitler and even myself. Father, forgive them....[19]

Oddly, it was not the direct casualties of war that most concerned her. "The orphans, what will become of them?" she mourns. For some reason she is especially affected by the orphans of Japan. Perhaps it is because they, too, like her beloved Indians and Negroes, are of another race. Katharine sends the archivist a photograph of an American soldier trying to cheer up an Asian child.[20]

Death was a reality, and Katharine, considering her age and physical condition, presumed it was approaching.

On Palm Sunday in 1944, she wrote:

> The Palm is a sign of Christian victory. I am going to have it in bed
> with me as I receive Holy Communion today, which I intend to receive
> today as if on my death bed. May it be a happy death! Lord into Thy
> hands I commend my death — come it must — I dread it — it is the
> punishment of sin. At 84 years, it must be near. The Martyrs bore the
> palm of victory. May I be victorious in the martyrdom of the death
> struggle — conscious or unconscious.

An assumption of approaching death is not the same thing as a death wish.
"Even in her extreme old age and weakness, no one ever heard her say, 'I wish
God would take me,'" observed Sister Francesca McCusker. "She seemed com-
pletely abandoned to God's will."

"How wonderful are God's ways, so full of Mercy," Katharine mused. "My
life is a moving picture of scenes which recall His wonderful providence in my
regard."

Prayer occupied both her day and night. If she could not sleep, it was no loss,
she would simply recite rosary after rosary during the long night, and if she
began to grow sleepy in the middle of a rosary, she would raise her arms from
the bed as a means of staying awake.

The nurse-Sister who would sleep in her chamber would share in these prayers.
One night she was surprised when Katharine said, "Well, offer this rosary for
the dying Sister." The nurse was taken aback; there was a seriously ill Sister in
the infirmary across the hall, but she did not appear to be dying. In fact, the ill
Sister did die just a few hours later.[21]

On good days Katharine was brought downstairs to be among her Sisters, and
it was always a treat to the community to have their revered foundress in their
presence. "The text is illuminated if read in Reverend Mother's presence," one
Sister remarked. "It is difficult to explain but there is something supernatural
which enhances the ordinary in Reverend Mother's presence. Rarely is Reverend Mother dejected or distressed."[22]

At Christmas 1946, she wrote what would be one of her last letters to the
far-flung missions.

> From my little Nazareth here at the Motherhouse many times in the
> day I speak through the little chapel window, to tell our dear Lord,
> exposed on the altar, about my dear daughters who are now scattered
> far over our country and ask Him to bless you one and all and help you
> in your labors for Him, and the souls dear to Him, and I am confident

He has done this.

The years pass quickly and our lives with them. The older members of the congregation are passing — three of our dear ones have been called this year — so the younger Sisters must come to the fore and continue the work of those who have gone before them. Lean much on your Guardian Angels, for God has given them charge of you "to guide you in all your ways."23

During these sunset years, Louise Morrell remained a source of comfort to her older sister. She would visit St. Elizabeth's Convent weekly, and kept a constant eye on the needs of Katharine and her Sisters. When Katharine had first become seriously ill, it was Louise who paid to have an elevator installed in the convent. It was Louise who also paid for the special nursing services. In earlier years some of the Sisters may have resented Louise's apparent freedom of visitation, because Katharine had always emphasized the necessity to break home ties upon entry into religious life. But it had been Archbishop Ryan who had directed that Louise should have access, because she was more than a relative, she was a collaborator in mission and a benefactress of the works of the Sisters, especially in their work in the black apostolate.

In any case, Louise was a formidable person. At St. Francis, a mile away from St. Elizabeth's, the Christian Brothers knew better than to cross her will. When the order removed Brother Edwin as director because he had served two terms, Louise, through Cardinal Dougherty, appealed to Rome. Brother Edwin returned.

A state inspector came calling and sent Louise a list of possible improvements for the school. Louise icily replied that St. Francis was a purely private charity. She accepted no state money and wondered why the state would concern itself with its operation.24

Louise's St. Francis is interesting in another respect. Her St. Emma's School in Virginia was segregated for most of its history for the same reason Katharine's schools were segregated — it was founded specifically for the advancement and education of black youth.

St. Francis in Eddington, the charity inherited from Elizabeth, had been founded simply for poor, homeless boys. Under Louise's guidance it was a pioneer in integration; black students were not excluded. To be sure, there was never, during her lifetime, a large number of black students at the school, for the simple reason blacks made up but a tiny portion of the Catholics in the Philadelphia area. Today, when most of the residents of the school are no longer Catholic, a majority of the students are African Americans.

In their outreach to the community, both Katharine and Louise were motivated by a zeal for evangelization and a passion for social justice. In Katharine's case, evangelization was definitely the overriding consideration. The balance between the two is much more apparent in Louise's charities.

On one of her last visits to Katharine, she could joyfully report that black children and white children were studying catechism together at St. Emma's. Both she and Katharine were prime financial supporters of the Catholic Interracial Movement, headed by Father John LaFarge.

Louise was a woman of wealth, yet, especially after Ned's death, possessions had little hold on her. During the Depression, through her attorney, Emanuel Friedman, she quietly sold family jewels — not because she needed money, but because the poor needed bread and shoes and coal. In all things, she was her mother's daughter. "Ministry to the poor was dear Mamma's legacy to me," Louise would say. Louise kept a warehouse at San Jose just for the clothing purchased for the poor. (San Jose was the Torresdale estate that adjoined St. Michael's.) There were always shoes because Emma had said, "The feet of the poor should never be cold."25

Like Katharine and her mother before her, Louise's charity was done without ostentation. But within her there also was that evangelical thrust. People associated with Louise tended to become Catholic. There was Ned, of course; then in her old age, Ned's mother. Leona Colby, Louise's nurse-companion in later years, also succumbed to her example by entering the Catholic faith.

This is not to suggest Louise did not respect the faith of others. Emanuel Friedman was Jewish, but, by his own admission, not always observant of the laws of his faith. He had a son who was approaching the age for bar mitzvah; Louise took it upon herself to gently remind the father of his religious duty to see that his son received proper instruction in the Jewish religion.

Just as the world whispered, "Katharine Drexel is a living saint," the Blessed Sacrament foundress thought the same of her sister.

"Mrs. Morrell would not like me to say it," Katharine remarked one day, "but I think she will be canonized."

"Oh, there is no doubt about it," responded the Sister who was visiting her sickroom.

Katharine reflected on this. "Well, there is a doubt," she said, "but her saintly life is, I think, wonderful."26

While Louise, in later years, seemed the more robust of the two, she would not outlive Katharine.

The two sisters had their last visit on November 2, 1945. Katharine had been bedridden for several months, but on this particular day, she was seated in an armchair in the little oratory, alone with God, when Louise came to her. It was a good visit, and typical of their visits, just about a half hour. Louise promised to return the next week.27

It was not to be. Five days later, Louise suffered a cerebral hemorrhage at San Jose. She received the anointing of the Church she had served so well and died peacefully several hours later. Katharine had been told her sister was sick, but it was decided not to break the news of her passing until the next day. When Mother Philip Neri entered her room, Katharine asked, "How is my little sister?"

"Your little sister will never be sick again," Mother Philip gently told her.

Katharine was absolutely devastated, and at the same time torn between faith and very human emotion. "Oh my God! My God! I cannot believe it," Katharine exclaimed. "It is not that I want anything different than God wants...I cannot believe it."

It was a bitter pill; Louise was that last link to joy-filled days at 1503 Walnut and St. Michel. Yet, as the day wore on, she came to accept this latest cross. By nightfall, her gentle smile had returned.28 Louise was clothed in the habit of the Third Order Franciscans, a congregation she was affiliated with many years before, and she was laid to rest in the family vault she had built at St. Michael's.

* * * *

At Louise's death, her personal estate had not been especially large — $287,000 — because she, like Katharine, had been spending her income on charity as it was received. The estate was divided mostly among her charities and the Blessed Sacrament Sisters. But with her death, Katharine's annual income doubled — at least for the moment. Of course, once she died the income would cease, because the trust fund would be distributed to the charities specified by Francis Drexel. The congregation had been trying to prepare for this day by gradually placing the various schools conducted by them on a solvent footing, capable of operating without a subsidy. But given the nature of the apostolate, this was not an easy task. Archbishop (later Cardinal) John F. O'Hara, Cardinal Dougherty's successor as Archbishop of Philadelphia, came up with a plan to soften the blow. A number of the charities were actually controlled by the Archdiocese. With the consent of the Vatican, Cardinal O'Hara set up a plan by which the bequest to these charities would be placed in a new trust fund. Income generated beyond the needs of the charities would be given to the Blessed Sacrament Sisters. Cardinal O'Hara also wrote to the other beneficiaries asking that they also make a contribution to the Blessed Sacrament Sisters.

When Louise erected St. Michael's it was her intent that all the Drexels — including Katharine — should be entombed there. Katharine herself had expressed the desire to be buried quite simply with her spiritual daughters in religion in the little cemetery at St. Elizabeth's convent. Neither would have their way.

Katharine was special; her Sisters knew it very well. Even then the thought of her eventual canonization was not out of the question. Those who lived with her daily and knew her best believed she was a saint.

In 1949, upon the request of Mother Mary of the Visitation, Cardinal Dougherty granted permission for a tomb to be prepared for Katharine under the chapel at St. Elizabeth's Convent. Of course, she was not quite ready to inhabit it. Her contemplative life would continue for a few more years.[29]

These were difficult years. Katharine became almost totally bedridden and suffered several heart attacks and strokes. There was also, according to testimony given by Sister Consuela Marie Duffy, a mastectomy. The Sisters and physicians were extremely protective of her, perhaps excessively so. One cannot help but wonder if her suffering might have been more bearable if she were at least wheeled around the convent's beautiful grounds, weather and health permitting.

In her youth Bishop O'Connor had restricted the number of hours a day she could spend in prayer. No need for that now; her rosary and other devotions became constant companions. She worried about the little ones. "Are the children cold?" she would ask. "Take my blanket and give it to them." There were periods of vision — or delirium — depending upon one's level of faith.

"Did you see them?" she asked a Sister on nursing duty, pointing to a spot on the ceiling. "See what?" the Sister asked.

"The children," she replied. The next day she explained there had been many children going by, and there was the Pope, too, in all his regalia. It was as if God had granted her a vision of the many children she had served.

During this last decade of her life, Katharine would be anointed many times, but somehow she continued on. Mass was celebrated in her room daily, but she was gradually drifting into silence. Only her serene smile spoke for her.

"My dying is eternal life with Christ. To the extent which I comprehend Christ in faith, to the same extent I shall embrace Him in love."

SAINT KATHARINE DREXEL

Chapter 13
In Paradisio

In 1952, on February 12, the 61st anniversary of her profession, Katharine was well enough to receive six postulants in her room. They were in awe of this tiny, very old nun, and pitied her in her obvious suffering.

In early 1955, she seemed to rally, and seemed more alert, but only by degrees.[1] Her chaplain asked if she wished to receive Communion. She could not articulate clearly, but opened her mouth. A look of anxiety crossed her face. Did he understand? Yes, he did. As she received the Host, gratitude clearly showed on her face and she closed her eyes contentedly.

Loss of clear speech should not suggest a total loss of mental faculties. A few days later, on February 15, according to the convent annals, she requested a Mass be said for her father. It was the 70th anniversary of Frank Drexel's death.

Katharine herself was fading; the Sisters knew this but could do little but pray. On February 20 she developed pneumonia, but this too apparently cleared up.

Then, on the evening of March 2, her breathing became labored. Although paramedics installed an oxygen tent, her condition worsened, and by morning it was quite evident that Reverend Mother Katharine Drexel was dying. It was about 8:30 a.m. when Mother Mary Anselm was informed the foundress's condition was very grave. When she arrived, Katharine's breathing was labored and her face was blue. "She is dying," Sister Clement said. Father John Nugent, the convent chaplain, and Dr. John F. McFadden were there, as were several members of the community. Mother Anselm led the other Sisters in prayers for the dying, but she could not bear to look at Mother Katharine. Finally, at 9:07 a.m., someone said Reverend Mother had died. Mother Anselm looked. Suffering had been erased by an expression of peace.[2] At age 96, Katharine Drexel had gone home to the Spouse she had served so faithfully.

The word quickly spread through the convent and was telephoned to the missions. In New Orleans, at Corpus Christi School, Sister M. Thomasita Daley was teaching class when the P.A. system crackled. "Attention, Sisters and students. Mother Katharine Drexel fell asleep in Christ at seven minutes after nine," Sister Alacoque McVey announced. Sister Thomasita stood frozen. The boys in the class, without prompting, went down on their knees and started to recite the rosary.[3]

Thousands braved stormy weather to attend Katharine's wake at St. Elizabeth's convent. Some had been educated or helped by the Blessed Sacrament Sisters, others knew her only by reputation. Police directed traffic and Sisters stood guard as the mourners filed past, gently preventing them from touching the body. The Sisters would take religious articles from the people and touch them to Katharine's remains, thereby creating a relic. One poor man presented a book to be touched to Katharine. "That's all I have," he said. Another held up his little boy. "Take a look at the nun, son," he said. "Some day you can say that you looked upon a saint."[4]

Even the Sisters, especially those young in religion, were taken aback by the outpouring of affection for their foundress. While the older Sisters were well aware of Katharine's importance, these young Sisters had little inkling of her impact.

"When I entered in 1952 Mother Katharine was an invalid," said Sister Juliana Haynes said. "I didn't realize the import of who she was. She was one of the very elderly Sisters being taken care of, and she was the foundress. She did have Mass celebrated in her room but there were not extraordinary things done for her that other Sisters would not have done for them.

"I didn't realize who she was, really, the extent of her influence, until she died.... When the whole world came here to the motherhouse at the news of her death, at her wake and for her funeral, that's when it came to me what a tremendous person she must have been."[5]

At the request of Archbishop O'Hara, Katharine was brought to the Cathedral of SS. Peter and Paul for her Mass of Requiem. The throng of mourners was beyond the capacity of the great cathedral as members of the three races — red, black, and white, united in love for Katharine, bore her remains up the long, polished marble aisle. Archbishop O'Hara celebrated Katharine's final liturgy; Auxiliary Bishop of Philadelphia Joseph McShea preached. He captured the spirit of Katharine in his homily:

First and foremost, in youth and old age, in health and in sickness, with friends and with strangers, the beloved soul of Mother Katharine was activated, inspired and impelled by an insatiable love of God and a complete subjection to His adorable Will. Hers was not a humanitarianism that stoops where true love should begin. She was not a mere social reformer, educator or philanthropist striving to better the condition of her fellow man while permitting him to ignore God. Hers was a love primarily of God, practiced with her whole heart, her whole soul and her whole mind....[6]

After the impressive Mass, the funeral cortege, under police escort, slowly returned to St. Elizabeth's convent. There was one detour. The road took them by Eden Hall, where the Sacred Heart Sisters, because of their semi-cloistered state, had been unable to attend the funeral. The procession entered the convent gates. This was where Emma, Katharine's beloved stepmother more than a century earlier, had learned to know, love, and serve God. This was the very convent where Katharine as a toddler would visit Aunt Louise. This was the convent where, as young women, she and her sisters would often ride by buggy or horseback to Mass.

Children from nearby St. Katherine School recited the rosary; Eden Hall students sang "In Paradisio," and the Religious of the Sacred Heart stood in solemn file, holding lighted tapers.[7]

After this final courtesy, Katharine was laid to rest beneath the chapel at St. Elizabeth's Convent. It was quite a different convent from what she and her little band of pioneers had first entered in 1892. Her tiny seed had grown to a great, flourishing vine.

By this time there were 501 professed Sisters, 30 novices, and 8 postulants scattered through 48 convents and ministering to 61 institutions — 48 elementary schools, 12 high schools, and one college.

With Katharine dead, the Blessed Sacrament Sisters — or more correctly the institutions founded by Katharine — lost a major source of income. Under the terms of Francis Drexel's will, his estate was distributed to the charities that had received the tenth of the estate at the time of his death.

When Frank Drexel died in 1885, this residual estate had been roughly $15.5 million. One would assume it would have grown in the 70 years that elapsed before his last daughter died. Just the opposite was true. The final distribution amounted to $12,913,799.32.[8] This was not only less, but vastly diminished in purchasing power because of inevitable monetary inflation over seven decades. What happened? While it can be argued the funds were not particularly well managed, the trustees had honored Frank Drexel's wishes. The trust fund had been invested for safety and income, not growth. Further, no investments had emerged unscathed from the Great Depression. Finally, all income was distributed as earned; nothing was reinvested to counterbalance inflation. In spite of these limiting factors, the trustees could report they had distributed well in excess of twice the initial value of the trust — $39,829,927, or an average of $550,000 a year.

Because Elizabeth had died young, Katharine received half of the annual income for most of her life, and the entire income during her final decade. Her share over the years was in the neighborhood of 55 percent of the total. The Blessed Sacrament Sisters' estimate of her lifetime charitable expenditures of $20 million may be slightly low.

Had she chosen to place 10 percent of her income into an endowment every year, simple compounding of interest would have produced a sum larger than Francis Drexel's entire estate. Of course, Katharine refused to do this. It was her firm belief that God provided; it was her duty to spend His bounty on her apostolate and on nothing else. God would provide for the future.

Many of the beneficiaries under Francis Drexel's will quietly made donations to the Blessed Sacrament Sisters, and true to his word, Cardinal O'Hara made annual contributions from the portion bequeathed to archdiocesan-controlled charities. In 1965, these voluntary donations on the part of the Archdiocese of Philadelphia ceased.

The congregation was not totally without resources. There was a small endowment, coupled with grants from the Bureau of Catholic Indian Missions. During Katharine's final years, when possible, schools, through tuition, had been placed on a break-even or near break-even basis. Inevitably, some schools closed and Katharine's beloved St. Michel had to be sold. The bodies of the Drexel dead were reinterred at the cemetery on the motherhouse grounds. Had Katharine lived to see this, she would have been saddened, but she would have accepted it. Buildings, no matter how beautiful, were not really important. The evangelization mission of the congregation was important. The needs of the poor were important.

Money was not the real challenge that faced Katharine's congregation after her death. First came *Brown v. the Board of Education*, the Supreme Court decision that forced integration of public schools all over the country. The Blessed Sacrament Sisters, along with all people of good will, applauded the justice of the decision. With enforced integration of public schools came voluntary integration of nonpublic schools. Some Blessed Sacrament Schools that had served black children combined with previously all-white schools, but the Sisters remained a presence in schools that were located in heavily African-American communities, as well as schools closely associated with Native Americans.

The second great challenge to the Sisters was one faced by virtually all religious congregations — the precipitous decline in religious vocations in the second half of the 20th century. This was coupled with turmoil within the Church in the immediate post-Vatican II years that caused a number of Sisters — including Blessed Sacrament Sisters — to resign from their congregations.

One bright new chapter for religious vocations had begun for the Blessed Sacrament Sisters before Katharine's death. The congregation reversed its tradition of not accepting candidates from the groups they served. Rose Haynes (Sister M. Juliana) had entered in 1952, and on March 9, 1955, six days after Katharine's death, was professed. She had the distinction of being the first African-American Sister of the Blessed Sacrament. At the time of Katharine's beatification, she was the first African-American president of the Blessed Sacrament Sisters and proudly led the delegation of Sisters to Rome for their foundress' beatification.[9] Sister Anna Cox, also African American, entered in 1953 and she, too, perservered to profession. Somewhere in heaven, Louise and Ned were probably telling Katharine and Elizabeth, "We told you so."

"...All is vanity except knowing,
loving and serving God.
This alone can bring peace
to my soul."

SAINT KATHARINE DREXEL

Chapter 14
Miracles of Faith

This idea of canonization for Katharine Drexel isn't something that sprang up after her death. From the time, many years earlier, when Elizabeth had quipped, "It's hard having a saint in the family," there had been those who whispered, "Katharine Drexel is a living saint." It wasn't just the brave women who joined her in her noble apostolate. There were the bishops whom she served. Archbishop Ryan thought it. Archbishop Curley of Baltimore believed it, too. Bishop Joseph McShea, who preached at her funeral, flatly testified, "I think she was a saint. I am convinced she was a saint and have no knowledge of any other dedicated woman, lay or religious, no personal knowledge, that would exceed her in sanctity."[1]

And finally — and most important — it was the little people, the men, women and children who had been ministered to by her Sisters. Perhaps they saw her only once or twice a year on visitation, but they knew what they saw, and that was a saint. Then too, there were the lay men and women who were employed by her and saw her, not as a distinguished visitor, but in everyday life.

A key ingredient to canonization in the Roman Catholic Church is the existence of a persistent cult — a body of people who believe the Servant of God is a saint. Katharine Drexel had such a cult, whispered during her lifetime, spoken loudly and often after her death. In that sense, she was very much like Mother Teresa of Calcutta in more recent years; except Mother Teresa's cult was — and is — worldwide. Katharine's was less well known abroad. There are similarities between the two women, quite beyond the fact that both founded religious congregations. Both chose to minister to the poorest and most despised populations they knew. Both had the greatest respect for the authority of the Church, especially in the person of the Pope.

But there are differences, too. These nuances make neither more worthy than the other, but simply point to differing understandings of God's will. Teresa's apostolate was more public; Katharine's was hidden. Both lived austere lives and expected their Sisters to follow their example. But while the poor in Teresa's hospices would not have television either, Katharine told her Sisters not to watch motion pictures, but to let the children see them. Blessed Sacrament Sisters were not permitted to attend social functions hosted by white neighbors. On the other hand, if such functions were conducted by Indian or black neighbors, attendance could be a form of missionary outreach.

Both Katharine and Teresa practiced a blend of the spiritual and corporal works of mercy. Perhaps Teresa, a 20th-century woman, looked more to the corporal works of mercy; Katharine, with a 19th-century mindset, always had religious conversion as the primary goal.

In any case, canonization in the Roman Catholic Church cannot be reduced to a popularity contest. It is by necessity a complicated process — the Church prefers to be cautious on a matter of such gravity. In fact, canonization, the final step to sainthood, is taken so seriously that it is considered to carry the weight of an infallible pronouncement of the Pope. The process itself, under current Church legislation, usually cannot begin until five years after the death of the Servant of God. As a process, it is much more likely to take centuries than decades. It is no accident that many modern saints are foundresses of religious congregations. Convents have the resources, skills, and patience necessary for a task that is rarely completed within the lifetime of the persons who initiate the cause.

In some respects, Katharine's cause began well before her death. It was certainly in the mind of Mother Mercedes O'Connor when she instructed the Sisters to preserve all correspondence they had with their foundress.[2] Every item of clothing, every book, every possible artifact that could be connected to Katharine from the time of her infancy until death, was carefully preserved. And again, the Sisters gave special reverence to their foundress when they received permission to prepare a separate tomb for her, not in the convent cemetery, but beneath the chapel of St. Elizabeth's Convent.

Katharine was dead less than four years when, in January 1959, Cardinal O'Hara, at the request of Mother Anselm, gave his imprimatur to a prayer card beseeching God that His servant Mary Katharine "may one day soon be raised to the honors of Thy altar." Nearly 100,000 cards were distributed in less than a year.

One of the first tasks was the preparation of an official biography. A previously written but unpublished biography titled *Compassion* had been prepared by Sister Francesca McCusker in 1950 and updated after Katharine's death. However, documentation of sources had not been completed, and in truth, the style was somewhat florid for modern standards. Katherine Burton, a laywoman who wrote several popular biographies of saints, wrote *The Golden Door*, a biography of Katharine published in 1957. While Burton's book was very good, it lacked the detail and documentation of sources that would be needed for the official biography. At first, through Cardinal O'Hara, a priest-historian had been asked to write the biography, but when circumstances prevented him from completing the work, the Sisters assigned the task to Sister Consuela Marie Duffy. She had edited "The Mission Fields," the congregation's outreach publication, and she had known Katharine very well.

Sister Consuela was more than equal to the task, and her *Katharine Drexel, a Biography*, published in 1966, was key to publicizing Katharine's cause and formed a foundation for documentation that would follow. Sister Consuela's task was made easier because of the wealth of resources in the convent archives; there were letters dating back to childhood, diaries of various members of the family and the congregation's annals, which told much of the Blessed Sacrament beginnings. For the early life of Katharine, Sister Consuela — as have all of Katharine's biographers — borrowed heavily from *The Francis Anthony Drexel Family*, a privately published authorized biography of the family commissioned by Louise Morell and written by Blessed Sacrament Sister M. Dolores Letterhouse. As in the case of most authorized biographies, it is totally uncritical but nevertheless a charming book full of insights into the home life of Katharine and her two sisters, ending with the death of Elizabeth and Katharine's embarking on a new life at St. Elizabeth's Convent.

Sister Consuela built upon this beginning and carried through to Katharine's death. Her biography would be a major source for the biographical portion of the positio, the official document prepared for Katharine's cause and submitted to Rome. In the positio Father Joseph (now Bishop) Martino had to add additional material and to retrace and document all of Sister Consuela's citations.

On February 27, 1964, Katharine's cause for canonization was formally introduced in Rome by Cardinal John Krol. At that time Redemptorist Father Nicholas Ferrante was named postulator for the cause in Rome. Father Francis J. Litz, also a Redemptorist, was named vice postulator in Philadelphia.[3] Both priests had the necessary experience — they were serving on the cause of Philadelphia Bishop John Neumann, who had been beatified the previous year. (He would be canonized in 1977.) A major difference between the two causes was that Neumann had been dead a century, a more customary time frame, unlike Katharine, in the grave but nine years.

One of the first steps was to forward copies of all of Katharine's known writings to Rome — and they were voluminous. The writings filled 41 cartons. These were approved by the Sacred Congregation for the Causes of Saints in 1973. Testimony was taken from a total of 54 witnesses in Philadelphia and elsewhere, in two periods — the ordinary process in 1966-67 and the apostolic process in 1980-81. Because Katharine had been dead but a short time, most of the witnesses knew her personally; some well, others slightly or by reputation. In 1980, Cardinal Krol issued a decree which recognized the public cult at Katharine's Bensalem tomb. This decree would not permit an undue cult but recognize the phenomenon that had been happening for the quarter century since her death.

The process was by no means a straight, smooth path. In 1982, the anniversary of Katharine's death was celebrated through a Mass at the Cathedral Basilica of SS. Peter and Paul. Cardinal Krol was the celebrant, Bishop McShea preached, just as he had at Katharine's funeral. As expected, his was an upbeat homily extolling the virtuous life of Katharine Drexel. Cardinal Krol, as celebrants normally do, spoke briefly after the Mass. His remarks were somewhat of a shock. Most saints are never canonized, he advised the congregation, and they should not be disappointed if Mother Katharine Drexel was not canonized.

Why was Krol so seemingly pessimistic at this point? For one thing, the entire canonization process was revamped, not once, but twice, in the post-Vatican II years. Each revision, even though it may have been a simplification of the process, was a temporary setback to the cause.

Under the former rules governing the process, there were striking similarities to a case in law. On one side, there was a postulator and his advocates whose task it was to prove the Servant of God was a saint. On the other, there was the Promoter of the Faith — the Devil's Advocate — whose team of lawyers would pore over the testimony and writings of the candidate to ferret out reasons why he or she should not be canonized.

This cumbersome process, centered in Rome and controlled by lawyers, was one of the reasons canonization processes moved at a snail's pace. In 1983, under new rules promulgated by Pope John Paul II, the office of Promoter of the Faith was abolished, and historians, not lawyers, were given the chief responsibility for developing the cause.

By this time, Jesuit Father Paul Molinari had succeeded Father Ferrante as postulator in Rome, and Msgr. James V. McGrath had succeeded Father Litz as vice postulator in Philadelphia.

In 1984, Jesuit Father Kurt Peter Gumpel was named relator, guiding the documentation process in Rome. Altruism, Father Gumpel said, "is especially admitted today, but often it is based on purely humanitarian motives. Inquiry into what inspired Mother Katharine in her work with the blacks and Indians will show that Mother Katharine operated out of no other motive except the love of God."

Father Martino was given the now critical role of external collaborator, working for the most part in Philadelphia. "Think of the collaborator as an editor," he explained. But it involved much more than editing. Working under the direction of the relator, Father Martino wrote a formal biography which, including documentation, encompassed more than 1,100 pages. He also extracted relevant material from the witness testimony and concluded with a summary of the cause. He brought a special expertise to the process — his own doctoral thesis had been on Katharine's good friend, Archbishop Patrick J. Ryan.

The witnesses represented persons from all walks of life, and quite naturally, most knew Katharine during her years of active ministry and as superior of the Sisters of the Blessed Sacrament. Because the testimony was taken more than a century after her birth, none could speak with firsthand knowledge of her childhood and formative years. The witnesses included bishops, priests, relatives, Blessed Sacrament Sisters and members of other congregations, humble employees and Native-American and African-American men and women. The interrogations covered many aspects of her life and work, focusing especially on her practice of heroic virtue.

As might be expected, virtually all the testimony was positive. For the most part, these were people who clearly believed Katharine Drexel was a saint in heaven and did not hesitate to say so.

"Black Catholics who knew her feel that she should have been canonized long ago," said Dr. Norman Francis, president of Xavier University. "...She saved the Church."[4]

"...We know she is in heaven and we know she is a saint," said Sister Marie Enfanta Gonzales, superior general of the Oblate Sisters of Providence.[5]

"Mother Katharine saw Christ in the souls of neglected people, and she taught the Sisters to see Christ in these people," said Mother Mary Anselm McCann, who had been Blessed Sacrament Superior General at the time of Katharine's death. "She had a passionate love of Christ and wanted everybody to know and love Him."[6]

Murray Lincoln, a Navajo Indian who gave testimony, had first met Mother Katharine as a school child in 1927, and saw her many times after that. When he first encountered Katharine, he had lost his own mother and was in despair. Suicide was not out of the question. "When I came across her, something that

I was left without came back to me," he said. "Mother Katharine never spoke as though she was looking down on someone," he testified. "She was always lifting, lifting."

One of the nuns was wearing an old patched habit. "Why don't you get a new one?" Mother Katharine asked. Lincoln found this amusing. "She had many patches on her own," he said. "So she had no desire for Cadillacs or eating in these fancy restaurants. She was not that kind."7

Kenneth Woodward, in his absorbing 1990 book *Making Saints*, critiqued the Katharine Drexel cause. While Woodward's comments are certainly fair, he brings up two points which might be addressed. In Woodward's opinion, the biographical portion of the positio is well developed up until age 30 or so. Afterward, it is more a history of the Blessed Sacrament Congregation.8

This is certainly true, but it is an unavoidable weakness of every biography of Katharine written thus far. During her happy childhood in an almost perfect family, we see absolutely charming letters (written under the gentle, watching guidance of Mary Cassidy). As a young adult there is the death of her beloved parents and the beautiful letters to Bishop O'Connor to whom we must be grateful for so thoughtfully saving them. Katharine's protracted search for vocation is undoubtedly her finest writing. After she founds her congregation, there is a bit of an anticlimax as she is relegated to the role of administrator, certainly not a role of her choosing. The real drama is in the lives and experiences of the brave young women she sends out into the African-American and Native-American missions, and how through them, she affected the lives of the children, women and men to whom they ministered. Katharine's writings which are generally quoted from these years as Reverend Mother tend to be instructional: Christmas letters and retreat talks written for the edification of her spiritual daughters. For a true window into the soul of the mature Katharine, the best are her personal notes, but they are not as plentiful. Some of the best are the last — those written during the first decade of enforced retirement before the infirmities of extreme old age stilled her pen.

Woodward's second criticism of the process concerns the testimonies. He thought the questions were not as probing as they ought to have been and the witnesses were almost universally favorable to Katharine's cause.9 Woodward is probably correct; one would expect sharp questioning in a process such as this, if not in the ordinary process which is controlled by the diocese proposing the candidate for beatification, then at least in the apostolic process, which is supervised by Roman officials.

For instance, Question 10 put to Bishop Harold Perry during the apostolic process would be considered in a court of law leading the witness. "When she broke barriers which up to that point had not been broken, for example, in the

South where churches were designated as Catholic churches just for blacks and those few churches that allowed blacks to be only in the back part of the church, the blacks were permitted to receive Communion only at the end of the line, as it were, and she was different, she did things that others wouldn't do. What can you tell us about that?"[10] Granted most questions were more concise and less partisan, but this example does give the impression that the interrogator had a preconceived bias in Katharine's favor.

As to the observation that the witnesses were almost uniformly favorable, that is perhaps unavoidable. If Katharine Drexel were indeed worthy of sainthood, it is perfectly logical that the people who knew her best believed it to be so.

Yet among all the witnesses who testified to Katharine's sanctity, Father Martino's positio clearly shows there were those who noted tiny flaws. That, by the way, is perfectly acceptable to the process. Saints may be a cut or two above the common run of mortals, but they are still human.

Some witnesses' perceived faults in Katharine may not have been real faults. For instance, there were hints she could have been unnecessarily stern or she was unwilling to address just grievances by junior Sisters against their superiors. To the first complaint, Katharine took her own vows very seriously and she expected the congregation to do likewise. As to the second, Katharine's own fidelity to her vow of obedience was extreme. She obeyed her parents, her confessors, her bishops, anyone in lawful authority. To Katharine, it was only natural that junior Sisters should obey their lawful superiors.

One interesting comment was given by Mother Mary Agatha Ryan, one of her closest associates: "My own opinion was that Mother Katharine had no great love for children as such. However, she was kind to them when occasion arose." It must be noted others testified "she had a special love for children," or "she just loved little children."[11]

Mother Mary Agatha, by the way, also testified: "She had a consuming love of God. All she wanted was souls to give back to God. She had given up everything — her money, herself, her prestige, her friends. She said there was nothing left to give. All she wanted was to give souls to God."[12]

There are also isolated incidents of impatience, noteworthy mostly because they were so rare. Another slight imperfection — if it is an imperfection — is her continued attachment to family, something a pre-Vatican II religious was expected to renounce. In religion Katharine kept her birth name; her other Sisters did not. Sisters normally had visitors once monthly; Louise visited weekly. At least two cousins, Josephine Drexel and Ulrica Dahlgren, accompanied Katharine on Western visitations. A number of Blessed Sacrament foundations honored Drexel family members by being named for their patron saints.

At the very time when a Sister was denied permission to visit a seriously ill relative, Katharine attended the funeral of Walter George Smith, the husband of her deceased sister.[13]

Each of the above criticisms can be answered individually. Katharine kept her birth name under the direction of Mother Sebastian of the Sisters of Mercy, her superior at the time. It made sense to do so, given the need for publicity for the new congregation. Louise was granted wide visitation rights, under orders from Archbishop Ryan, because she was more than a relative, she was a collaborator in mission. Katharine took her young cousins west in the hope of introducing them to a possible religious vocation, or at least interest in the missions. Blessed Sacrament missions honored Drexel saints because they were built with Drexel money. Smith was more than a brother-in-law; he was also the Blessed Sacrament Sister's attorney, donating his services without charge. In this sense, Katharine was quite right to attend his funeral.

According to Blessed Sacrament historian Sister Patricia Lynch, Mother Katharine was reluctant to attend Smith's funeral. She did so only at the urging of one of her general councillors who said she should forget he was a brother-in-law and remember he was a great benefactor of the congregation.

But even if each of the above can be individually explained, it is the cumulative weight of the whole which suggests a minor violation of the Blessed Sacrament rule. If Katharine expected this of the other Sisters, should she not have done the same?

Naturally, the rule today is quite different — like the rules of many other congregations. All of Katharine's actions would be quite acceptable, and love of family, if an imperfection, is truly understandable.

The acceptance of Katharine's writings and proofs that she had practiced virtue to a heroic degree, were still not enough for beatification. For this, except in the case of martyrs, a miracle is required. Although the Pope may dispense with this requirement, he rarely does so.

Literally thousands of people informed the Blessed Sacrament Sisters of favors received through intercession to Katharine, and these were sifted in search of the miraculous. Favors can be anything — employment obtained, marital difficulties overcome, a healing from sickness. Few of them would past muster with the very demanding medical and theological boards that would review them as a possible miracle.

Miracles proposed for beatification or canonization are almost always miracles of physical healing. To be accepted by the physicians, the doctors — who may or may not be Catholic — must be convinced there is no natural explanation for the healing. Further, the healing must be spontaneous — it cannot be over a protracted period of time. The theologians then determine whether or not the cure is attributable to the intercession of an individual Servant of God. For example, if half of one's friends and relatives prayed to Katharine Drexel for a cure while the other half prayed to the Virgin Mary, no matter how dramatic a cure, it could not be accepted as attributable exclusively to Katharine.

While favors received and reputed cures were reported from around the country and around the world, Katharine's miracle accepted for beatification was from her own back yard, almost literally. The Guthermans — George, Bea, and their 11 children — were devout Catholics living in Bensalem. Several of the boys served Mass at St. Elizabeth's Convent, a pleasant duty because the Sisters served a very good breakfast. In 1974, the fourth child, Bob, age 14, was hospitalized with a serious ear infection. At worst, it was life threatening; at best the damage was so severe he would almost certainly lose his hearing.

One of the Blessed Sacrament Sisters suggested the family pray directly to Mother Katharine and exclusively to her. Bob Gutherman's fever abated and the infection disappeared, as did the already documented inner ear damage. His diseased inner ear bones, which had been surgically scraped, regenerated. The Guthermans were convinced they had received a miracle through the intercession of Mother Katharine. Its announcement took 13 years, but in the end Bob Gutherman's cure could not be explained either naturally or scientifically. The December 6, 1987 ruling of the Roman medical board was a major breakthrough in Katharine's cause.[13] She had been declared venerable on January 26, 1987 by Pope John Paul II, that is, worthy of veneration by the faithful. Father Martino's positio was approved by the Congregation for the Causes of Saints at this time, too.[14]

On March 15, 1988, the Board of Theologians found that Gutherman's cure was a direct result of prayers to Katharine, and their finding was passed on to the Cardinals of the Congregation for the Causes of Saints. This body reviewed the work of the physicians and theologians, and after accepting Gutherman's cure as miraculous through the intercession of Mother Katharine, it petitioned Pope John Paul II to beatify the Blessed Sacrament foundress. The Pope gave his formal consent on July 20 and designated November 20 as the date for her beatification.[15] Philadelphia's new Archbishop, Anthony Bevilacqua, led a pilgrimage of 1,200 people to Rome for the ceremony. Cardinal Krol was there, and many Blessed Sacrament Sisters were joined by former pupils from the black and Indian schools.

"We knew she would be a saint," said Sister Mary Louis Nestler, who came from New Orleans in spite of her 91 years. "But she always said it would cost too much money."

There were any number of Drexel, Hookey, and Bouvier relatives too — many not Catholic but still aware that this was a singular honor for their distinguished relative. Practically the entire Gutherman family was in Rome, their presence somewhat poignant because Bea Gutherman, Bob's mother, was confined to a wheelchair and slowly dying of cancer. The family's faith was nonetheless strong. Every evening in their Roman hotel, they would pray the rosary, just as they did at home. Bob Gutherman was in awe that his cure had played a little role in this drama. "If I hadn't gotten the miracle I don't know what my life would have been," he said. "I don't think I could ever waver from my faith now."

During the impressive ceremony, Pope John Paul II spoke of the Church's newest "Blessed." Katharine Drexel, he said, was "a woman of lively faith, deeply committed to the truth revealed by Christ." American Indians and blacks "in the United States suffered great injustice as a result of racial prejudice," he said. "Seeing clearly the evil of this situation she set out with determination to combat and overcome it."

Sister M. Juliana Haynes, as president of the Sisters of the Blessed Sacrament, spoke on behalf of the congregation during the ceremony. Katharine Drexel, she said, gave the total gift of herself to God and God's people. "We, as Sisters of the Blessed Sacrament, are proud today and pledge ourselves to continue the work of Blessed Katharine. We need more Blessed Katharines."[16]

Beatification is the final way station on the road to canonization or sainthood. But in truth, most beatified never achieve canonization, even though, technically, all that is required is the approval of one more miracle and the recommendation by the Congregation for the Causes of Saints to the Pope. It is a dramatic step, and even though Pope John Paul II has been more prone to create saints than his predecessors, it is by no means assured that it will happen in any particular instance.

In Blessed Katharine's case, the process of finding and forwarding to Rome a probable second miracle began almost immediately. This task was initiated by Msgr. McGrath as vice postulator, and continued by Msgr. Alexander J. Palmieri after Msgr. McGrath retired.

Philadelphia's Cardinal John Krol, who had taken great interest in the advancement of the cause for canonization of Blessed Katharine, died peacefully on March 3, 1996. Coincidentally, it was Katharine's feast day and the 41st anniversary of her entrance into eternal life.

Meanwhile, her cause for canonization had remained alive, slowly wending its way through the thicket of Roman bureaucracy. Such causes are by necessity and deliberately complex. Rome, where eternity takes precedence over immediacy, remains reluctant to move hastily in matters of such importance. Saints, once named, will be held up as exemplars for the uncounted generations to come.

Sister Monica Loughlin, president of the Sisters of the Blessed Sacrament, reminded the people at the 1999 Feast Day Mass, "Blessed Katharine's message is not one of miracles but of mission. Her message speaks of Christ, simple everyday action that contributes to accomplishment of goals." That mission, she said, "is a long way from being accomplished," and she asked people to support not just the cause of Mother Katharine, but her work.

What was that work? Cardinal Bevilacqua in his homily said, "Like her Lord and Master she served the needs of everyone... she remembered the forgotten, ministered to the lowly and loved the unloved."

Meanwhile, the Sisters did just as their president pledged at the beatification ceremony. They returned to their schools in the ghettos and reservations of America and continued the arduous task begun by their foundress — the evangelization of the African- and Native-American races. Katharine would not have used those exact words. "Indian and Colored races," she would say, using the correct terminology for her era.

The Blessed Katharine Drexel Guild has continued to receive correspondence from people who believed they had received favors through Katharine's intercession. "About 15 a week," estimated Sister Ruth Catherine Spain, director of the guild.[17] Most would not qualify as "miraculous," perhaps employment found, loved ones reunited, family difficulties settled. Others did indeed sound quite extraordinary, and the most promising were submitted to the vice postulator for investigation as the possible second miracle needed for canonization. For one reason or another each was rejected. Then in 1994 the Sisters learned about a little girl, Amanda (Amy) Wall, who had been born deaf, and according to her mother, Connie Wall, the child was able to hear after the family and friends prayed to Blessed Katharine.

The alleged cure was thoroughly examined by a team of Philadelphia doctors who could find no medical explanation for Amy's sudden onset of hearing. It was submitted to Rome in 1997, and on October 7, 1999, the Rome board of physicians also voted that there was no medical explanation.

On January 5, 2000, the Vatican's board of theologians decided the healing was due solely to the intercession of Katharine Drexel and reported it to the cardinals and bishops of the Congregation for the Causes of Saints. In turn, on January 18 the cardinals and bishops recommended the cure as miraculous to Pope John Paul II. The Pope, on January 27, 2000, issued a decree formally declaring that Amy Wall's cure was miraculous. This was the final requirement for canonization; only a date needed to be set.[18]

There seemed to be unusual similarities between the Gutherman and Wall miracles. Both miracle beneficiaries were children, and at that Caucasian children, not of the two races Katharine and her Blessed Sacrament Sisters served.

Both children lived in Bucks County, the site of Katharine's motherhouse. Both miracles involved hearing, even though nothing in Katharine's life seemed to be connected with physical handicaps.[19]

It was not total coincidence; there was a connection between the two miracles.

Bea Gutherman, Bob Gutherman's mother, had known the Blessed Sacrament Sisters well and had a devotion to Mother Katharine Drexel. When she asked the Sisters to pray for her son, in her words, "It was like going to a neighbor for a cup of sugar." It was the most natural thing in the world for Bea Gutherman and her very devout family to pray for a miracle.

However, the Wall family, further north in Bucks County, had no connection to the Sisters and little knowledge of Mother Katharine. When it was discovered little Amy had an incurable hearing impairment — the nerves in her ears were dead — Connie Wall did not immediately pray to Mother Katharine.

As she recalls, one evening in November 1993, she noticed a special television program on the life of Mother Katharine Drexel would be airing on PBS. She remembered her grandmother had affection for Katharine and used to contribute small sums of money to the Blessed Sacrament Sisters. There had been little trinkets around her grandmother's house, items from the missions the Sisters had sent to her. It was out of fond memory of her grandmother that Connie Wall decided to watch the show.

During the course of the program, Bob Gutherman recounted how his ear infection had been cured through Katharine Drexel's intercession and his hearing restored. Connie Wall decided to pray to Katharine, too, but not for a cure.

"When we first started praying to Mother Katharine Drexel we didn't pray that her she would hear," Connie Wall explained. "We prayed that we would be able to communicate with her. She started to learn sign language and could sign she wanted her bottle. I was thrilled."

The Walls had two other children — Jack, who was in parochial school studying for First Communion, and Jeanette, little more than a toddler. Jack learned about miracles in school and came home and said, "Mom, I'm not thrilled. I want Amy to hear. I want to pray to Blessed Katharine so that Amy can hear." Little Jeanette piped in that she wanted to pray too, so that Amy could hear, and if not that she would lose her own hearing so she and her little sister would be the same.

Connie Wall was taken aback. "I had to pray to have the faith so that my son could pray for a miracle," she confessed. She contacted family and friends, obtained a medal of Blessed Katharine and a prayer card that had a tiny piece of her habit — a second class relic — enclosed in it. The whole family prayed as did their circle of friends and relatives. It was just about a week later, near the March 3 feast day of Blessed Katharine, when a teacher in the school where Amy was learning sign language noticed the toddler suddenly could hear.[20]

Dr. Matthew Bucko, a Norristown, Pennsylvania, ear, nose, and throat specialist, was a member of the team of doctors who were brought in to study Amy Wall's case. Was her now-perfect hearing some kind of coincidence? Had the child heard all along and been simply unresponsive? "No," Dr. Bucko explains, the tests administered to Amy before her miracle were very thorough and not dependent on a voluntary response from the child. For example, under anesthesia she had been subjected to sounds and her brain waves measured. There were no brain responses to the sounds. She did not hear them.

Another aspect of the case struck Dr. Bucko as very unusual. As a non-hearing toddler, Amy had not begun to learn speech. Now, at 17 months, she began to speak in distinct words and sentences. "Children usually start with baby talk, she never spoke baby talk," he observed.[21]

To have a family member touched by a saint has to have an effect on family life, although the Walls have tried to keep Amy out of the limelight so she can have a normal childhood. Connie Wall is a birth-Catholic; her husband John came from a Baptist background and considered himself non-denominational Protestant. At the time of their marriage he had agreed to allow his children to be raised Catholic. Intellectually, John Wall could accept miracles, but when it hit home, it seems to have changed his life.

"I converted (to Catholicism) two years ago. My son and I took confirmation at the same time," John Wall said at the January 27 press conference when Philadelphia's Cardinal Anthony Bevilacqua announced Pope John Paul II had signed the decree on Amy's miracle. "After the miracle occurred," John Wall said, "it changed our whole family, we are closer."[22] St. Katharine, who worked her entire life to promote the love of God through her Catholic faith, has to be pleased with this later development in the Wall family.

Bob Gutherman also felt his life was touched by Katharine Drexel's miracle. Now married and the father of two children of his own, he remains a devout Catholic. He has taught Rite of Christian Initiation for Adults (RCIA) programs in his parish and sometimes wondered how effective his words were. "Was anybody really listening?" he wondered. Gutherman said it is especially humbling to know Connie Wall heard his explanation of his personal miracle on a television program and was moved to pray to Blessed Katharine. "To think someone prayed and received a miracle because of something I said," he marveled.

That both accepted miracles of St. Katharine Drexel involve hearing, Gutherman does not find the least bit strange. "I think this is her way of telling us we should listen to the Word of God," he said.[23]

All that was left was a date of formal canonization, and this was established during a consistory of cardinals and bishops (including Cardinal Bevilacqua) presided over by Pope John Paul II on March 10, 2000. Mother Katharine, along with several other beatified from around the world, would be formally canonized in Rome during the great Jubilee Year, on October 1, 2000.[24]

* * * *

Who was this woman, this Katharine Drexel whom we now call St. Katharine Drexel? If you believe she was first and foremost a social activist, you miss the point. If you believe she was a feminist icon in a male-dominated Church, you misunderstand her. If, to you, Katharine Drexel was primarily an educator, you have seen but a small part of her gift and none of her soul.

Yes, Katharine, through her work, was on the cutting edge of social change in the treatment of minorities. And yes, through the application of her natural ability and with the leverage of a large fortune, she was able to push her Church and society toward social change as few women (or men) could.

And yes, Katharine was a pioneer in minority education; her schools, especially Xavier University in New Orleans are living testimony to that. Putting all this aside, the essence of Katharine Drexel was a pure and never-diminishing love of God that manifested itself through a particular devotion to Jesus Christ in the Blessed Sacrament.

What has been her impact? It is difficult to say. Most African Americans and many Native Americans have not embraced the Catholic faith she so longed to share with them. But if this is so, we cannot know what would be the case had she not lived. We know only what she accomplished, and with God's grace, learn from her example. The strong faith that exists among the African Americans and Native Americans in the parishes and missions she helped build and staff is St. Katharine Drexel's true monument.

Katharine wished to serve God, and how better to do so than to follow the Gospel message of Jesus — "Whatever you did for one of these least brothers of mine, you did for me." In Katharine's milieu, the least of His brethren were the Native Americans and African Americans. Yes, she would fight for them, and yes, she would bring them education. But most important, she would try to give them the gift of her Catholic faith, the faith she truly and sincerely believed was the surest road to Heaven. This, St. Katharine believed, was the greatest gift of all.

Principal Sources Cited

Annals, Sisters of the Blessed Sacrament (Annals ASBS) (Original Annals ASBS)

Archives, Sisters of the Blessed Sacrament (ASBS)

Canonizationis Servae Dei Catherinae Mariae Drexel (1858-1955) Rome, Congregatio pro Causis Sanctorum, 1986 (Positio)

Century Book, Sisters of the Blessed Sacrament, Bensalem, 1991

Davis, John H., *The Bouviers: Portrait of an American Family*, New York: Farrar, Straus & Giroux, 1969 (John Davis)

Davis, Cyprian, *The History of Black Catholics in the United States*, New York, Crossroad Publishing, 1990 (Cyprian Davis)

Duffy, Sister Consuela Marie, S.B.S., *Katharine Drexel: A Biography,* Cornwells Heights, 1941 (Duffy)

Golden Jubilee 1891-1941, Sisters of the Blessed Sacrament, Cornwells Heights, 1941 (Jubilee)

Letterhouse, Sister M. Dolores, S.B.S., *The Francis Anthony Drexel Family,* Cornwells Heights, 1939 (Letterhouse)

Letters, Mother M. Katharine Drexel, Archives, Sisters of the Blessed Sacrament (Letters MKD)

Lynch, Sister Patricia, S.B.S., *Sharing the Bread in Service, Sisters of the Blessed Sacrament, 1891-1991,* Bensalem, 1998 (Lynch)

Tarry, Ellen, *The Third Door: The Autobiography of an American Negro Woman,* Tuscaloosa, the University of Alabama Press, 1955 (Tarry)

Woodward, Kenneth L., *Making Saints*, New York, Simon and Schuster, 1990 (Woodward)

Baldwin, Lou, *A Call to Sanctity*, Philadelphia, 1988

The Catholic Standard and Times, Philadelphia

ENDNOTES

Chapter One   The Challenge
1. Retreat Talk, Mother Katharine Drexel, Dayton, Ohio, August, 1921 (ASBS).

Chapter Two   In the Beginning
1. Letterhouse, Sister M. Dolores, S.B.S., *The Francis Anthony Drexel Family*, Cornwells Heights, 1939, p. 1.
2. Ibid., p. 3.
3. Ibid., p. 4.
4. Ibid., p. 7.
5. Annals, ASBS, v. 1, p. 4.
6. Letterhouse, p. 5.
7. *Retrospective Holy Trinity Parish, 125th Anniversary*, Philadelphia, 1919, p. 88.
8. Letterhouse, p. 7.
9. *In Memoriam, Francis Anthony Drexel*, Philadelphia, Collins, 1884, p. 16.
10. Letterhouse, p. 8.
11. *Annals, Sisters of the Blessed Sacrament* (Annals ASBS), v. 1, p. 117.
12. Annals, ASBS, v. 1, p. 6.
13. Letterhouse, p. 16.
14. Letterhouse, p. 11.
15. Baptismal Records, Assumption B.V.M. Church (now held at St. John the Evangelist Church, Philadelphia).
16. Old Annals, ASBS, 1946, p. 53.
17. Ibid., p. 83.
18. Francis Drexel papers, ASBS.
19. Letterhouse, p. 12.
20. Ibid.
21. Davis, John H., *The Bouviers: Portrait of an American Family*, New York: Farrar, Straus & Giroux, 1969, p. 20.
22. Ibid., p. 30.
23. Letterhouse, p. 15.
24. John Davis, p. 55.

Chapter Three   Prayers and Industry
1. Letterhouse, p. 17.
2. Annals, ASBS, v. 1, p. 11.
3. Ibid., v. 4, pp. 36-40.
4. Duffy, Sister Consuela Marie, S.B.S.; *Katharine Drexel: A Biography*, Cornwells Heights, 1941, pp. 35-6.
5. Letterhouse, p. 16.
6. Oral Memoir, Mother Katharine Drexel, November 29, 1935, Archives of the Sisters of the Blessed Sacrament.
7. Ibid.
8. Letterhouse, p. 16.
9. Annals, v. 1, p. 117.
10. Ibid.
11. Oral Memoir, Mother Katharine Drexel.
12. Letterhouse, p. 126.

13. Ibid., p. 125.
14. Ibid., p. 164.
15. Ibid., p. 43.
16. Ibid., p. 114.
17. Ibid., p. 115.
18. Ibid., p. 47.
19. Duffy, p. 41.
20. Letterhouse, p. 70.
21. Ibid., p. 17.
22. Ibid., p. 24.
23. Ibid., p. 45.
24. Duffy, p. 34.
25. Letterhouse, p. 45.
26. Ibid., p. 25.
27. Will of Catherine Drexel, ASBS.
28. Letterhouse, p. 21.
29. Annals, ASBS, v. 1, p. 23.
30. Mother Katharine Drexel papers, ASBS.
31. Annals, ASBS, v. 1, p. 12.
32. Letterhouse, p. 46.
33. Mother Katharine Drexel papers, ASBS.
34. Ibid.
35. Mother M.E. Tobin, R.S.C.J., to Mother M. Anselm, S.B.S., June 8, 1964, ASBS.
36. *Canonizationis Servae Dei Catherinae Mariae Drexel (1858-1955)* Rome, Congregatio pro Causis Sanctorum, 1986 (Positio) v. 1, p. 156.
37. Retreat Notebook, Mother Katharine Drexel, v. 8, pp. 76-7, ASBS.
38. Annals, ASBS, v. 1, pp. 19-20.
39. Letterhouse, p. 123.
40. Ibid., pp. 58-9.
41. Ibid., p. 96.
42. Ibid., pp. 91-2.
43. Ibid., pp. 97-8.
44. Annals, ASBS, v. 1, p. 35.
45. Duffy, pp. 57-8.
46. Katharine Drexel to Bishop O'Connor, ASBS.
47. Bishop O'Connor to Katharine Drexel, ASBS.
48. Katharine Drexel to Bishop O'Connor, May 21, 1883, ASBS.
49. Positio, v. 2, p. 164.
50. Annals, ASBS, v. 1, p. 58.
51. Letterhouse, pp. 107-8.
52. Ibid., p. 171.
53. Katharine Drexel to Bishop O'Connor, January 27, 1884, ASBS.

Chapter Four   Trials and Meditation
1. Duffy, pp. 68-9.
2. Positio, v. 1, p. 2.
3. Letterhouse, p. 67.
4. Ibid., p. 187.
5. Annals, ASBS, v. 1, p. 230.
6. Letterhouse, p. 195.

7. Katharine Drexel to Bishop O'Connor, January 27, 1884, ASBS. Katharine told him when she and her sisters were children Emma would say, "I do hope God will not give you, my children, a religious vocation. If He does, I must submit; but I shall never permit you to enter a convent until you are at least 25 years of age."

8. Katherine Burton, *The Golden Door: The Life of Mother Katharine Drexel,* New York, P.J. Kenedy and Sons, 1957), p. 49.

9. Duffy, pp. 80-88.

10. Duffy, pp. 84-86.

11. Annals, ASBS, v. 1, p. 52.

12. Ibid., v. 1, p. 48.

13. Ibid., v. 26, p. 57.

14. Duffy, p. 59.

15. Ibid., p. 60.

16. Ibid., p. 62.

17. Ibid., p. 63.

18. Katharine Drexel to Bishop O'Connor, May 21, 1883, ASBS.

19. Ibid.

20. Bishop O'Connor to Katharine Drexel, May 26, 1883, ASBS.

21. Katharine Drexel to Bishop O'Connor, May 21, 1883, ASBS. The exact wording is, "Does it not appear my own corrupt nature leads me to the married state?" She may also be simply implying a lack of perfection.

22. Bishop O'Connor to Katharine Drexel, August, 1883, ASBS.

23. Annals, ASBS, v. 2, p. 136.

24. Duffy, p. 62.

25. Bishop O'Connor to Katharine Drexel, October 25, 1883, ASBS.

26. Katharine Drexel to Bishop O'Connor, November 20, 1883, ASBS.

27. Ibid.

28. Katharine Drexel to Bishop O'Connor, January 27, 1884, ASBS.

29. Letterhouse, p. 210.

30. Ibid., p. 213.

31. Annals, ASBS, v. 2, p. 170.

32. Positio, v. 1, p. 181.

33. Letterhouse, pp. 220-23.

34. Ibid., pp. 223-24.

35. Archbishop P. J. Ryan Correspondence, Archives, St. Charles Borromeo Seminary, Wynnewood, Pa. Although the Drexel and Childs families were best of friends, Emma Bouvier Drexel was not related to Emma Bouvier Childs. In this letter (April 29, 1890) Emma Childs invited the Archbishop to dinner and a drive to inspect a property in Wayne.

36. Letterhouse, p. 232.

37. *In Memoriam, Francis Anthony Drexel*, Philadelphia, 1885, p. 70.

38. Annals, ASBS, v. 2, p. 170.

39. Will of Francis A. Drexel, ASBS.

40. Letterhouse, p. 235.

41. Duffy, p. 77.

Chapter Five   The Most Attractive of the Three

1. Annals, ASBS, v. 23, p. 287.

2. Letterhouse, p. 243. Francis Drexel chose St. Francis de Sales for his patron saint because "he was noted for his sweetness of manner and his meekness, which I need and must strive to acquire." (Letterhouse, p. 270).

3. Letterhouse, p. 337. In 1888 Louise funded Epiphany College in Baltimore for the Josephite Fathers, who worked exclusively among African Americans. Her initial donation was $60,000.
4. Letterhouse, p. 316.
5. Annals, ASBS, v. 3, p. 232.
6. Katharine Drexel to Bishop O'Connor, August, 1885, ASBS.
7. Bishop O'Connor to Katharine Drexel, August 29, 1885, ASBS.
8. Letterhouse, p. 242.
9. Ibid., p. 247.
10. Ibid., p. 250.
11. Ibid., p. 265.
12. Ibid., p. 266.
13. Bishop O'Connor to Katharine Drexel, March 3, 1887, ASBS.
14. Ibid., March 10, 1886.
15. Ibid., April 21, 1887.
16. Letterhouse, pp. 316-22.
17. Ibid., pp. 326-33.
18. Annals, ASBS, v. 2, p. 214.
19. Katharine Drexel to Bishop O'Connor, November 11, 1888, ASBS.
20. Ibid., November 26, 1888.
21. Bishop O'Connor to Katharine Drexel, November 30, 1888, ASBS.
22. Katharine Drexel to Bishop O'Connor, December 15, 1888, ASBS.
23. Barnie F. Winkelman, *John G. Johnson, Lawyer and Art Collector,* Philadelphia, University of Pennsylvania Press, 1942, p. 96.
24. Annals, ASBS, v. 23, p. 89.
25. Katharine Drexel to Bishop O'Connor, February 12, 1889, ASBS.
26. Annals, ASBS, v. 3, p. 24.
27. Father Stephan to Katharine Drexel, February 12, 1889, ASBS.
28. Bishop O'Connor to Katharine Drexel, February 16, 1889, ASBS.
29. Katharine Drexel to Bishop O'Connor, February 24, 1889, ASBS.
30. Bishop O'Connor to Katharine Drexel, February 28, 1889, ASBS.
31. Katharine Drexel to Bishop O'Connor, March 19, 1889, ASBS.
32. Ibid., April 6, 1889.
33. Ibid.

Chapter Six   Mother and Servant

1. Letterhouse, p. 359.
2. Ibid., p. 360.
3. Sister Katharine Drexel to Bishop O'Connor, May 31, 1889, ASBS.
4. Ibid., May 12, 1889.
5. Annals, ASBS, v. 2, p. 271.
6. Positio, v.1, p. 403.
7. Duffy, p. 151.
8. Ibid., pp. 151-2.
9. Ibid., p. 152.
10. Positio, v. 1, p. 410.
11. Memoir, Mother Mercedes O'Connor, S.B.S., ASBS.
12. Ibid.
13. Mother Katharine Drexel papers, ASBS.
14. Annals, ASBS, v. 2, p. 278.

15. Letterhouse, p. 337.
16. Sister Katharine Drexel to Bishop O'Connor, January 14, 1890, ASBS.
17. Annals, ASBS, v. 3, p. 13.
18. Ibid., p. 17.
19. Ibid., p. 18.
20. Ibid., pp. 21-2.
21. Ibid., p. 21.
22. Archbishop Ryan to Sister Katharine Drexel, September 23, 1890, ASBS.
23. Annals, ASBS, v. 3, p. 110.
24. Cardinal Gibbons to Archbishop Ryan, Ryan Correspondence, Archives, St. Charles Borromeo Seminary, Wynnewood, Pa.
25. Annals, ASBS, v. 21, p. 138.
26. Ibid., p. 123.
27. Ibid., p. 126.

Chapter Seven   Pioneers with Patience

1. Annals, ASBS, v. 3, p. 220.
2. Ibid., p. 237.
3. Ibid., p. 238.
4. Ibid., p. 173.
5. Annals, ASBS, v. 31, p. 242.
6. Annals, ASBS, v. 3, p. 242.
7. Ibid.
8. Ibid.
9. Ibid., p. 323.
10. Ibid., pp. 183-7.
11. Sister Patricia Lynch, S.B.S., *Sharing the Bread in Service, Sisters of the Blessed Sacrament, 1891-1991,* Bensalem, 1998 (Lynch).
12. Ibid., p. 58.
13. Sister Patricia Lynch, S.B.S., *Collective Biography of the Founding Sisters of the Blessed Sacrament*, U.S. Catholic Historian, v. 10.
14. Letterhouse, p. 368.
15. Annals, ASBS, v. 3, p. 189.
16. Ibid., p. 205.
17. Ibid., p. 203.
18. Ibid., p. 209.
19. Duffy, p. 180
20. Annals, ASBS, v. 3, p. 219.
21. Ibid., p. 273.
22. Ibid., p. 290.
23. Annals, ASBS, v. 10, p. 295.
24. Cyprian Davis, *The History of Black Catholics in the United States,* New York, Crossroad Publishing, 1990, pp. 110-114.
25. Annals, ASBS, v. 3, p. 290.
26. Cyprian Davis, p. 160.
27. Mother Consuela, superior of the Oblate Sisters of Providence, hinted to the Blessed Sacrament Sisters that Theresa Maxis may not have been blameless when she was forced to leave their congregation (Annals, ASBS, v. 3, p. 58). However, Bishop Lefevre's comment and Bishop Wood's response were both patently racist. Lefevre wrote (August 2, 1859): "If you take the pains to go and see this Mother Theresa and Sister Ann, and

converse with them a little, you will soon discover in them, notwithstanding their advanced age, all the softness, slyness and low cunning of the mulatto." In his response (August 6, 1859) Bishop Wood said of the light-skinned Mother Theresa Maxis, "...I tremble to think of the impression that will be made when our good people discover that their daughters have been sent to a place under the care of a mulatto superior." See *Apostolate of the Archives*, Sister Diane Edward Shea, I.H.M., and Sister Marita Constance Supan, I.H.M., The Josephite Harvest, Summer, 1983.

28. Annals, ASBS, v. 3, p. 296.
29. Annals, ASBS, v. 4, p. 51.
30. Ibid., pp. 53-4.
31. Ibid., p. 75.

Chapter Eight   Mission Days

1. Annals, ASBS, v. 4, p. 75.
2. Ibid., p. 85.
3. Ibid., p. 100.
4. Ibid., p. 127.
5. Mother Katharine Drexel to Sisters of the Blessed Sacrament, ASBS, September 6, 1894.
6. Annals, ASBS, v. 4, p. 161.
7. Ibid., v. 4, p. 200.
8. Annals, ASBS, v. 5, p. 17.
9. Ibid.
10. Ibid., p. 203.
11. Ibid., p. 274.
12. Memoir, Mother Mercedes O'Connor, ASBS.
13. Annals, ASBS, v. 6, p. 32.
14. Ibid., p. 41.
15. Ibid., p. 42.
16. Ibid., p. 282.
17. Tarry, pp. 29-54.
18. Annals, ASBS, v. 5, p. 75.
19. Ibid., p. 81.
20. Annals, ASBS, v. 6, p. 131.
21. Ibid., p. 24.
22. Annals, ASBS, v. 5, p. 188.
23. Ibid., p. 278.
24. Annals, ASBS, v. 6, p. 149.
25. Annals, ASBS, v. 7, p. 66.
26. Annals, ASBS, v. 5, p. 177.
27. Annals, ASBS, v. 6, p. 300.
28. Ibid.
29. Annals, ASBS, v. 5, p. 85.
30. Annals, ASBS, v. 6, p. 257.
31. Annals, ASBS, v. 7, p. 21.
32. Ibid., p. 55.
33. Ibid., p. 29.
34. Ibid., p. 267.
35. Ibid., p. 273.
36. Ibid., p. 295.
37. Ibid., p. 144.

38. Ibid., p. 176.
39. Annals, ASBS, v. 8, pp. 111-36.
40. Ibid., p. 137.
41. Ibid., p. 246.
42. Ibid., p. 250.
43. *The Indian Sentinel*, Washington, D.C., 1904-5, p. 31.
44. Annals, ASBS, v. 17, p. 91.

Chapter Nine   Go to Rome Yourself?
1. Duffy, p. 275.
2. Ibid., p. 276.
3. Ibid., p. 278.
4. Ibid., p. 282.
5. Annals, ASBS, v. 9, p. 98.
6. Ibid., p. 121.
7. Ibid., p. 123.
8. Ibid., p. 132.
9. Duffy, p. 285.
10. Annals, ASBS, v. 9, p. 144.
11. Ibid., pp. 185-6.
12. Ibid., p. 187.
13. Ibid., p. 266.
14. Annals, ASBS, v. 10, p. 222.
15. Annals, ASBS, v. 8, p. 171.
16. Annals, ASBS, v. 11, p. 21.
17. Annals, ASBS, v. 10, p. 289.
18. Annals, ASBS, v. 12, p. 78.
19. Ibid., pp. 240-4.

Chapter Ten   Firm Faith, Confident Hope, Ardent Charity
1. Annals, ASBS, v. 14, p. 221.
2. Ibid., p. 226.
3. Ibid., p. 23.
4. Ibid., pp. 244-6.
5. Ibid., p. 88.
6. Ibid., p. 133.
7. Ibid., p. 88.
8. Ibid., p. 236.
9. Annals, ASBS, v. 15, p. 210.
10. Lynch, *Sharing the Bread in Service,* p. 313.
11. Annals, ASBS, v. 14, p. 284.
12. Ibid., p. 298.
13. Duffy, p. 303.
14. Annals, ASBS, v. 15, p. 60.
15. Ibid., p. 106.
16. Ibid., p. 107.
17. Sister Brendan O'Brien, S.B.S., taped memoir, ASBS.
18. Annals, ASBS, v. 15, p. 107.
19. Ibid., p. 103.
20. Ibid.

21. Ibid., p. 262.
22. Ibid., p. 222.
23. Ibid., p. 223.
24. Annals, ASBS, v. 16, p. 81.
25. Duffy, p. 322.
26. Lynch, *Sharing the Bread*, p. 204.
27. Ibid., pp. 209-222.
28. Duffy, p. 323.
29. Annals, ASBS, v. 15, p. 127.
30. Lynch, *Sharing the Bread*, pp. 228-52.
31. Annals, ASBS, v. 20, p. 13.
32. Annals, ASBS, v. 23, p. 60.
33. Annals, ASBS, v. 26, p. 59.
34. Positio, v. 2, p. 333.
35. Ibid., p. 319.
36. Ibid., p. 5.
37. Testimony box 2, ASBS.
38. Positio, v. 2, p. 118.
39. Annals, ASBS, v. 4, pp. 36-40.
40. Annals, ASBS, v. 17, p. 223.
41. Annals, ASBS, v. 18, p. 8.
42. Annals, ASBS, v. 17, p. 223.
43. Annals, ASBS, v. 22, pp. 224-5.
44. Annals, ASBS, v. 29, p. 126.
45. Mary Powell to Mother Katharine Drexel, ASBS.
46. Annals, ASBS, v. 17, p. 275.

Chapter Eleven   Bigotry and Blessings

1. Annals, ASBS, v. 18, p. 4.
2. Ibid., p. 139.
3. Ibid.
4. Ibid., p. 208.
5. Annals, ASBS, v. 19, p. 156.
6. Ibid., p. 215.
7. Ibid., p. 216.
8. Cardinal Dennis Dougherty to Mother Katharine Drexel, November 1, 1923, ASBS.
9. Annals, ASBS, v. 20, p. 50.
10. Ibid., pp. 131-45.
11. Annals, ASBS, v. 22, pp. 109-11.
12. Positio, v. 2, pp. 249-50.
13. Ibid., p. 326.
14. Annals, ASBS, v. 23, p. 162.
15. Lynch, *Sharing the Bread*, p. 395.
16. Testimony box 2, ASBS.
17. Annals, ASBS, v. 23, pp. 83-7.
18. The author was born in St. Agatha Parish, where the practice was common knowledge. For documentation of parish policies aimed at excluding African Americans, see John T. McGreevey, *Parish Boundaries,* Chicago, University of Chicago Press, 1996. While McGreevey focuses on Gesu Parish as his Philadelphia example of black exclusion, the St. Agatha methods were similar and it was probably the case in some other (but certainly not

all) Philadelphia parishes. Playwright Charles Fuller, a Philadelphian and African American, relates how he and his wife tried to register at St. Francis de Sales Parish in West Philadelphia in the early 1960s. They were advised by a parish priest that they could attend but they "wouldn't be welcomed." They chose to attend Mass at St. Ignatius Church, almost two miles away. (*The Catholic Standard and Times*, February 11, 1999).

19. Annals, ASBS, v. 24, p. 112.
20. Annals, ASBS, v. 26, p. 116.
21. Ibid., p. 225.
22. Ibid., p. 183.
23. Annals, ASBS, v. 22, p. 38.
24. Msgr. Ketcham to Mother Katharine Drexel (August, 1921), ASBS.
25. Annals, ASBS, v. 20, p. 56.
26. Annals, ASBS, v. 21, p. 112.
27. Duffy, p. 253. See *Statutes at Large, United States of America 68th Congress, Section 1, Chapter 234, Section 1.*
28. Annals, ASBS, v. 15, p. 161.
29. Testimony box 2, ASBS.
30. Annals, ASBS, v. 26, p. 16.
31. Annals, ASBS, v. 23, p. 309.
32. Positio, v. 2, pp. 3-4.
33. Testimony box 2, ASBS.
34. Annals, ASBS, v. 21, p. 8.
35. Ibid., p. 82.
36. Annals, ASBS, v. 23, p. 117.
37. Annals, ASBS, v. 25, p. 212.
38. Annals, ASBS, v. 26, p. 207. Possible mistake in transcribing. Villanova beat Boston College in football that year, 7-6.
39. Lynch, *Sharing the Bread,* p. 217.
40. Taped memoir, Sister Ancilla Goerschner, S.B.S., ASBS.
41. Duffy, p. 291.
42. Positio, v. 2, p. 30.
43. Ibid., pp. 282-3.
44. Annals, ASBS, v. 29, p. 176.
45. Cyprian Davis, p. 254.
46. Annals, ASBS, v. 26, p. 173.
47. Cardinal Dennis Dougherty to Mother Katharine Drexel, January 25, 1932, ASBS.
48. Cardinal Dennis Dougherty to Mother Mary of the Visitation, March 19, 1941, ASBS.
49. Positio, v. 1, p. 944.
50. Ibid., pp. 962-3.
51. Annals, ASBS, v. 29, p. 14.

Chapter Twelve   Please Dear Lord, Spare Her

1. Annals, ASBS, v. 29, p. 84.
2. Original Annals, ASBS, 1947, p. 32.
3. Annals, ASBS, v. 29, p. 41.
4. Ibid., p. 245.
5. Ibid., p. 236.
6. Annals, ASBS, v. 30, p. 50.
7. Annals, ASBS, v. 31, p. 7.
8. Ibid., p. 73.

9. Cardinal Dennis Dougherty to Mother Katharine Drexel, January 8, 1936, ASBS.

10. Annals, ASBS, v. 31, p. 95.

11. Ibid., p. 162.

12. Duffy, p. 353.

13. *Jubilee Book, 1891-41*, ASBS.

14. Duffy, p. 361.

15. Annals, ASBS, v. 32, p. 156.

16. Annals, ASBS, v. 33, p. 66.

17. *The Catholic Standard and Times*, Philadelphia, November 17, 1988, p. 21.

18. *Reflections from the Life on the Vine: Quotations from Mother Katharine Drexel* (Cornwells Heights, Sisters of the Blessed Sacrament, 1982, p. 17).

19. Duffy, p. 371.

20. Original Annals, ASBS, 1944, p. 188.

21. Duffy, p. 374.

22. Original Annals, ASBS, 1944, p. 169.

23. Original Annals, ASBS, 1946, p. 136.

24. St. Francis in Eddington, Bensalem, Pa., 1988, ASBS.

25. Emanuel Friedman, *Louise Drexel Morrell: A Reminiscence.* Philadelphia, The American Catholic Historical Society, Records, March, 1965.

26. Annals, ASBS, v. 32, p. 75.

27. Original Annals, ASBS, 1945, p. 155.

28. Ibid.

29. Cardinal Dennis Dougherty to Mother Mary of the Visitation, March 22, 1949, ASBS.

Chapter Thirteen   In Paradisio

1. Letter, Mother Mary Anselm, Original Annals, 1955, p. 33.

2. Positio, v. 2, p. 139.

3. *The Catholic Standard and Times*, November 17, 1988, p. 21.

4. Positio, v. 1, p. 1017.

5. Baldwin, Lou, *A Call to Sanctity*, Philadelphia, 1988, p. 95.

6. *The Catholic Standard and Times*, March 11, 1955.

7. Annals, v. 38, p. 138.

8. Baldwin, Lou, *A Call to Sanctity*, Philadelphia, 1988, p. 86.

9. Ibid., p. 92.

Chapter Fourteen   Miracles of Faith

1. Positio, v. 2, p. 219.

2. Annals, v. 23, p. 81.

3. *The Catholic Standard and Times*, February 28, 1964, p. 1.

4. Positio, v. 2, p. 373.

5. Ibid., p. 324.

6. Ibid., p. 133.

7. Ibid., pp. 348-50.

8. Woodward, Kenneth L.; *Making Saints,* New York, Simon and Schuster, 1990, p. 246. Pages 221-252 comprise an excellent critique of Mother Katharine's cause, at least as it stood up until her beatification.

9. Ibid., p. 237.

10. Positio, v. 2, p. 250.

11. Ibid., p. 8.

12. Ibid., p. 14.

13. Positio, v. 2, p. 13, 98.
14. *The Catholic Standard and Times*, December 17, 1987, p. 3.
15. Ibid., January 29, 1987, p. 1.
16. Ibid., July 28, 1988, p. 1.
17. Ibid., November 24, 1988, p. 1, pp. 19-22.
18. Interview with Lou Baldwin, January 27, 2000.
19. *The Catholic Standard and Times*, February 3, 2000, p. 1.
20. *Peacemaker*, the Blessed Sacrament Sisters' newsletter of the Blessed Katharine Drexel cause, reported on another alleged hearing-related miracle for a child in its summer 1999 issue.
21. News conference, St. Elizabeth's Convent, January 27, 2000.
22. Ibid.
23. Ibid.
24. Archdiocese of Philadelphia news release, March 10, 2000.

ABOUT THE AUTHOR

Lou Baldwin, a staff writer for *The Catholic Standard and Times*, wrote *A Call to Sanctity*, a 1988 biography about Mother Katharine Drexel.

As a youth Lou attended St. Francis Vocational School in Eddington, Pennsylvania, an institution founded by Elizabeth, Katharine and Louise Drexel.

A native Philadelphian, he also attended St. Bernard School and graduated from Northeast Catholic High School in Philadelphia. Lou attended the University of Pennsylvania and has worked at various times as a librarian, a cryptographer in the U.S. Army, a stock trader and an accountant.

As staff writer for *The Catholic Standard and Times*, he has won numerous writing awards from the Catholic Press Association, Philadelphia Press Association and the Society for Propagation of the Faith.

Lou is married to the former Rita Crawford, and they have nine children.